D1648563

"Sometime ago I watched Bokara's enchanting one person show and I appeared on her television show "Lunch with Bokara" since then I plumbed deep into Bo's spiritual side. She is a very dear and valued friend who has lived a fascinating life which she relates with great humor. I share this book enjoyfully."

Ram Dass author of Be Here Now

In this brilliant and engrossing book, Bokara Legendre intimately shares her life-long adventures as she searches for the family and home she never really had. Highly recommended.

Michael Harner author of The Way of the Shaman

Bokara Legendre sure knows how to tell a good story. A journalist, raconteur, and spiritual seeker, Bokara has led a life full of adventures. "Not What I Expected" is a wonderful memoir and a delight to read.

Wes Nisker, author of Crazy Wisdom

By turns funny, touching, and a sparkling romp across the globe. A marvelous life and a great ride.

Jack Kornfield author of A Path With Heart

Bo's life brings together worlds that might be in collision but instead blend and fuse, held by her great heart and wise perspectives. Born into life's luxuries, she pursues the inner life (with room service). Educated to live in a world populated by privilege, she makes friends everywhere, including artists, writers, spiritual teachers, and monks. Her humor is infectious. Her adventures are bold, and her book takes you along for the exhilarating ride.

Mirabai Bush author of Compassion in Action

Not What I Expected is a delightful page turner. Through it, we share in Bokara's many adventures, spanning the globe and the decades. Written in a beautiful, clear voice, this very personal book provides a fascinating, rich view into a search for transformation that has affected an entire generation.

Sharon Salzberg, author of Lovingkindness and Real happiness

Not What I Expected

Bokara Legendre

BALBOA
PRESS
A DIVISION OF HAY HOUSE

Balboa Press books may be ordered through booksellers or by contacting:

Balboa Press
A Division of Hay House
1663 Liberty Drive
Bloomington, IN 47403
www.balboapress.com
1 (877) 407-4847

Because of the dynamic nature of the Internet, any web addresses or links contained in this book may have changed since publication and may no longer be valid. The views expressed in this work are solely those of the author and do not necessarily reflect the views of the publisher, and the publisher hereby disclaims any responsibility for them.

The author of this book does not dispense medical advice or prescribe the use of any technique as a form of treatment for physical, emotional, or medical problems without the advice of a physician, either directly or indirectly. The intent of the author is only to offer information of a general nature to help you in your quest for emotional and spiritual well-being. In the event you use any of the information in this book for yourself, which is your constitutional right, the author and the publisher assume no responsibility for your actions.

Any people depicted in stock imagery provided by Thinkstock are models, and such images are being used for illustrative purposes only.
Certain stock imagery © Thinkstock.

Printed in the USA

ISBN: 978-1-5043-7339-5 (sc)
ISBN: 978-1-5043-7341-8 (hc)
ISBN: 978-1-5043-7340-1 (e)

Library of Congress Control Number: 2017900832

Balboa Press rev. date: 05/31/2017

DEDICATION

To Don Hanlon Johnson, Daidie Donnelley and Jack Kornfield
without whom this book would never have been published.

And to my family of friends worldwide
with whom I've had
adventures, laughter, tears and wild times.

In memory of my beloved governess
Mamie
Miss Violet Evans.

CHAPTER

Crashing the Coronation

In 1975 I accidentally crashed the coronation of the king of Nepal.

Of course, I didn't mean to. I thought I was invited.

In fact, I *was* invited.

A few months earlier, I'd gone for cocktails with a couple of other people at the San Francisco home of Jack and Lita Vietor. Jack was, among other things, the honorary consul to Nepal. Over vodka and tonics, which must have been too strong, he said, "Why don't you join Lita and me at the coronation of the king of Nepal in March?"

I looked at the two other people in the living room, and we all said, "Absolutely! Let's go."

"I'll arrange it," Jack replied.

So *boom*—just like that we were going to a Himalayan coronation.

My marriage was falling apart, and my dog had just died. Some clear mountain air and a royal jamboree sounded like just what I needed.

I took Jack at his word and assumed that a lovely manila envelope with a printed invitation would be forthcoming. I booked a flight to Kathmandu and delightedly told my mother—who imagined herself the Queen of Glamorous Adventures—that I was off to the coronation of the king of Nepal. My friend Harold Talbott, a devout Buddhist with connections worldwide, arranged for me to stay with Gene Smith (an eminent Buddhist scholar) and his wife. It all sounded perfect.

Naturally, there were a few hitches. I never did receive a printed invitation, for instance. I kept thinking it would come in the mail before I left, but since Jack would be in Kathmandu, I assumed that either the invitation would be at the gate or that he would be there to escort me in.

I was sure it would all work out.

I carefully packed a coronation costume, complete with gold high-heeled sandals, evening dresses for royal balls, and Arnold Scaasi suede pants for "casual lunches." Just in case, I packed my Nikon and its foot-long lens and a heavy reel-to-reel tape recorder—vestiges of my early career as a reporter—so I could pose as a member of the press corps if I had to. Maybe I'd actually get a chance to interview the royal couple or at least take a photo or two that might appear in a glossy magazine.

I waved good-bye to my husband and hopped on the plane.

The Kathmandu airport, which had only a dirt road for an airstrip and a tin shack for a terminal, buzzed with private jets. Coming down the airplane steps, I pushed my dark glasses on top of my head in what I fancied was a grand movie-star gesture.

The taxi into town crawled through narrow streets crowded with people, cows, and elephants. I noticed that all the elephants' toenails had been lacquered red, just like mine. The huge curling horns of the cows had been painted red too, and everywhere red dust had settled on the stone statues of elephants, monkey gods, naked goddesses, and assorted fierce-looking deities that lined the roads.

When the taxi finally drew up to the house where Harold, my Buddhist friend, had arranged for me to stay, I was greeted hurriedly by a housekeeper and rushed to the very back to a tiny room with a shared bath. My hosts at that moment were entirely occupied with their main guest, the queen of Bhutan, who had only just arrived with a sizable entourage.

As I looked around my cramped room in some despair, my host popped by for a moment. "I hope you'll be comfortable," he murmured distractedly. "I'm sure you can take care of yourself." Then he hurried back to the queen.

I saw right away I'd better go out for lunch.

I strolled along the streets, exhausted from my trip, remembering the last time I'd been there, when I'd gone around the world with my mother in 1961. Huge white bulls with red horns and hooves blocked the roads, while little bands of Nepalese musicians played among tiny stalls selling everything from sweets to religious statues to cold cream. At length, I found a stall selling lentils and rice, which I ate standing in the street while being jostled by the constantly moving crowd of natives and tourists. Later, I stopped for some tea in the shade of a *stupa*—a type of monument representing the enlightened mind of the Buddha—that was strung with multicolored prayer flags. The streets were an Asian opera, with men and women wrapped in fabulous colored costumes that were their everyday clothes—so much better looking than the black suits of New York. On their heads, they carried everything from chickens to brass pots to cakes.

At last, tired and overwhelmed, I made my way back to the scholar's house to rest and to ask my host about getting into the coronation. I had no idea when or where it actually was going to happen. How, I wondered, could I broach the question of the missing invitation?

Unfortunately, my host was not at home, so I called the hotel where I knew the Vietors were staying. They weren't in either, so I left a message with the concierge to ask the consul general from San Francisco if he had my invitation. Should I pick it up from him? Or should I just meet him at the coronation?

Later, I was passed a reply message: "We'll see you there."

I sat on the edge of my narrow bed pondering my dilemma. So far, this trip was not turning out to be the glamorous adventure I'd imagined. I'd made some meager effort at unpacking, but the room was so small that I had to hang my ball gown on the wall light in the hall. The tiny sink opposite my bed was completely buried under all the creams and sprays I'd brought with me. Water had soaked my face powder.

Finally I emerged from my room to look for my host, and I found him chatting with the queen outside her door. I wondered if I should curtsy. Since it was an informal encounter, I decided against it and instead simply smiled and waited for my host to acknowledge my presence.

"When you have a second," I said finally, "I wonder if I could ask you one tiny thing?"

He looked put out by the interruption, but I plunged ahead.

"I wonder if I could trouble you for a lift to the coronation. Somehow," I equivocated, "I think the Vietors must have my invitation with them. I thought they would have dropped it off here, but it seems they didn't," I finished with a flourish.

My host appeared uninterested rather than concerned.

"You'll have to get in on your own," he said, shrugging. "We'll drop you off."

I assumed that he meant he would drop me at the entrance gate and I could slip in with them. After all, the queen and her entourage were a pretty good cover.

I was actually relieved.

The coronation celebrations began the next morning at five. A parade of dignified elephants decorated with silk tassels, eye makeup, and—of course—splendid red toenails made their way through town. Cows, sacred to Hindus, meandered lazily through the traffic and the parade. The multitude of stone statues—enormous monkeys representing the Hindu god Hanuman, Buddhas, and deities of every kind—were wrapped in red or white silk prayer scarves. The temples and houses of Kathmandu were plastered with onlookers clinging, along with the monkeys that ran wild through the city, to any cranny or crevice that would support them. Street vendors had been up all night creating delectable fried dumplings and sweet cakes for the watching crowds, and musicians filled the squares and courtyards with a charming, if somewhat cacophonous, musical accompaniment. Luckily, the weather was clear and the ambiance was extremely friendly.

On the way to the official entrance, my host unceremoniously dropped me off beside a wood rail fence around Kathmandu's centrally located cow pasture—masquerading as a parade ground, masquerading as a palace garden. I could see the coronation tents far off across the huge muddy field.

"You'll have to get in on your own," my host curtly informed me as the queen looked on impassively.

"Thank you," I murmured out of well-brought-up habit.

I watched the car slowly disappear into the procession before turning my attention to the immediate problem of making my way to the tents. Dressed in a tie-dyed, multicolored silk evening dress with long full sleeves and a quilted vest, I battled a harness of binoculars and cameras strapped crisscross on my shoulders like hunters' game bags—ready to join the press corps instead of the royal court if I had to. Then, glancing around to be sure no one was looking, I carefully placed one high-heeled gold sandal on the bottom fence rail and, as gracefully as possible, climbed over. At each step my high heels sunk into the mud and the cow pies. I felt like a soldier crossing enemy territory waiting for a bullet, but nothing happened and no one seemed to notice.

The atmosphere within the royal enclosure was a cross between those of a country fair and the opening day of the Royal Ascot: windy, sunny, and countrified, but *dressy*. Visiting male dignitaries from Europe and America, their pockets bulging with binoculars, wore morning coats and high collars, which contrasted strangely with their dark glasses and cameras. Western women were in full evening dress—satins and flowing silks, their necks wrapped in jewels and the straps of binoculars and cameras. Bhutanese ladies wore long brightly colored wrapped skirts with formal striped aprons and silk blouses in brilliant lapis and ruby silks. Silver necklaces set with huge lumps of turquoise and coral hung from their necks, and giant turquoise ornaments adorned their foreheads. The Tibetans wore traditional *chubas*—long ornate robes wrapped around the waist with silk cords—their arms lost in endless sleeves. Saffron-robed monks from Southeast Asia and maroon-clad Tibetan lamas mingled with maharajas in long brocade coats and satin jodhpurs and maharanis wearing brilliant saris and glittering jewels.

People bowed and smiled as I passed, and since I was already inside, nobody asked to see my invitation. Nevertheless, I was hugely embarrassed and kept my gaze to the ground, convinced I'd be discovered as the gate-crasher I was. When I looked up I saw, seemingly miles away, a small red tent for the king and queen and two large white ones, which I assumed had been erected for invited guests.

When I came upon the first of the guest tents, I rushed in and sat down without raising my eyes from the muddy grass. After a few minutes I looked up—only to discover that I was surrounded by a sea of Nepali men, all clad in white *dhotis*, black Nehru coats, and white turbans. There wasn't a woman or a Westerner to be seen. No one moved; no one said a word. I felt as though I'd stepped into a classroom where everyone was taking an exam.

I exchanged a polite but surprised glance with my nearest neighbor, who quickly withdrew his gaze to the middle distance. Then I fled, a bolting rainbow of tie-dyed silk battling my cameras and binoculars, and headed for the other white tent.

To my inestimable relief, it was full of Western women in evening dress and men in morning coats. I slid gratefully into an empty chair beside a woman in a green-satin dress with three strands of pearls and a camera around her neck.

"Did you know," she murmured after I'd settled into my seat, "that the queen's coronation wig was eaten by a *yak* yesterday?"

"Really?" I replied with some relief as I adjusted my folding metal chair, which had begun to sink into the soft earth.

Such a confidence, I imagined, proved that I'd been accepted by the right people.

"It was at a hairdresser's in one of those open street stalls," the woman continued. "The yak just reached right in and took it!"

The royal couple were sequestered so far away in their little red tent that even with our binoculars we couldn't see them very clearly through the open flap. Nevertheless, we craned our necks for a glimpse of the queen's hair. But at that moment, the king must have given the signal for a "photo opportunity." A herd of press photographers tore out of their enclosure like horses from a starting gate, all snapping and flashing like mad, completely blocking our view.

To prove that I knew a thing or two also, I offered up a bit of gossip I'd heard the day before. "Did you know," I asked, "that the king had all the stray dogs and hippies trucked over the border to clear the streets for the coronation?"

Before my neighbor could reply, a warm spring wind from the Himalayas blew into Kathmandu, causing the roof of the tent to flap against the hastily planted metal tent poles. In the distance, Kanchenjunga—the third highest mountain in the world—floated like an iceberg in a sea of blue haze, and just outside the tent the March sun glinted on the golden embroidery of a maharaja's cream silk coat.

A flurry of trumpets sounded, which I suppose signaled the main event of the coronation. But the view was completely blocked by the press of photographers and reporters. I was outraged. Here I'd traveled thousands of miles, brazened my way across a cow field in full evening dress to see a king and queen receive their jeweled crowns, and when the view finally cleared, all I could see were two rather short people on seats wearing something vaguely glittery on their heads.

"Are those their crowns?" I asked my green-satin neighbor.

"I think they're fake," she replied. "I heard that the real coronation was this morning in the palace and only a few very important dignitaries were invited. This was just a celebration for the rest of us."

"You mean this was just a show for foreigners?" I asked, looking around at all the glittering people gathered under the tents.

"Yes, and I suppose for the people of Kathmandu, so they would feel it was for the public."

"By having it in a cow field? That seems a bit much."

My neighbor shrugged noncommittally, and I readjusted my chair, which had begun to sink again into the mud.

I'd come to a coronation, and I had ended up at—what, exactly?

After the ceremony finally ended, I ran into the Vietors as we all emerged from the tent. They greeted me delightedly as if there had been no difficulties or misunderstandings at all, and they asked me to join them for lunch. We made our way on foot to the Palace Hotel, where we sat in the sun in the courtyard drinking Bloody Marys. Perhaps twenty or so people were gathered around a long table. Our jewels sparkled in the sun, and the men in tails reminded me of an illustration from the cover of *The New Yorker*.

Apparently, none of us were invited to any more coronation "dos," for at one end of the table, Peggy D'uzes—at one time, society's leading debutante and by then a duchess—announced, "I'm giving a party tonight. I've taken over the Yak and Yeti. And there'll be a *band*."

"How did Peggy get a band here?" I whispered to the man to my right, the maharaja of Jaipurh. "That's rather incredible, isn't it?"

"Imelda Marcos flew it in with a bunch of her friends," he answered, laughing. "Sounds like quite a party, knowing Peggy. Have you been to the Yak and Yeti?"

"Actually, I went ages ago," I replied. "It was really tumbled down back then, but it was fun. I think the rooms had been converted from a stable!"

Just then, huge silver trays of curried chicken arrived. The maharaja turned to the lady on his right, and I to the Burmese ambassador on my left.

The Yak and Yeti had become *the* bar and restaurant in Kathmandu since last I'd visited. Imelda Marcos arrived with a planeload of jet-setters and the band. We sat at long tables decorated with candles and flowers and silk saris for tablecloths, and we drank toasts to everyone we could think of. I danced all night, twice with the king of Sikkim. When the party ended at three in the morning, I joined a small band of night owls for "just one more" drink at the Palace Hotel.

I don't recall much of the rest of the day—except that the Vietors invited me to accompany them to a party later that night on the outskirts of Kathmandu, where the owner of Tiger Tops had his "town house." I cleaned the mud off my gold sandals and decked myself out in a leopard printed chiffon caftan. I arrived with Jack and Lita but lost them at some point during the evening. As the party drew to a close, I realized I couldn't recognize a single familiar face among the dwindling crowd of guests. I made my way outside, where I accosted a plump ambassador-type just as his car drove up.

"How do you suppose I can get back to town?" I asked, with just a hint—I hoped—that an offer of a lift would be most welcome.

"Oh, just grab a cab," he replied, with a dismissive wave as he jumped into his car and was driven away.

Of course, there *were* no cabs to be grabbed this far from the center of town.

I set out on a long, dark, and chilly stroll, alone at the hour of the wolf. In my chiffon caftan, sparkling with jewelry, I tottered down deserted, unlit streets, past ragged shacks and piles of refuse. Lost, unable to speak the language, I wandered toward the dim and distant lights of Kathmandu. The cold night air—and the fear of being accosted by street toughs—sobered me up pretty quickly, and I began to have a bit of a think.

What was I doing here? Escaping my marriage? Playing the part of the carefree jet-setter? Chasing adventure for the sake of … adventure? Whatever veneer of self-confidence I'd achieved as an adult began to crumble. The "stiff upper lip" that WASPs cultivate started to slip.

I was hungry for something, but I wasn't sure what.

My world had been rather out of balance most of my life. I was always looking for an elusive combination of family, home, community, and *raison d'etre*. I looked for it in love, in work, and in society. My childhood had prepared me for a party, for "keeping my end up" in a conversation, and for traveling. But growing up with always *en voyage* parents—who had given away my beloved dog and sent away my beloved nanny—had caused me to shut my heart against the threat of any pain that comes with the exchange of love. I was looking, without really knowing it, for a way to find connection that wouldn't hurt so much. I lived, without admitting it, in a deep depression, which I stuffed down with food and alcohol. It was those very obstacles of loneliness and the need to find meaning that eventually sent me on a life quest. The illusion that I could escape them was over. I longed to belong—a feeling that, years later, my friend Brother David Steindl Rast, would tell me was a "longing for God."

Now what? I wondered. I was tired of thinking, tired of planning, tired of running. But was I running away from something or toward something?

I woke late the next morning, hungover and my feet aching from the long walk home in high-heeled sandals. I tried to figure out what my next move might be. I remembered that my friend Harold, who had arranged for my stay here, had given me the telephone number of an acquaintance of his, a woman named Jane, who was staying at a little trekker's lodge in Kathmandu. I slapped some water and cream on my face and put on some red floppy pants, an Indian shirt, and a straw hat. I gave her a call and made arrangements to meet her at the lodge for lunch.

The place was called Tashi Delek, which means "good luck" in Tibetan. It was owned by Tibetan brothers who sold the rugs that had been piled to make seats around the low, rough-hewn wooden tables in the tiny restaurant on the ground floor of the lodge. Jane, an attractive woman with reddish-blond hair and green eyes, greeted me as though we were old friends, and led me to a table where she introduced me to her companion, a slight young Vietnamese man named Nian. He merely nodded and muttered something that may have been a greeting. As Jane settled next to him at the table, I deduced from their body language that they were more than just companions.

Jane and I chatted for a while and discovered that, in addition to Harold, we knew many of the same people. Though we'd traveled in more or less the same circles, it seemed odd that we'd never previously met. When I mentioned this, Jane replied cheerily, "Well, things happen in Kathmandu."

"I couldn't agree more," I said—and then I regaled her with a decidedly insouciant account of my misadventures since my arrival. Despite my attempt at breezy nonchalance, Jane picked up on my melancholy undertone. Tilting her head quizzically, she said, "You know, I'm setting off on a kind of pilgrimage in a few days."

"Oh?"

I remembered Harold telling me that Jane was a dedicated practitioner of Tibetan Buddhism.

"Yes," she continued. "I'm going to visit my teacher, Tulsi Rinpoche, at his monastery. I'm taking Nian to see him, and then I'm staying on to start my *ngöndro.*"

"Oh, Harold goes to someone in England to practice his," I said.

"It basically means preliminaries," Jane explained. "They're practices you do before moving on to more advanced meditation techniques. We start with a hundred thousand full-body prostrations."

"Yes, I remember Harold struggling though that."

"Oh, don't worry," Jane interrupted. "I'm not saying *you'd* have to do them. But I was thinking, why don't you at least come to visit the monastery and meet Rinpoche? I think you'd find it an interesting adventure, to say the least. I'll be staying on, but you can come back with Nian."

She didn't have to try hard to convince me. The point was to let this trip change my life. Anyway, I didn't have anything else to do.

"Absolutely, yes!" I said. "That sounds wonderful."

Over Tibetan noodle soup and beer, Jane laid out the basic plan of the trip. First, we'd take a flight to the Himalayan foothills and from there hike up the mountains for a couple of days to reach the monastery, stopping overnight at a village along the way.

"It's pretty cold up there, so you'd better have some warm clothes … and shoes for hiking. The trails are rough."

"Fine," I said. "I can do that."

As the lunch drew to an end, I was exultant. I didn't have to plan or plot my next move. Some other force or destiny had taken over—which was fine by me, as I wasn't doing so well on my own.

The only uncomfortable aspect of the afternoon was the utter unresponsiveness of Jane's friend Nian. Maybe he didn't want a third party along on the trip. Or more likely, I hoped, he simply wasn't fluent enough in English to follow our conversation.

I'd come to Kathmandu prepared for a party, but here I was going on a pilgrimage. *Perfect!* I thought.

After lunch I wandered through the Boudhanath district, which is dominated by one of the largest Buddhist *stupas* in the world. The stupa is surrounded by Tibetan Buddhist monasteries, small stores, stalls, restaurants, hostels, and guest houses. As I wandered through the bazaar, I found a pair of five-dollar sneakers and a yak-wool jacket in a little stall. None of the hiking slacks I looked at fit comfortably, and in the end I decided I would wear the pants I'd packed for "elegant lunches."

Since I'd worn out my welcome from the moment I'd arrived at the Buddhist scholar's house, I loaded my belongings into a taxi and moved into the Tashi Delek. My little room with a fireplace and overlooking the garden cost the equivalent of seven dollars a night. I felt deeply relaxed for the first time since I'd arrived in Kathmandu, suddenly free of the need to make plans, afloat on a river I could rest upon without thrashing.

Two days later, Jane, Nian, and I boarded a tiny plane, piloted by a dark-haired, wiry bush pilot named Peter, who had been hired to carry supplies to Sir Edmund Hillary for a hospital he was building in the Himalayan foothills. During the flight, Peter complained that he found life in Nepal too dull; he missed the good times back in Borneo in the sixties, when he'd sat in an armored cockpit and dropped munitions to the communist revolutionaries while fighters on the other side took potshots at him. We plunged and spiraled over icy chasms, but I was less concerned about our safety than about Nian, whose silence had begun to take a sulky turn.

A jeep was waiting for us at the landing strip, and as soon as the supplies had been unloaded, Peter took off again, dipping his wings before quickly becoming a dot in the blue infinity between two peaks. Sir Edmund met us at the edge of a small camp of tents set up on a hillside near the partially completed hospital. He was an angular pillar of charm, who greeted us like old friends, crinkling his bright blue eyes.

"You can set up in there for the night," he told Jane and me, pointing to a small blue nylon tent fitted with tiny twin cots. "Nian, I hope you won't mind bunking in with the Sherpas, as we don't have another spare tent."

12

Nian exchanged an unreadable glance with Jane, and then he clumped off behind one of the sturdy, impassive Sherpas who had appeared when we arrived.

"Please join me at six in my tent," Sir Edmund urged us. "It's right over there." He pointed to a khaki tent a few feet away. Before heading off, he instructed another of the Sherpas to bring us hot water to wash.

As dusk fell, we gathered in his tent, which was just big enough for a card table and four folding chairs. In the glare of a Coleman lantern and enveloped by the fragrance of wet wool and campfire smoke, we shared warm gin poured from an old plastic face lotion bottle that Jane had brought. Over a dinner of rice and lentils, Sir Edmund spoke about the plight of the rural Nepalese.

"These are wonderful people up here in the mountains," he said, "but the government hasn't provided for them. I don't think it even occurs to the people to ask for assistance. These mountains breed strong, independent men and women—so brave, self- sufficient, and uncomplaining. This far from Kathmandu, they don't have any access to professional medical treatment. They just manage their hurts and sicknesses as best they can. So many die who wouldn't in a town with doctors and hospitals. The children are especially vulnerable. They need a hospital desperately, so I'm building one right here."

"With whom and what?" I wondered aloud. He was, after all, living in a tent among the bare mountains with a handful of Sherpas.

"Peter brings me supplies in his plane every few days," Sir Edmund explained. "And I pay the people in the villages near here to help build. They'll be the ones using it." His voice had an almost wistful note as he continued, "This country has brought me more than I could ever repay. I want to try to give something back."

As I listened, I was struck by the contrast between the glittering swirl of events surrounding the coronation and the path Sir Edmund had chosen. The cost of the private jet that had carried a load of socialites to Kathmandu could, on its own, have built a couple of hospitals. Yet I was part of that glamorous world—a world of pleasure for its own sake, a world in which donating a tiny percentage of one's income made the donor feel almost holy. I had no right to judge.

I noted that Nian hadn't paid any attention to the conversation but sat like a grim lump eating his lentils. Sir Edmund didn't seem any more taken with him than I was, but he managed to overlook his presence without seeming rude.

Full of gin and good conversation, Jane and I sank into the small cots in our tent.

The next day dawned clear and cold. After a breakfast of coffee, eggs, and *chapatis*, we set out in the company of two Sherpas from Sir Edmund's camp, who would serve as guides on our trek up to the monastery. For the first leg of our journey, the hills were a riot of wild rhododendrons, filling the mountainsides with bushes of bright red flowers. As we made our way to the foothills, our path ran by a stream that sauntered down from the high peaks. At each mountain pass we encountered piles of "mani stones"—rocks carved or painted with the letters of the Tibetan Buddhist mantra of compassion, *Om Mani Padme Hung*—to mark the way for pilgrims; frequently, we came upon tiny stupas, too small to enter, but which Jane said were filled with sacred texts and objects.

The path grew ever steeper as we passed through numerous small villages for which this narrow earthen way served as the main thoroughfare. Twice, women emerged from their huts and encouraged us to buy huge turquoises and coral beads strung together in rough necklaces and headpieces. I thought they were gorgeous, and the prices the women asked were absurdly low.

"Shall we buy some?" I asked Jane.

"No," she said. "They sell them too cheaply. We'd be virtually stealing their worldly goods."

I thought of the shops in Kathmandu that would sell such heirlooms for fortunes these women would never see—and of the vast spiritual gulf between these hill people praying at their stupas and working hard for their *chappatis*, and the relatively well-off dealers in the valley below. I felt guilty for even buying these baubles, although occasionally I had.

And just as Sir Edmund's conversation the night before had made me see things in a new light, I knew I was on the right path—though actually I wanted both baubles and Buddhism.

As we continued along the winding path up the mountain, we passed villagers swinging prayer wheels and others winnowing small fields of wheat. Jane and I hiked along chatting and lamenting the fact that we hadn't thought to bring any food or water with us. Finally, I gave into temptation and drank from a stream that looked innocently clear. I'd been warned about parasites and hoped I wouldn't end up getting sick.

Nian, meanwhile, clumped on ahead of the Sherpas. His continued silence was unfriendly.

As the afternoon wore on and the light began to fade, one of the Sherpas shouted, "Jumla! Stop! Jumla!"

Apparently, we had arrived at the place where we were to spend the night—the village of Jumla, which consisted of seven small huts. I was grateful to stop for the day. I was exhausted, entirely unprepared for hiking in the Himalayas in my sneakers and suede pants.

Our guides led us into the hut of a Nepali man. In the front room were two small bunk-like beds where Jane and I would sleep. A pile of rugs would serve for Nian, and the Sherpas would sleep on the bare floor. After a dinner of fried eggs, *chapattis,* and tea, I crawled gratefully into bed. As I drifted off to sleep, I heard Nian and Jane talking outside the house and wondered why in the world they weren't as tired as I was.

A shrill scream woke me in the middle of the night. In the glint of my flashlight I caught a glimpse of Nian wielding a huge knife over Jane, who was cowering in her bed. I quivered in my own bunk, sick with terror and nauseated from the water I had drunk straight out of the mountain stream. One of the Sherpas leapt from the floor and grabbed Nian's arms while the other gripped his legs; together, they threw him to the floor and held him until the owner of the house appeared from the back room rubbing his eyes. He took in the situation and hastily produced a rope with which to tie Nian up before the Sherpas dragged him outside, where they kept a watchful eye on him through the rest of the night.

What I'd thought would be a healing spiritual pilgrimage had turned into a murderous nightmare. I felt overwhelmed. What should I do? What *could* I do? Hike back down the mountain on my own? Find some way back to Kathmandu, where I could get on the first and fastest flight I could find back to the States? And then what? Get divorced? I felt tears rolling down my cheeks and my throat closing as panic gripped me.

As the hours till daylight passed, my thoughts cleared a little bit and I remembered reading something by Joseph Campbell: that we're each on a hero's journey and there were always obstacles to such deep explorations. I didn't feel like much of a hero, choking back tears, shivering with cold and fear, and sick to my stomach; but I'd certainly met some obstacles. And since, realistically, there was no way I could make the journey back down the mountain on my own, there wasn't much choice except to move forward. This idea was cold comfort, and not especially inspiring, but it was at least a plan.

The next morning, the Jumla village chief confined Nian in one of the seven houses. Jane and I, exhausted from an almost sleepless night, nibbled at a breakfast of *chapattis* and tea before setting out on our trek up the mountain. Jane was silent and depressed, not in the mood to explain what had happened, although, of course, I was aching with curiosity. After an hour or so of going on this way, it occurred to me that Jane might open up a bit about her life if I explained a little about mine.

"You know, I came on this trip to decide whether or not to leave my husband. I'm absolutely certain now that that's what I need to do. I'm not really sure if that's because anything special happened. It's more a combination of everything."

"Yes?" Jane replied absently.

Obviously, she was still thinking about her own problems. But I forged ahead anyway.

"I came for the coronation and a party—whereas in fact none of us could actually see the event, and the parties afterward just forced me to see that my life is lonely and without a center. Not only because of my marriage, which just makes it worse, but because I don't really like who I am. Or maybe I don't like how I'm living my life. Anyway, there's something wrong with the picture.

"Now I'm on a pilgrimage with you. Actually, ever since I met you, things have seemed to be moving in the right direction. I don't even know what's going to happen next. Last night I was so frightened, I seriously considered going back. But here I am because I think we are somehow on a better track."

Jane nodded but didn't reply. I thought perhaps I'd said enough and walked in silence behind her.

Here and there on the trail we passed maroon-robed monks swinging prayer wheels or bent under baskets filled with brush piled as high as they were tall. They shuffled along chanting mantras in a deep singsong growl. The path wound along the side of a steep hill, and across the valley the blue waves of the foothills rose into foaming crests. In the distance were the snow-capped peaks of the high Himalayas. The air, so clear it felt like sharp crystals in the lungs, had grown colder as we ascended the hills. The few scraggly trees that dotted the landscape explained the monks' need to gather brush for firewood.

The final stage of the ascent was extremely steep, but at its summit stood the great white wall surrounding Thubten Chöling, one of the largest monasteries in Nepal. We could see, above the wall, an island of red roofs that formed the monastery compound, festooned with prayer flags whipping against the crisp blue Himalayan sky. As we approached, the rushing wind echoed around the walls, almost drowning out the wisps of chanting from within.

An elderly monk with a wizened face unlocked a huge and ancient padlock that held a formidable chain binding a massive iron gate. I wondered how many donkeys or porters had collapsed transporting that gate up the mountains. The main building that housed the shrine room stood in the center of a carefully swept earthen courtyard. It was surrounded by long, narrow white buildings with shuttered windows and low dark doorways: dormitories for the monks, Jane explained.

A young maroon-swathed monk led Jane and me to our quarters—a solitary structure with a small room beneath the eaves, which we could reach only by climbing a long, nearly vertical ladder. It was lit and warmed by a metal brazier set in the middle of the room. Faded red Tibetan carpets covered the floor, while smaller carpets had been piled five or six deep along the wall to serve as our beds. From the small window, we could make out the snowy Himalayan peaks reflecting the pink of the setting sun. Slowly the peaks faded to gray, the sky grew dark, and thousands of stars emerged. With no reflected urban lights to dim the view, the universe was transformed into solid glitter, stretching out like a sea of phosphorescence. Unfortunately, the cold night wind forced us to close the shutters.

As we settled in, Jane dug out the lotion bottle from her knapsack. After a few nips of moisturizer-flavored gin, she finally spoke up about Nian.

"I was really attracted to him when I first met him," she explained. "I liked his silence. I thought he was polite and strong. It took a while for me to realize that it was really a sign that he was emotionally disturbed." She sighed. "I'd hoped Tulsi Rinpoche could help him, but I guess that wasn't his destiny."

Her confession was interrupted by a rap on the door. The young monk who'd led us to our room entered bearing a large tray. I wondered how he'd managed to climb up that ladder and tried to visualize him, clad in long heavy robes, holding the tray in one hand and letting go of each rung to grasp the next as he made that long, steep ascent to our room. We dined on lentil soup and boiled potatoes in their jackets with coarse brown salt and salty Tibetan tea. I was so hungry that this simple dinner gave me more satisfaction than all the champagne and caviar I'd had in Kathmandu.

Jane's assessment of Nian made me think about my husband, Richard, and his occasional rages and odd behavior. I'd been violently physically attracted to him when we first met, and I was titillated by the idea of being with an older man and by his rough sexiness. Had I taken the time to get to know him better instead of rushing into marriage, I might have recognized his temper and how different our worlds and expectations were. But rushing had been more or less a way of life for me, and I hadn't figured out what I'd gotten myself into until it was too late.

Seeing Jane confront her dilemma, I realized how desperately I wanted my freedom. I was absolutely determined not to go back to Richard.

Exhausted from our trek and all the emotions that had come up along the way, we fell asleep, despite the howling of the black mastiffs that guarded the monastery. One of these monsters was fastened by a heavy chain to his huge spiked collar near the bottom of the ladder to our room. Unfortunately, during the night I had to pee; but given a choice between being crushed in the dog's huge jaws and waiting till dawn, I elected to hang out from the ladder and dampen the dust below. *This must be how birds feel*, I thought, hanging tightly to the ladder. I crawled back beneath the welcoming warm rugs and drifted off to sleep.

Maybe it was the incense of the brazier's wood smoke, or the uncanny atmosphere of the minds and spirits of so many monks pressing themselves toward another level of reality, that seduced a delightful dream my way. In it, I was surrounded by the most beautiful music imaginable: a great symphony and, at the same time, a charming melody. A man, a woman, and a child stood at the door of a flower shop waving good-bye as I danced down a cobbled street to the music that surged around and through me. I felt as though I was dancing in tune with life, finding a chord in the music of the universe that felt right for me.

The dream brought me a profound feeling of happiness and belonging, and I sank back on a cushion of peace in the middle of the jagged journey of being thirty-four and wishing I knew what my life was really about. In the atmosphere of the monastery I felt connected to some ancient, profound truths about the meaning of life, though I couldn't articulate them. All I knew was that I hadn't planned to come here, and now it felt right that I had. I didn't know why. I didn't know yet that I was looking for a home in myself, a place to rest my head and relax.

The next morning as we sipped our salty tea for breakfast, I told Jane about my dream. "Maybe I was seeing a past life," I suggested.

"I don't know," Jane replied. "What's important is that you had it here, in this monastery. I think it means you have a connection to Tibetan Buddhism. Here," she added, "have a potato."

I had three, dipped in the coarse Tibetan salt.

When the young monk who had been assigned to attend us came to take our breakfast tray, he told us we had an appointment to see Tulsi Rinpoche at ten thirty. For this audience, Jane had brought white silk scarves, called *katas*, which she explained were traditionally offered to a teacher as a sign of respect. At the appointed time, the monk led us into the red-lacquered shrine room, and Jane and I bowed and presented our *katas*.

Tulsi Rinpoche indicated we should sit on two of the round cushions on the floor in front of him. Wrapped in burgundy robes, he sat on a pile of silk cushions beside a low table covered with silver bowls, brass bells, a ritual dagger, a china teacup with a lid, and—curiously—a Swiss army knife. Around his knees played two black-and-white Lhasa apsos, which he occasionally fed bits of sweet flaky pastries called *kapse*. Behind him was an altar, topped with glass cases filled with Tibetan texts wrapped in yellow-and-orange silk; a tall brocade throne stood to the side. The altar itself was draped with *katas* and lined with statues of the Buddha wrapped in white silk, as well as offerings of colored rice and butter sculpted in spherical and pyramidal shapes.

"It's so cold up here the butter sculptures last for weeks," Jane whispered.

Rinpoche welcomed us through another young monk who served as a translator and offered us tea. He gazed at us quizzically but said nothing further.

As this was my first experience of meeting a lama, I wasn't prepared for the feeling of being ill at ease with someone who appeared to feel no need whatsoever to make polite conversation. I'd been brought up with the notion that one should *chat* at tea, and I squirmed inwardly, trying to formulate some pithy spiritual question. Nothing came. Jane merely sat with her eyes half-closed, looking completely blissed out, while Rinpoche and the translator noisily sipped their tea.

After an agonizing few moments, Jane finally leaned over to say that "Rinpoche" was the respectful way to address her teacher, which I took as my cue to say something.

The translator looked at me expectantly.

I smiled hopefully and said—to my surprise—that I wanted to study Buddhism.

What else could I say? I really didn't know if I wanted to study Buddhism. I just knew I had to say something.

Rinpoche nodded calmly and produced two red strings, which he tied around our necks. Out of a small cloth bag he took some red pills and something that looked like coffee grains, which the translator slowly and deliberately wrapped in small paper wrappers before handing them to us.

"Ground lama bones," Jane whispered.

"The red pills are for mental ills," the translator explained, "and the grains for physical ones."

Rinpoche also presented us each with an ancient Tibetan coin and then indicated through the translator that the interview was over. As we rose to leave, he suddenly asked if I would take a sack of *tsampa*—roasted barley flour, a staple of the Tibetan diet—to his friend Dudjom Rinpoche when I returned to Kathmandu.

After we left the shrine room Jane explained that *tsampa* from this monastery was "stronger" than that found in the valley. I had absolutely no idea what she meant. I was much more intrigued by her suggestion that, for some reason, Tulsi Rinpoche must want me to meet Dudjom Rinpoche. An odd tingling sensation crept over me when I heard that. I hadn't necessarily felt a strong response to meeting her teacher or that my life had suddenly changed, but I knew somehow that some sort of connection was being made, that I was in the right place at the right time.

Over the next two days, the Sherpas and I hiked back down the mountain to Sir Edmund Hillary's camp. I was astonished to find that

21

Peter arrived with more supplies at exactly the right moment to fly me to Kathmandu in time for lunch. *Are these people psychic or what?* I wondered. They certainly weren't in radio contact. How did they know when I'd return to the camp—or was it just coincidence? But then, ever since I'd met Jane, my trip had begun to feel like one grand series of coincidences.

Back in Kathmandu, I spent the following morning in Boudhanath, site of the famous stupa with the big eyes looking in all four directions that one sees on Nepalese postcards. It is just outside of Kathmandu near Pashnuparti, where the dead are cremated or their bodies are sent floating down the Bagmati River. Boudhanath was a little village, with the main stupa surrounded by large monasteries of different Tibetan traditions. At the foot of the stupa were little street stalls selling Tibetan jewelry, religious objects, brocade Tibetan coats, and sweaters of oily yak's wool like the one I had bought for our hike. I climbed up to the highest platform surrounding the dome of the giant stupa. Strings of huge, brightly colored prayer flags flapped in the wind. The whole Kathmandu valley was spread out before me, and as I gazed out over it I experienced a great wave of freedom and happiness, as though something heavy had been lifted. I felt ready to embrace the future, suddenly looking forward to whatever was ahead.

In the afternoon, I visited Dudjom Rinpoche to deliver his tsampa. He was, at that time, the head of the Nyingma lineage, the oldest of the four main schools of Tibetan Buddhism. To my surprise, he lived in a simple white cottage with a small lawn of dry grass out front. A monk in maroon robes answered the bell and led me into a bare white room covered with red-and-blue Tibetan carpets, where Dudjom Rinpoche sat on a large pile of silk cushions. We both bowed with respect, and then I settled onto a smaller pile of cushions. A low table stood between us, on which were laid out a bell, a *dorje*—a ritual object symbolizing "the thunderbolt of enlightenment"—two texts wrapped in yellow silk, and two cups of tea. Rinpoche was wearing dark glasses, which he took off after a few minutes but shortly put on again.

There was no problem with teatime conversation here. To my immeasurable relief, Rinpoche began chatting right away, proceeding without any preliminary to tell me the whole history of the Boudhanath stupa. When I asked him how he knew I'd just been there, he merely smiled. We talked of Buddhism, Tulsi Rinpoche, the Thubten Chöling monastery, and other things I can't remember—because something else was happening. I was sinking into the glorious feeling of what I would later learn Tibetans call "being in the great oceanic presence": a profound and spacious sense of peace that can arise when one encounters a great lama or some other highly evolved spiritual being.

As I basked in this feeling, I found myself able to look back on my time in Nepal with greater clarity. In dealing with suffering, there is always a choice: I could run, escape to a party or some other diversion, or embrace the pain as an invitation to begin a journey toward a whole new perspective. It occurred to me, too, that although I hadn't *really* been invited to the coronation and its attendant festivities, I'd felt welcomed by my friends (some of whom had crashed it, too!). I'd felt welcomed at the monastery. And when I'd met Jane at the Good Luck Hotel, my life had really begun to change.

Good luck, indeed!

A warm serenity suffused my being as I sat with Dudjom Rinpoche. The entire world seemed to rest in perfect balance.

It hadn't always been so.

PHOTOS

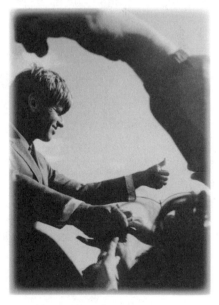

Scarlett O'Hara Lives Again In Carolina

NEW YORK—Good-looking Bokara (Bobo) Legendre, the snappy society girl to end all snappy society girls, will take the plunge in mid-May—date to be announced. Bobo has been popular with the boys since, oh, before boarding school, the cute thing.

She met her fiance, Dick Mack, for the first time when she was 10, and Dick and his first wife (he's had two) were off on an expedition to Nepal for the National Geographic with Bobo's mother, Mrs. Sidney Legendre. Legend has it Bobo was wearing a pinafore at the time.

Born on Medway Plantation, one of the largest in South Carolina, and reared in the traditions of a Southern belle (her mother Gertrude, is the daughter of the late multimillionaire carpet manufacturer John Sanford; her late father was a member of one of the most aristocratic families of the Old South), Bobo started writing articles before she was even out of Foxcroft, and is still scribbling away. She has always been politically and intellectually involved — traveling with the Bobby Kennedy entourage and things like that. Her friends just adore to have her run on in her Southern drawl. Sounds just as if Talulah B a n k h e a d wrote the script, really it does.

Suzy

Plans for the wedding sound dreamy. It will be Scarlett O'Hara all the way, with Bobo (or Miss Bokara, as the servants still call her) wearing one of her great-grandmothers (either maternal or paternal, she has both to choose from) lovely costumes which have been carefully preserved in attic trunks and a floppy hat wreathed in field flowers.

The ceremony will take place in the garden at Medway beneath the wisteria and the magnolias. Guests will roam the plantation's 8,000 rolling acres of manicured gardens, private lakes, bridle paths, paddocks and pastures and will be put up in the guest cottages that dot the estate.

The main house—the oldest in the state and built a hundred years before the Civil War—will be turned into a virtual flower bower. Despite all the gorgeous preparations, Bobo says it will be a teeny-tiny en famille reception with her uncle and aunt, the Stephen Sanfords, flying up from Palm Beach and a few brain trust pals of the groom, like William F. Buckley Jr., flying down from New York. After the ceremony, the Macks will honeymoon in the Soviet Union (it's the only place, really) and then will return to the barefoot, blue-jean life at Big Sur in California, where Dick has built a dream house.

Dick, a Yale graduate, has been a member in good standing in the society of achievement almost since college and is currently producing high-level films in cooperation with an Iron Curtain country. Co-author of the Whole Earth Catalogue, he is also an inventor and holds 24 patents. He is also president of an architectural and environmental design company and the head of Peregrine Films Publications—not to mention Himalaya Industries, which has to do with mountain-climbing equipment, what else?

This romance really got off the ground (never mind the initial encounter at Medway with our leading lady sucking a lollipop or whatever) when Bobo went to California on a magazine assignment and rediscovered the Prince Charming of her childhood dreams shooting serious documentaries at Big Sur. May they live happily ever after.

Monterey Peninsula Herald Saturday, May 1, 1971.
Peninsula Notebook

Romantic Plans For Richard Mack

Next Sunday, in the lush setting of a South Carolina plantation, Richard Gerstle Mack and Bokara Hennan Legendre of New York City will be married. Dick is the son of Col. and Mrs. Harold Mack of Carmel, and Bokara is the daughter of Mrs. Sidney Legendre of Medway Plantation, S.C., near Charleston.

The bride will wear her great-grandmother's wedding gown and a floppy-brimmed hat wreathed in field flowers for the ceremony, which will take place in the plantation's 200-year-old main house — the oldest in South Carolina — surrounded by 8,000 rolling acres of manicured gardens, private lakes, bridle paths, paddocks and pastures, with some 20 guest cottages sprinkled around the acreage.

Dick has a 15-year-old son, Jeffrey, who has been living here the past year while attending Carmel High School. Jeffrey is in New York now with his father and will accompany him to South Carolina for the wedding.

Dick's mother will leave Carmel Thursday for South Carolina, and she and Jeffrey and the newlyweds plan to return here together soon after the wedding. The couple will live in Dick's Garrapata Creek home down the Coast, which Bokara says she is eager to get busy "fixing up" right away.

The bride-to-be, whose late father is a member of one of the aristocratic families of the Old South, attended Foxcroft School in Virginia and is a free-lance writer for several New York area newspapers and publications. She worked for a time as a writer traveling with the late Sen. Robert Kennedy's campaign entourage. She was on the Monterey Peninsula for a visit about a month ago, and the senior Macks say they are "charmed and delighted" about the wedding.

Bokara was in pigtails when Dick first met her in 1949, when her mother was a member of a scientific exploration trip to Nepal headed by Dick, who has traveled and explored in many parts of the world and was with the first party of Caucasians to see the south face of Mount Everest. His bride will accompany him on his next journey, to Siberia to look for saber-toothed tigers for the Smithsonian Institution and National Geographic Society.

Dick attended Yale and until last year was associated with Himalayan Industries on Cannery Row, which was sold to The Leisure Group Inc. This is the first marriage for his 30-year-old-bride-to-be, and his third. His first wife, Linn, Jeffrey's mother, is now Mrs. Edward Bayne. She lives in Rome with her husband, who is associated with the American Field Service there. Linn was in Carmel just before Christmas for a visit with Jeffrey while her husband was on an AFS tour.

Dick was divorced 16 months ago from his second wife, the former Jinx McLucas Baldwin, who now lives in Hawaii.

William F. Buckley Jr., the conservative editor, writer and TV personality, and a friend of Dick's, will be flying from New York to the plantation with his wife to attend the wedding.

CHAPTER

In the Beginning

When my father died, it made me feel important because everyone in the family suddenly noticed me. Before then, I had felt pretty much invisible.

It was March 8, 1948. I was seven years old and living in Aiken, South Carolina, with my governess, Mamie. The telephone rang, and as Mamie listened to the voice on the other end, two tears ran down her wrinkled face. After putting down the receiver, she turned to me and gently said, "Your father died of a heart attack this morning, Bo. He was a wonderful man."

I looked at her blankly. I didn't feel anything. To me, my father was practically a stranger. All I could remember of him were the maroon velvet sleeves of his dinner jacket, which appeared at my eye level when I approached his chair to say good-night on the occasions I was invited to visit my parents at their home at Medway plantation. If I tried, I could summon up an image of him from his portrait by the English painter Simon Elwes, which hung in the dining room at Medway. In it, he wore a loose shooting jacket over a blue turtleneck sweater and carried a gun on his left shoulder. His hair was black and curly. He had a strong jaw and brown eyes that looked kind.

"That's one of them gone," I said, shrugging. "They never liked me, but of the two of them, I wish it had been Mummy. Daddy seemed nicer."

I'm not sure why I felt that way, since I'd never spent an entire day together with him in my life. In fact, my parents lived in a world I could hardly imagine: a glamorous round of travel, parties, shooting, tennis, and friends. Watching their lives was like looking at a movie in installments—most of which I never saw.

My mother, Gertrude Sanford Legendre, was a socialite turned Great White Hunter. At eighteen she killed her first elk in the Grand Tetons with a bullet through the heart, and her passion for hunting game continued for the rest of her life. It was her way of connecting to nature. Everyone called her Gertie, a nickname that suited her impetuous nature and ferocious energy. My sister and I, in typical WASP fashion, called her Mummy.

She was born in 1902 in Aiken, South Carolina, which at the time was a rural village lined with a few sandy roads. Her father was a tough businessman who owned the Sanford-Bigelow Carpet Mills in Amsterdam, New York. He was passionately devoted to his stables, buying and breeding racehorses and polo ponies. He wintered them in Aiken, where during the twenties and thirties, a life sprung up that revolved around horses, hounds, hunting, golf, and parties. Then he brought them north for the summer to a stud farm in Saratoga Springs, not far from the racetrack and near the family's main residence in Amsterdam.

The family also had a New York town house on East 72nd Street, which was later transformed into the Lycée Francaise. During her late teens and early twenties, Mummy spent most of her time there with her sister Jane and their brother Stephen, whom everyone called Laddie. Mummy and Aunt Jane were chauffeured about town in a Rolls Royce, and Lars, the butler, bought theater tickets every day, which he placed on the hall table just in case one of members of the household might feel a spur-of-the-moment mood to see a play or a musical.

Once a week in the ballroom on the second floor of the town

house, Mummy, Aunt Jane, and Uncle Laddie threw a party they called Businessmen's Night, which ended at midnight so those who did have to go to the office the next morning would not be too tired. On other nights, when the family wasn't at the opera or the theater, the parties often went on until just before dawn. The Sanfords' glamorous life in their New York house was the inspiration for *Holiday*, a play by Philip Barry that later became a film starring Katharine Hepburn (whose role was based on Mummy) and Cary Grant.

Later in life, Mummy would say that in spite of her privileged upbringing she often felt trapped—a feeling that may be partly attributed to the stifling atmosphere created by her estranged parents; for at some point during their marriage, my grandparents simply stopped speaking to each other and instead communicated by sending notes back and forth on their private elevator in the72nd Street town house.

The larger factor was probably that she and her family were worlds apart in terms of their interests. Although Mummy delighted in the social whirl of the 1920s, her deepest pleasure came from being out on the range with a horse and a gun or freezing in a duck blind as the sun rose to get the first crack at the great *V* of black ducks descending over the marsh. It probably didn't help matters much that my grandfather clearly favored Laddie over his two daughters and showered him with largesse.

The whole family spent their summers in Europe so my grandfather could watch Laddie play polo. In 1928, they stayed in Osterly Park outside of London, which had lawns so expansive and well manicured that servants were obliged to move the lines for the grass tennis court every night to a fresh patch of lawn. Every morning, guests had to hunt to find the relocated courts.

Mummy and her siblings clowned around the Riviera with the Marx Brothers and the Philip Barrys. Judging from photo albums from that period, they spent a lot of time finding just the right gypsy flounces or Arab ragtops for costume parties. Mummy *adored* costume parties and threw some legendary ones. In one photograph from this period, she and a group of her contemporaries—ambassadors and doyens of society—were dressed as babies carrying rattles and wearing bonnets. Even "Chip" Bohlen, our ambassador to Russia, was dressed as a baby!

One weekend during that summer, two brothers from New Orleans were invited for a weekend of tennis. Sidney Legendre had dark hair and brown eyes; his brother Morris was sandy-haired, with fair skin and blue eyes. The brothers were inseparable: Morris, a Rhodes scholar, had delayed his studies at Princeton so he could graduate with Sidney. Everyone who knew Sidney said he was charming, handsome, and a good listener. He and Morris shared a killing sense of humor, though, and Mummy was smitten by them both. Ultimately, Mummy chose Sidney.

She had managed to persuade her father to give her thirty thousand dollars to help fund a hunting expedition to Abyssinia (now Ethiopia), organized by the American Museum of Natural History. Mummy invited Sidney and Morris to join her on the expedition, which was set for the winter months of 1928. It was a rare invitation by a woman, which was considered especially forward at that time. Mummy, Sidney, and Morris would hunt, and the museum provided mammalogists, skinners and taxidermists, and artists to provide detailed drawings of native wildlife habitats.

That expedition was the first of many for my parents. They were royally received in Abyssinia by Emperor Haile Selassie, who threw a lavish party and presented them with an elaborately appareled mule. It was considered such an honor that the mule remained clad in his beautiful costume throughout the entire expedition and was never burdened with a single thing. This was done although pack animals were sorely needed, considering all the tents, guns, food, liquor, and camp furniture to be transported. In return, Mummy presented the emperor with a white polar bear skin rug.

Toward the end of the expedition, it became clear that *someone* would have to travel ahead of the others to Addis Ababa, the capital, to arrange for shipping the skins of three hundred mammalian species and one hundred bird specimens back to New York. Sidney and Morris tossed a coin; Sidney lost and left for Addis. However, while he was away, Mummy realized that, despite the fun she had with Morris, she deeply missed my father and cared for him in a more romantic way than she did for his brother. Shortly after she joined Sidney in Addis, the two of them sailed on to Antibes, where they shared a villa and Sidney proposed.

They were married on September 17, 1929. Hundreds of their friends attended and afterward went back to the 72nd Street town house for dinner and dancing. "I was determined to survive the ordeal," she would say later. "Weddings are ghastly for brides. All I can remember is wishing for it to end."

My parents spent their wedding night at the Waldorf Astoria, and the next morning they left for their honeymoon in Alaska and British Columbia, stalking and shooting wild sheep and goats. Even though they were trapped in a blizzard and tent-bound for several days, Mummy described this trip as "heavenly." Their friends thought they were crazy.

After the honeymoon, their first priority was to find a place to live. New York, Florida, and New Orleans were all ruled out. Neither of them wanted to live in a city, and Mummy told me later that in Florida, she'd have to listen to "the thrashing of those damn palm trees." While staying with friends in South Carolina, my parents discovered Medway, a tumbledown wreck of a plantation with no heat, electricity, or running water. They were captivated—enchanted by Medway's potential—and in the spring of 1930, with help from my grandfather, they bought it.

The main house was the oldest in the Carolinas, built in 1686 on a tributary to the Cooper River, which was formerly called the "Meadway" or "Medway." One of only three South Carolina plantations spared by General Sherman when he marched his army down the Cooper River, Medway changed hands a number of times until it was purchased by my parents, who worked feverishly for a year to transform it into a viable and beautiful estate. My father took courses at Cornell to learn about agriculture and farming, while Mummy took courses in proper nutrition. Eventually they succeeded in converting what was essentially an abandoned hunting lodge into the glorious site it is today.

The estate is surrounded by seven thousand acres of longleaf and loblolly pine forests filled with quail, turkey, and deer. Medway's ponds are home to hundreds of migrating ducks, herons, ospreys, and eagles. Sixty miles of riding trails wind through the pine woods passing duck marshes and fields of dry golden cornhusks and millet planted for the quail and doves. The main house nestles among the low-slung branches of ancient oak trees draped with long gray wisps of Spanish moss, while the front lawn sweeps down to a black lake curving about the house and under a bridge. The bridge leads to the long U-shaped driveway lined with oaks and pink azalea bushes. Clustered near the main house are several vine-covered guest cottages, which in days past, previous tenants had used as the kitchen, schoolhouse, and smokehouse.

Running a plantation was an enormous challenge, and neither of my parents had any experience with such a project. The troubles of money danced into their life as they found themselves entangled in the enormous expense not only of rebuilding a house, but also of landscaping enormous lawns, meadows, and gardens. In my father's journal of the early days there he wrote, "Now that Gertrude has taken over the management of the plantation, she no longer shouts at me for staying in the office and writing letters to do this and that, and be certain the crops are taken in and not left in the fields to spoil. Now she has to this herself and is beginning to realize how really long it takes to manage Medway."

Three years after my parents settled into Medway, my sister Landine was born, a fact that Mummy neglected to mention in either of the two memoirs she would later publish. It's not surprising. She never referenced my own birth, either, even though I was born on my parents' eleventh wedding anniversary, September 17, 1940. However, I would later find in a journal that my father kept of life at Medway, a reference, albeit brief, to my entrance into the world: "My daughter Bokara was born today. In her little hands are already the tiny lines that tell the story of her whole life."

Because my mother was so enamored of the exotic, I was named for a faraway place: Bokhara, a city in Uzbekistan where blue mosques rise from the desert sands in the southern steppes of Russia. Apparently, my name was chosen one evening while my parents were having drinks in the Gun Room at Medway and spun the globe to find a place they had never visited. Mummy thought Bokhara with the *h* was too long, though, so she took it out to make my name, Bokara.

I was not yet two years old when my parents disappeared from my life. Six months after Pearl Harbor was attacked and America entered the war, Daddy and Uncle Morris enlisted in the navy. They were stationed together in Hawaii, while Mummy, who simply *had to be* where the action was, took a job with the OSS. She was first posted to Washington, DC, where she managed the cable desk, monitoring what she would later claim to be "sensitive and top secret transmissions."

My sister and I were billeted for a while in New Orleans with my father's brother, Armant. Later, we were moved to New York, where we celebrated Christmas with a friend of Mummy's, who had her two Labradors drag our presents into her living room on a children's sleigh. No adult had ever taken that much trouble to delight me. Not long afterward, Landine was sent to live in Virginia with her own nanny, and from then on we lived with separate nannies in separate houses in separate cities.

In 1943, Mummy was sent to London, where she found a flat and a Swiss cook and—rationing restrictions and bombing be damned— began hosting dinner parties. The frequent air raids didn't faze her. During the summer of 1944, she moved to Knightsbridge, which was known as Buzz-Bomb Alley because of the frequency of German air strikes that employed jet-propelled missiles known as buzz bombs. By late July, though London had been hit with two hundred daily buzz bomb attacks, Mummy kept the parties going. During one soiree, where she played hostess to twenty-eight airmen and high-ranking brass, a buzz bomb barely missed her flat.

"To think," she wrote afterward, "that one buzz bomb could have destroyed most of the American high command!"

She was reassigned to Paris after the city was liberated in August 1944. Early one September evening, she persuaded her friend and fellow OSS officer Bob Jennings to take a trip to the Allied front lines to see the shooting. I imagine very few people would think of visiting the front lines of a war as fun; but she probably didn't even consider the risk.

She and Jennings joined Major Max Papurt, who was en route to interview some German prisoners, and they accidentally drove into enemy territory. Papurt and his driver were shot and killed. Mummy and Bob Jennings were captured and interrogated as spies. The first American woman captured in France, Mummy spent six weeks in a cell and another two months in a thirteenth-century castle that had been turned into a makeshift prison. Eventually she was turned over to the custody of Lieutenant William Gosewich, a German who had spent eighteen years in the United States and was accidentally caught up in the war when he visited his native land to see his family. Gosewich helped arrange for Mummy to be billeted with a German family for the final stretch of her captivity, and he was pivotal in coordinating her escape shortly before the end of the war in March 1945.

Mummy was put on a train bound for Switzerland. But when the train stalled in the middle of the night, she ran for the border in the glare of the Nazi spotlights. She was pursued by a guard, who yelled at her several times to halt. But she didn't stop, the guard didn't shoot, and within moments Mummy made it across the border to safety. The American government was furious over her recklessness and rescinded her passport for a year.

For my permanently en voyage mother, the punishment was dreadful. However, she was so grateful to Lieutenant Gosewich that she was eventually helped him come to America and start a new life.

I was five years old when I consciously met my mother for the first time.

Mamie and I were living in a gloomy apartment in New York City. The dreary living room was furnished with brown velvet chairs draped with lace antimacassars, and the whole stuffy apartment smelled of the kind of beige flannel upholstery that used to make me carsick in limousines. One afternoon, long red fingernails tap-tap-tapped against the frosty glass of our front door. Mamie opened the door to a strange woman with dark hair and small brown eyes, dressed in a black suit. I ran to hide, but Mamie caught my arm.

"Say hello to your mother, Bo," she gently urged. "She's home from the war."

I tentatively offered to kiss her cheek, but I could feel my stomach turn watery with fear. Life with Mamie had been predictable and cozy. Though she had played no apparent role in my life until this point, somehow I knew that this strange, dark woman could change all that.

A few days later she left to meet my father in Hawaii, and after he was discharged, they returned to Medway. I was *not* invited to join them.

In fact, as a child, I never lived at Medway. My mother didn't much like children around and brought us up in the style of the British aristocracy who had nannies. I spent the first fourteen years of my life living almost exclusively with Mamie, being shuttled between various rented cottages and apartments, generally in towns my parents did not frequent. I spent the holidays with them and occasional weekends when I lived somewhere close to Medway. But even during those brief visits, I spent my days and evenings primarily with Mamie.

Mamie's real name was Violet Evans. She had wispy gray hair that she kept pulled back in a net, and pale blue eyes in a very English face dominated by a prominent nose. She typically wore shirtdresses—simple cotton dresses with buttons down the front and short sleeves—which she wore with a brown leather belt, stockings, and oxfords. Because one of her legs was shorter than the other, her shoes had to be specially crafted to order. I later discovered that they cost her four hundred dollars—an entire month's salary. When she told me this, I was so appalled by Mummy's stinginess toward the woman—whom she had hired to fill a role for which she herself had neither the inclination nor the aptitude—that I burst into tears. Of course, Mamie said it was all right and tried to convince me that Mummy was really very generous.

Mamie, however, *was* generous, a kind, gentle woman who consistently offered me the only love I really knew as a child. She was an orphan who had started working as a nanny as a teenage girl. Mummy had hired her on the recommendation of the family pediatrician, Dr. Schloss, who knew another family that Mamie had worked for. I think she was very happy with that family, as she mentioned them quite often. Her previous charge had been a girl named Pauline, whom she called "P"; sometimes, she called me "P" by mistake. I have always regretted never making an effort to find Pauline and talk with her about Mamie. I never inquired about her life at the orphanage, either, and Mamie rarely mentioned it. Amazingly enough, considering she had never had a home of her own, she had a unique ability to create warm and comfortable sanctuaries in the series of dreary little furnished cottages Mummy rented for us.

Shortly after the war ended, Mamie and I were moved from New York to Aiken. It boasted a country club called the Green Boundary, which served tea and elaborate cakes with deep swirling frosting on Sunday afternoons. The members were mainly golfers clad in linen trousers and alligator shirts and polo players in white jodhpurs. Their wives wore pastel dresses or Bermuda shorts and straw hats. In the fall, everyone donned hunting clothes and a bag of fox scent was dragged through the woods, which the hounds followed, trailed by hunters in pink coats and black bowler hats.

I liked the cakes, but I didn't pay attention to the rest.

In Aiken, everybody rode—it was considered part of life—so I *had* to ride, whether I liked it or not. Every Wednesday, Mamie poured me into jodhpurs and a riding jacket, settled a velvet hard hat on my head, and brought me to Captain Gaylord's Riding Academy—where the horses invariably ran away with me. I would cling to the English saddle, flattened against the horse's back to avoid being scraped off by passing tree branches. When finally I let go and fell, my stomach felt as it does after riding an elevator going down too fast. Captain Gaylord, dressed in a German army uniform, would ride up on his towering stallion and scowl down at me. "Achtung!" he ordered. "Get back on and show him who's boss."

He terrified me. I didn't like horses, and I hated riding. The whole thing made me miserable. I begged to give up riding lessons, and I even persuaded Mamie to intervene on my behalf. Daddy wrote me a letter saying everyone had to learn to ride.

Mummy added, "If Miss Evans keeps spoiling you this way, I shall have to let her go."

The threat of losing Mamie, the only person I loved and who loved me in return, was too horrible to bear. I went on with my riding lessons.

However, for my sixth birthday, my parents gave me a black mutt with white paws, whom I called Timmie. I had just read *The Little Prince* and was especially moved by the prince's love for his rose and by the encounter between the prince and the fox. The fox tells the prince, "Taming is creating ties. If you tame me, we'll need each other … You must have patience and come to visit at the same time every day. If you come at four, I shall begin to be happy by three." I longed for the feeling of anticipation of devoted friendship, and so Timmie became my "fox"—waiting for me to come home from school, when I would give him water (like the Little Prince, who watered his rose regularly) and hug him frequently.

Secretly I wished my parents would tame me the way I tamed Timmie. My parents just didn't behave that way. I could see that they loved their dogs almost the way I loved Timmie, but children were an entirely different matter.

When I was invited to Medway, Mamie, Timmie, and I were put up on the top floor of the house, where Mummy's lady's maid had her room. I was supposed to keep out of the way of the grown-ups, so I rarely saw Mummy and Daddy save for a regularly scheduled appearance during evening cocktails. I dressed especially for this event in black patent leather Mary Jane shoes, white silk socks, and a freshly ironed dress.

The men wore velvet smoking jackets and dress trousers, and the women wore exotic dressy costumes of pants and tops or flowing silk tea gowns. All the ladies had beautiful jewelry, and their satin shoes matched their outfits. To me, they looked like movie stars. Mummy favored long Indian brocade coats and brightly colored, tight-legged Indian silk pants. She cut an exotic figure with masses of Indian jewels, a silk turban, and a long black-and-gold cigarette holder. She was only five foot five, but to me she was a towering presence. I was terrified of her. I was so afraid I would make a fatal mistake that would cause her to send me away forever.

Under her watchful eye, I curtsied to each of the adults and occasionally received a kiss from those who were more familiar or were frequent guests. Dutifully, I kissed each of my parents. Then Mamie and I had supper at a card table in the dining room, which had been set up next to the grown-ups' table; then the maids whisked away all vestiges of our presence before everyone else was served. Sometimes, I would listen from the top of the stairs to the sounds of laughter and the clinks of glasses.

During my visits, I would try to flatter Mummy in hopes that she would show me some sort of warmth or affection in return. So after watching her play a set of tennis, I would offer, "Oh, Mummy, what a great shot that was you played!" Or after she returned from a shoot, I would ask, "How many ducks did you get today?" "That was such a beautiful dress you wore last night," I'd venture if I caught her on the fly to some sporting experience, dressed to the nines in her shooting suit, golf costume, or tennis skirt.

She never responded to me directly. Instead, she would turn to her friends and say, "Bo's my little fan."

I also loved the idea of wearing costumes, so I invented some of my own. One morning, I padded by wearing a blue dress with a white apron. My hair was in pigtails, and I was carrying a wooden bowl and leading Timmie, who was sporting a bell.

"Where are you going in that *ridiculous* outfit?" Mummy asked.

"I'm Heidi, and Timmie is my goat," I explained. "I'm getting some milk to put in my wooden bowl."

"Who in the world is Heidi?" Mummy asked.

"You know—the book *Heidi*," I replied. "It's about a little girl who lives in Switzerland! She's an orphan."

"Well, you aren't an orphan, and we don't live in Switzerland. What an *imagination* you have!" Mummy exclaimed, as though it was a bad thing. "We are on a plantation, and you should wear jeans and a plaid shirt like everyone else."

Actually, the only person I ever remember wearing a plaid shirt was my sister, and it certainly was not a regular thing.

On the day we received news of my father's death, Mummy sent Robert, the family chauffeur, to drive us from Aiken to Medway. Mamie asked him if many people had come. "Yes, ma'am," he replied. "I been meeting planes all morning."

We arrived shortly after five o'clock in the evening. The cypress-paneled living room, lined with shelves of leather-bound books, was full of people, some in shooting clothes, others in city suits. A tea table was set up in front of a cowhide chair where Mummy calmly poured tea from a large, ornate silver pot into pale blue cups that were stacked on a special little tiered table designed exclusively for them. Brownies and sandwiches were piled in silver salvers.

My sister Landine, whom I hadn't seen in ages, had come down from boarding school in Virginia and was sitting next to our aunt Mary, who was married to Uncle Laddie. Aunt Mary motioned to me to sit next to her on the long cushy sofa upholstered with thousands of tiny beige thread loops. A former movie actress, Aunt Mary was easily the most glamorous person I knew, smelling of gardenias and always dressed in soft cashmeres and silks. I cuddled next to her, and Aunt Janie, Mummy's sister, gave me a sweet smile. Then she reached out her long, thin fingers covered with huge jeweled rings and beckoned me to give her a kiss. Uncle Laddie, who smelled of leather and horses, said he wanted one too.

A cedarwood fire filled the room with its warm, rich scent, and the flames glittered off the silver and porcelain ornaments that covered the tables and shelves. Everyone seemed terribly glad to see me. I was passed around the room from lap to lap and kiss to kiss. Timmie, who was never allowed to be with the grown-ups, managed to slip into the room, and to my great surprise Mummy actually patted him.

The funeral took place the next morning. I was dressed in a gray chambray dress, which had red piping. I was terribly worried about the inappropriateness of wearing red piping for a funeral. As I stood waiting anxiously in the living room with Landine and my aunts and uncles, I wished desperately that I had a black dress.

Finally Mummy appeared dressed in a black silk suit, low-heeled black suede pumps, and a black wide-brimmed fedora of the type she favored. A large gold broach shaped like a fish, which Daddy had given her, was pinned to her lapel. Panic constricted my throat, but she didn't mention the red piping on my dress. I doubt she even noticed.

To my amazement, she took my right hand. Uncle Morris took my left, and we walked slowly out under the ancient oaks to the grave that had been dug on a hillock above the black lake that curved in front of the house. Dozens of relatives and friends of my parents had gathered around already, and suddenly I noticed something startling: everyone was looking at me as I stood between my mother and Uncle Morris.

For the first time in my life, I was at the center of things, at the center of my family. As the coffin was lowered into the grave, I had to struggle to keep from grinning over the fact that, at last, I was a part of my family.

Jenkins, the head carpenter at Medway, was also a Baptist minister. He stepped forward and led the servants in singing "Give Me That Old Time Religion." The men and women who worked at Medway, dressed in their finest clothes, sang spirituals that dated back to the slave era as well as hymns they had learned in the churches around Charleston. At the end of the service, someone handed my mother a shotgun. She raised it, sighted, and shot—a final tribute to her husband.

As we walked back from the grave, I asked Mummy what I should wear for dinner. Earlier in the morning, I had seen the maids putting extra leaves in the dining table and laying out what seemed like the entire set of my favorite turquoise-and-gold china. Naturally, I assumed I would be staying. It would be one of the first —if not *the* first—time I would dine with everyone else.

"You have to go back to Aiken, darling," Mummy replied, staring straight ahead. "Tomorrow's a school day, and anyway there are guests in your room."

I was so stunned I almost stopped in my tracks. Of course, I should have realized that Mummy's taking my hand as we walked and having me stand beside her at the grave had been nothing more than a performance. I wasn't part of the family after all.

The afternoon passed in a haze. I don't remember anything that was said. I don't even recall saying good-bye to Mummy, my sister, or anyone else when the time came to leave for Aiken. Mamie and I just walked outside to the drive, Robert opened the car door for us, and we climbed into the backseat. I gazed up at the house one last time. Lights twinkled in the upstairs bedrooms as my family and parents' friends dressed for dinner. I grasped Mamie's hand tightly, and she gave me a comforting squeeze in return.

As we rode down the five-mile driveway between walls of pine trees to the main road, I glimpsed the sunset streaking the sky with pink-and-orange clouds. "Daddy must be walking on those beautiful clouds," I murmured.

"I'm sure he is," Mamie replied, holding my hand tightly.

During the drive back we stopped at a Walgreens drugstore, where we ordered grilled cheese sandwiches and chocolate milk shakes. I prayed that Mamie would never leave.

The next day at school, my teacher asked, "Did anything interesting happen to any of you over the weekend?"

My cousin Janet, Uncle Morris's daughter, instantly shot up from her desk and announced, "My uncle died."

Not to be outdone, I raised my hand and stood up.

"He was my *father*," I said proudly before resuming my seat.

For one day I'd had a taste of what it was like to be important, to be visible, and I wasn't about to give that up.

Two years after my father's death, Mamie, Timmie, and I were sent to Charleston, where we lived in a little brick cottage on Hazel Street, part of a compound of houses that belonged to the Kittredges, who owned the neighboring plantation to Medway. Carola Kittredge, two years my senior, lived next door in a similar cottage with her nanny, and she became my dearest friend. We fed her poodle the Whitman's chocolates we didn't like from the yellow box that identified the flavors on the lid. The poor poodle ran in circles and howled afterward, but he seemed to enjoy them. Carola and I dressed up in costumes to visit her grandmother, who lay in bed all day dressed in pink satin and pearls.

She gave us cookies and listened attentively to what occurred at our local day school, where we were considered rich Yankees beneath contempt. Carola's governess was an astrologer, and I remember her telling me I would always have enough money but a lonely emotional life.

I was, in fact, soon to begin a lifelong quest for home.

CHAPTER

3

The Girls' Confederate Army

In the fall of 1954, I stood alone with Mamie on a platform at Grand Central Station, while a pack of girls about my own age giggled and chatted excitedly farther down the platform, protectively observed by their parents, who chatted cozily amongst themselves and occasionally with their daughters. I'd prepared carefully for the upcoming journey, choosing what I imagined as a very "grown-up," tight-fitting black-and-white tweed suit and medium-heeled pumps. I'd recently had my hair cut, too, in a short bob popularized by my then-idol, Audrey Hepburn. But as I surreptitiously studied the other girls—dressed almost identically in kilts and cashmere sweaters, with black velvet hair bands holding back their pageboys—my heart sank. My deliberately cultivated sophisticated look, and the conspicuous absence of my parents, marked me as "different." This was an inauspicious and potentially dangerous precedent, as these were the girls with whom I would be spending most of the next four years of my life at Foxcroft, a private boarding school in Middleburg, Virginia.

Several weeks earlier, Mummy and I were having lunch in the summerhouse she had recently bought on Fishers Island. I worked up

48

the courage to ask her if I might possibly go somewhere else for boarding school. My sister Landine had gone to Foxcroft and hated the place so much that she ran away (although she was lured back by the promise of hot chocolate and eventually managed to adapt to the school's rigid militaristic culture).

Miss Charlotte Haxall Noland, the founder of the school, was also a close friend of Mummy's and a frequent visitor at Medway, where I'd had the chance to observe her a couple of times. A powerful woman with an angular face and a heavy jaw, she favored jodhpurs and severely tailored jackets, and she exuded the brisk, uncompromising, and very male attitude of a battle-tested veteran. In fact, she referred to herself as the governor general of Foxcroft. And I'd had a conversation with a girl on Fishers Island who was going to board at Farmington, and another at Garrison Forest—both of which sounded like much nicer places. "Please, Mummy," I begged, "let me go to Farmington or Garrison or anywhere else. Please let me go to Switzerland!"

"Everyone has to go to school," she replied. "Foxcroft is the best one. And anyway, you won't like any other better. You just don't like discipline."

Of course, Mummy thought Foxcroft was the best; she had gone there herself. But that had been in the school's early years, when the class schedule was rather vague, discipline was lax, and she and her classmates spent most of their time fox hunting and beagling. Since Mummy had gone to Foxcroft, and Landine as well, I really had no choice in the matter. I was duly packed off, while Mamie was sent to Medway as a housekeeper—along with Timmie, as an unwanted dog.

The train ride to Virginia was agonizing. All the other girls seemed to know each other, having summered together with their families in South Hampton or Newport. I, on the other hand, had been regularly uprooted for fourteen years and had just passed a lonely, uncomfortable summer at Mummy's new house on Fishers Island. At her insistence, I'd been chauffeured to the local tennis club every morning and left there till lunchtime to "make friends." I'd sat alone on the porch there for an entire month before anyone my own age spoke to me, and I was mortified when our black chauffeur arrived to drive me back home, because I couldn't even pretend that I was being picked up, like the other children, by a member of the family.

So I had nothing to contribute to the conversations around me, and I sat staring out the window at the towns and cities we passed, thinking nothing could be worse than this lonely, uncomfortable train ride.

I couldn't have been more wrong.

It was much worse.

Foxcroft School was less a girls' academy than a military camp, where Miss Charlotte trained and created her own private army of rich, socially prominent young ladies. Though her background and training had been in physical education, Miss Charlotte had become wholly captivated during World War II by the rules and rigors of military discipline. She believed it was essential for developing the character of her students, whom she frequently and publically denounced as "spoiled." Accordingly, the school's dormitories had been set up as barracks. Identical iron cots equipped with sleeping bags and rough flannel sheets were lined up on long communal sleeping porches open to the wind and snow. There were no chairs or tables—no soft, gentle place to relax or sit—just a small bureau for each girl and a closet for our uniforms.

Of course, there were uniforms, a not uncommon feature of private boarding schools. The Foxcroft uniforms, however, were military, consisting of green corduroy jackets, tan skirts, white or khaki blouses, beige kneesocks, and clunky oxfords. Hair nets were *de rigueur* even for girls with very short hair—and mine was *very* short. The crowning glory consisted of green Confederate army–style caps with gold braid and brown visors. For weekly military parade drills we were obliged to wear special "dress" green twill jackets with brass buttons and insignia of rank on the left lapel. A small concession was made for the warm months of the school term, during which our regulation outfit consisted of a plain blue or yellow dress that looked like a maid's uniform and short white socks.

Regimentation was strict, and inspections were frequent. Our closets had to be arranged in a specific order: First came our tan skirts, then our green jackets, followed by our white and then khaki blouses. Sneakers had to be lined precisely to the left of our oxfords and riding boots precisely to the right. If anything was out of order, the unlucky girl received a demerit. We were also obliged to scour our shared bathrooms with Bab-O cleansing powder and steel brushes. One spot of unpolished chrome in the bathroom earned a demerit. A single hair left in a hairbrush: one demerit. An uncapped toothpaste tube: one demerit.

Five demerits were punished by the loss the one "lunch privilege" we were allowed each term: a terrible blow, since lunch privilege was one of the few means of escaping the horrors of Foxcroft for a few brief halcyon hours. I usually enjoyed this privilege at the home of one of Mummy's friends, who owned horse farms near the school. I remember Mrs. Robert Phillips and Adele Astaire being especially kind. Eventually I made friends with Eliza Lloyd, who was a couple of years behind me at school. One afternoon, we had lunch at her parents' beautiful home, Oak Spring Farm. It was an especially memorable occasion, during which we were served sorbet in the shape of fruits, which Eliza's mother, Bunny Mellon, was trying out as a possible dessert for her older daughter's coming-out party.

I passed my first two weeks at Foxcroft in a state of almost unrelieved terror. Miss Charlotte turned a blind eye to the hazing the new arrivals suffered at the hands of senior girls, to whom we were bound as virtual slaves. We were required to clean their shoes, lie down in the mud before them to "scramble like an egg," and wear demeaning signs around our waists. Mine read, "I've got a swing on my back porch," because one of the senior girls had determined that I wiggled my hips when I walked. At the end of two weeks, we were led into a dark room to stand in the glare of blinding spotlights while the seniors interrogated us about our lives and the school. To further unnerve us under questioning, they would occasionally cross their legs in military unison with a crashing stamp.

As if the hazing, regulations, demerits, and inspections weren't enough, the uncongenial atmosphere at Foxcroft was encouraged by a division of the student body into two competing groups—Foxes and

Hounds. Miss Charlotte was a Fox; she'd even named the bungalow where she lived The Covert, a reference to a fox's lair. Mummy and Landine had been Hounds when they attended Foxcroft, so I was assigned to that group as well. Of course, since Miss Charlotte was a Fox, Hounds were considered second-class.

Miss Charlotte also referred to herself as "the boss," while we students were designated, for some unfathomable reason, as "hobos." At school assemblies, such as the big basketball game between the school teams, the Foxes and the Hounds, she would join us in singing a call-and-response chant. It began with her singing, "Who is the boss?" In response, we sang, "You are the boss! You are the boss! You are the governor general and no hobo. No hobo. You are the boss, and your name is Charlotte Haxall Noland." Miss Charlotte would then sing, "I am the boss! I am the boss! I am the governor general, but no hobo." The chant continued for a while in the same vein.

Classes could sometimes be quite tough. Though I had no head for math or most other subjects, I spoke and wrote well enough to be assigned to the "better" English class, taught by a brilliant and exacting woman by the name of Miss Cawser. Her idea of instilling excellence in composition was routinely administered criticism. "You are all *babies*," she would frequently pronounce. "You will *never* get published in *The New Yorker*"—which was the pinnacle of publication to which she thought we could aspire. (I'm happy to report that, despite Miss Cawser's dire prediction, my friend and classmate Frankie Fitzgerald regularly appears in that magazine.)

Then there were the drills.

Every Tuesday and Thursday we formed up in our drill uniforms, our shoes spit-and-polish clean. We carried heavy guns called "pieces," which didn't shoot but nevertheless had to be oiled and polished to perfection. Up and down the drill field we marched, executing various maneuvers memorized from complicated arms manuals.

On these occasions, Miss Charlotte would wear a more formal version of the Foxcroft uniform adorned with military decorations. Remarkably, she had enough pull in Washington to persuade four-star generals to come to the school to observe our maneuvers. What could these real military commanders who reviewed us have thought of an army of adolescent girls, only a breath away from their nannies and looking forward to their debutante parties, drilling in Confederate army uniforms? Did we look as foolish as we felt, shouting, "Present arms!" in Long Island accents and Southern drawls?

During my entire time at Foxcroft I was lonely beyond belief. Having been shuttled around from place to place for the first fourteen years of my life, I hadn't acquired the skills necessary to make friends quickly or easily. Most of that time, too, I'd spent in the company of adults, so I felt terribly insecure about contributing anything to whatever it was that other teenage girls talked about—their beaus, their families, the mysterious things they giggled over. Because we did everything together, I was isolated in a crowd, paralyzed by having to communicate with so many people every day. Eventually, I lost my voice completely, which was surely an expression of the school's senior class motto: "An outward and physical sign of an inward and spiritual state." My inward state was pretty wretched.

A doctor prescribed inhaling milk fumes to soothe my vocal chords, so I began visiting the infirmary regularly to hunch under a towel over a steaming pot of milk. Miss Shrammie, the nurse, took care of me. She was a kind, soft-spoken lady who reminded me of Mamie. I wanted to spend my life in the infirmary, but of course that was impossible.

To escape the exhaustion and discomfort of interacting with people around whom I felt shy and afraid, I sought privacy in the toilet stalls in the big school bathrooms. I sat on the toilet seat eating saltines, which I'd collected in my corduroy jacket pockets. I also took to sneaking into the supply closet during mealtimes, hiding among boxes of erasers and notebooks and stuffing down an assortment of stale tea sandwiches I'd saved from the day before. Thus began a fast friendship with food that would continue for the next twenty years.

Unfortunately, the teachers to whose dining tables I had been assigned for meals noticed my frequent absences, and eventually I was summoned to Miss Charlotte's office for a severe dressing-down. "From now on," she concluded, "the whole school will march to meals in platoons to ensure that this never happens again."

Sure enough, from then on we marched to meals.

Whenever possible, I took the hall phone—an old-fashioned black thing with a long cord—into the cloak closet and called Mamie for reassurance and to hear a loving voice. I buried myself amidst the macintoshes and polo coats so the sound of my voice would be muffled, as there would be hell to pay if anyone found out what I was doing. Mamie always made me feel better; telling me she loved me, that soon it would be vacation time—we would count the number of days—and that Timmie missed me as much as I missed him.

One terrible day when I asked her how Timmie was, my question was met with a long silence. At last, she replied quietly, "Mrs. Legendre has given him away."

I was devastated.

Timmie, my most beloved companion and trusted friend, the creature I had "tamed" like the Little Prince's fox, was gone. Only Mamie was left at Medway, and now I worried that she might be sent away, too. Although Mamie said Timmie had gone to a family in the navy yard, it dawned on me later that no one had bothered to find Timmie a home. No one ever mentioned Timmie when I went to visit Medway. Once I asked Mummy about him, and she curtly replied that, since I was away, he was better off somewhere else.

At midnight, I slipped into the bathroom to cry where no one would hear me. I quickly discovered that I was not alone. One of my classmates had also sequestered herself there, confessing, when I asked her, that she was considering suicide because of the alienation she felt from her own family. We sat commiserating on the floor all night, weeping and wondering whether to go on living ... and if we did, where and how that might be. I shall never forget the little squares of cold white tile on the floor, the hard white marble sinks, the curl of the metal pipes under them. There was no softness, no comfort, anywhere—not even a bath mat. That was how my life felt in that moment: bare and cold and hard.

I was so distracted by anxiety and desperation at Foxcroft it was impossible for me to ever concentrate. I sat in study hall in paroxysms of anxiousness or daydreaming about "when I grow up." Our desktops flipped open the way laptops do now, and I used mine as a screen behind which I could eat, cry, or dig holes in my head. I had developed a nervous tic—or more likely a form of self-mutilation, like children nowadays who slice themselves with razors—scratching holes in my head until they formed open sores. I was regularly sent to the infirmary to have gentian violet applied, and when I scratched again, my fingers turned purple and made purple streaks all over my papers.

Naturally, my grades were so terrible that I barely graduated. Just before commencement, in 1957, Mr. Merle Smith, the president of the school, took me into his office. "Bo," he said, frowning, "you never showed any enthusiasm or team spirit. You have been a great disappointment to us all."

I stared at him wordlessly. That remark sunk like a sword to my heart, confirming my conviction I was worth nothing to anyone, an inevitable failure in life. How could I confess to him that I was a big disappointment to myself?

I hadn't applied to college, the consensus being that since I would never be accepted, I shouldn't even try. Mummy had already told me, "You're no great brain," and Miss Charlotte, having looked at the size of my Confederate cap, opined, "Big head, small brains." The real issue for me, though, was that I imagined college would be just as much a nightmare as Foxcroft. Since no one had bothered to advise me otherwise, I wasn't keen about the prospect of four more years of school.

My time at Foxcroft was the lowest point in my life, and I have experienced some pretty low ones since then. Even today, when something truly terrible, beyond-the-pale painful happens, I think, *Well, at least I'm not at Foxcroft.* My four years as a member of the Confederate Girls Army, however, had left me hollowed out and hopeless. My only recourse, as I saw it then, was pretense, and I threw myself into creating the impression of a girl having a good time.

CHAPTER

Stepping Out

A Hindu sage once advised me that my mantra should be, "I exist." I wish he'd told me that in 1957, for during the eleven years following my graduation from Foxcroft, my life passed in a tumult of trial and error as I struggled to define my existence and discover who I was.

I was possessed by the fear of disappearing, and I looked for a way to transform myself from the unattractive, fat teenager I saw reflected in my mother's eyes (not to mention the figure of fatness and insecurity I imagined I presented to potential suitors) into a "person of charm and consequence." That I had no idea how to achieve such a transmutation merely darkened my mood further. I concealed my fear behind an outrageously buoyant exhibit of having a good time, desperately engaged in an effort to convince myself and everyone else that I enjoyed being a social butterfly.

Although debutante parties are now passé, they were still obligatory when I finished at Foxcroft, and I was afflicted with two. The first was held in June at our house on Fishers Island. Mummy insisted on a South Sea island theme, complete with a hula teacher. Mummy had become quite enamored of the hula when she met up with Daddy in

Hawaii after the war, and we'd acquired large numbers of coconut hats and paper leis the previous summer during a trip we'd taken to Tahiti.

The dress that had been chosen for me for the occasion was a white, V-waist organdy nightmare, with short cap sleeves like on a bridesmaid's gown and a billowing skirt. I literally had to squeeze myself into it, since by the time I'd left Foxcroft, I'd become quite the butterball. Instead of sending me to a slimming spa, as other parents of Foxcroft's overfed daughters had (I wasn't the only one who'd sought solace in food), Mummy simply said, "Your figure doesn't matter. It's character that counts." I suspect she said that because she was jealous of me, and keeping me fat also prevented me from becoming a potential threat.

My neighbor, a supremely popular and thin girl (and naturally greatly admired by my mother), generously asked two of her beaus to escort me to my own party, as I had no escort of my own. I talked incessantly and danced wildly to show I was having a good time.

In the middle of the summer—and the middle of the coming-out parties at which all my contemporaries were presented—Mummy suddenly whisked me off to a river in Montana with a group of her friends to go fly-fishing, a sport I neither knew nor had any interest in learning. The first night she accidentally put her sleeping bag on an anthill. She spent the rest of the trip making jokes about me, telling her friends that it was I who knew nothing about camping or the wilds and had put my sleeping bag on an anthill. It was the kind of gratuitous cruelty in which she specialized.

My second debutante party was held in September at Dunford, the Long Island home of my aunt Mary and uncle Laddie. It was quite a glamorous affair, as Aunt Mary was known as the "Queen of Palm Beach" for her parties. Uncle Laddie, by then exhausted and stiff from a life of polo accidents and excess, was confined to a wheelchair. But as the evening drew to a close, he became quite jolly and somewhat tipsy. He sang a song he had written called, "Poor Little Palm Beach Baby." I remember him, late in life, sitting in his wheelchair, singing this song and still loving it:

Poor Little Palm Beach Baby.
She has a sad, sad life.
Nothing to wear but diamonds and pearls.
Nothing to do but lunch with the girls …

Uncle Laddie lived a jaded life in some ways, spoiled by money and indulging in countless affairs, but he was wryly perceptive about the world of privilege he inhabited. He was the only one who gave me advice about love affairs, and it was awful: "Marry everyone you sleep with."

Despite the fact that I was outfitted in yet another unbecoming dress—a strapless cream satin number with a huge bow across the chest and no waist at all, which the saleswoman at Bergdorf's had convinced me to buy—I actually had quite a bit of fun, as I always did with the Sanfords. Aunt Mary's sense of glamour and excitement was contagious, and since she had no children of her own, she showered affection on me. She also let me have perfume from her *huge* bottle of Joy. It must have been a quart, though still in the traditionally shaped Joy bottle.

As the summer drew to a close and girls I knew packed for Radcliffe and Vassar, I bought a shaggy blue coat, which I imagined was the latest thing for Paris. Aunt Janie had arranged for me to spend the winter there with a high-bourgeois, low-income family who lived in the fashionable sixteenth *arrondissement*, just off Place Victor Hugo. Mamie saw me off at the airport, and during the entire flight I cried over leaving her. How could I leave her now that finally Foxcroft over and we had been reunited? Each time I left I was afraid to come back and find her gone. Yet the desire to find friends, to create a life of my own was also burning a hole in my heart. I was torn.

I arrived on a rainy, cold day and rode a birdcage of an elevator that inched its pokey way up to my hosts' apartment, which I discovered was the scene of deep mourning. The women were draped in black veils, while the men wore black suits and somber expressions. A dear friend of the family had recently lost her mother, and out of respect for her grief the family had offered her the room that had been arranged for me. Accordingly, I was settled into an adjoining anteroom, which required my asking permission of the bereaved each time I wanted to cross her room to get to the bathroom. And since everyone necessarily had to walk through my room to visit her, I had no privacy.

The situation was made even more uncomfortable by a peculiar habit practiced by the head of the household. At every meal, "Monsieur" would spin a lead pendulum on a string over his plate, to determine whether the food was appropriate for him to eat. If it spun to the right, all was well; if it spun to the left, something else had to be prepared. As if I were somehow to blame for his dietary predicament, he would look at me and shake his head saying, "*La petite Americaine* leaves the lights on and uses up all our money for *biftsek.*"

The family had a daughter, Bettina, about my age; but she had her own friends and wasn't particularly interested in dragging along a shy American girl who spoke halting French. There was also Charles Henri, their son, who appeared only for meals, as he was studying for *le bac,* the all-important exam that determines one's fortunes in the French university system. Much of the dinner conversation revolved around his progress or around the fate of the family's older daughter, who had her own apartment and was engaged to a very rich man.

Since gas heat was very expensive, the apartment was always cold. Each morning, "Madame"—a lovely, delicately boned red-haired woman—stood in front of a fire she'd built in the grate, holding up the back of her skirt to warm her legs. She always inquired if I wanted *dejeuner,* but soon after my arrival I'd begun taking my meals away from the family. I thought that by drinking and eating the same things as the romantic couples in the cafés I frequented, I would find romance myself. At one café, I remember, I watched a sexy red-haired girl in blue jeans with a small dog order a Campari and soda and a *croque monsieur.* Soon she was joined by a young man in a black leather jacket and dark glasses. I called to the waiter and ordered the same, but no young man magically arrived to join me.

I also found a place to take painting lessons in an unheated *atelier* in Montmartre (we wore wool hats and gloves to keep warm), and after class I choked over countless Gauloises hoping I would somehow be transformed into an artist, sitting with like-minded friends for hours over tiny demitasses. No such wondrous conversion happened, but I did learn my way around Paris.

When the woman who had lost her mother eventually departed, I moved to the room that had originally been arranged for me. The very next day, however, a new boarder arrived and was put up in the anteroom I had just vacated; so the endless traipsing through each other's rooms continued. This young woman was English—very pretty and outfitted with the latest fashions. She knew lots of young people in Paris and spent her days and nights drinking and dancing and having fun. She never introduced me to anyone, and compared to her I felt ugly and decidedly unchic in my shaggy blue coat.

Twice, the family escorted us to dances, where ancient women in black dresses sat along the wall keeping an eye on us. Since I knew no one, I rarely danced, and after we returned home, I would sneak into the kitchen late at night to eat cheese to stuff down the empty feelings of isolation and homelessness. Madame found out and accused me of stealing food, which I suppose I was doing, though I hadn't thought about it that way. I took again to the cafes, where I pretended to myself, and anyone who noticed, that I was having a good time.

I happily bid adieu to my French family after a friend of Mummy's—the well-known American photographer Toni Frissell—invited me to accompany her and her husband, Mac Bacon, on a ski trip to Zermatt. I moved into a tiny rooming house there, which provided a box lunch every day—which I ended up giving to my ski instructor, as one was expected to buy lunch as well as pay for the lessons. I used all my money to pay for lessons and rent skis, and I subsisted primarily on rolls I'd saved from breakfast and dinners with the Bacons.

The Bacons treated me like a daughter, including me in all their plans. I finally began meeting people and having fun. My ski instructor introduced me to his friends as well: other instructors and visiting Americans and Europeans. We all formed an impromptu family, skiing and eating and sitting around fires together. I felt I'd found, at least temporarily, a friendly hearth.

When the Bacons moved on to Courchevel in the French Alps, I went along too. By spring, however, I ran out of money and gloomily returned to Paris and the family with whom I'd originally stayed. I was momentarily excited by the prospect of a weekend visit to their country chateau—which turned out to be a huge stone affair set in a bare and dismal countryside, with no heat and only a single bathroom inconveniently located on the main floor. I took chilly walks on the bare dirt roads, which smelled of farm animals, and I bought Petite Marie biscuits in the village. The only other diversion was *goutee*—enormous teas with pastries and cakes that went on all afternoon. When we returned from the country, I began to eat my way through Paris.

Late that spring, Mummy arrived, suddenly showing up at the apartment wearing a 1930s Madame Worth corduroy suit, a felt hat, and sensible shoes. I watched with horror the astonished glances exchanged between Madame and her daughter, who had assumed that, however wilted a specimen of American society I was, I at least belonged to a rich and chic family.

Fortunately, I didn't have to endure their dismay very long, for Mummy whisked me off to Germany. Apparently, she'd ordered a Mercedes and just wanted company as she drove it to Italy, where she planned to meet friends in Rome.

In truth, I was relieved to put my European excursion behind me, for I realized that even abroad I couldn't escape the catalog of my deficiencies. I could neither shoot nor hunt, or even catch a fish with a hook and bait, much less with flies. I was a frightened and awkward horsewoman; my tennis and golf skills were, at best, mediocre; I'd barely scraped through school; and, an ungainly debutante, I hadn't attracted even a trickle of suitable swains. To cap it off, Paris, a city of gaiety and joy adored by everyone I knew, had been for me a scene of unrelenting loneliness.

Back in the States, I finally discovered a temporary focus for my life—in the theater. I'd moved to Charleston to stay with my sister, who had married a man of old Charleston society, a charming newspaper publisher who didn't seem to mind putting up his little sister-in-law in his guesthouse. Landine found me a job at the Dock Street Theater, which was run by her friend Emmett Robinson. I made a somewhat tenuous stage debut dressed in a hat of silk flower petals, entering via a trapdoor stage center and pronouncing, "They have made worms meat of me," before disappearing into the floor again. To celebrate this event I gave a party in Landine's guesthouse. It was a chilly night, so I bought a Japanese hibachi and closed the windows. By midnight, my guests had begun to pass out from asphyxiation. Alarmed by this turn of events, I summoned my brother-in-law, Peter, who solved the problem by opening the windows. My guests, fortunately, revived, and Peter went back to bed.

Partly on the strength of my being in that play (about which I vastly exaggerated the importance of my role), I earned a scholarship to the American Theater Wing summer stock program. In the fall of 1958, I moved back to New York and began taking acting lessons.

Mummy was horrified at the prospect of having a daughter in the theater. She solved the problem by renting her friend Ellen Barry's flat for me and moving Mamie in as my chaperone. I thought the situation was perfect! The apartment was full of plays by Ellen's husband, Philip, and other writers, as well as an enormous collection of books and a piano. I embarked on a steady round of throwing parties. Mamie cooked, and the cabaret singer and pianist Bobby Short—who became a friend after we were introduced soon after my arrival in New York— entertained my guests at the piano. For fun, I would change outfits several times during the course of an evening, trying out different personalities. I would sometimes start out in a black velvet caftan, then shift to a corduroy dress and wool hat with a rose on it, and finally change into a long black gown with a rose in the décolleté.

Eventually, I got a gig singing at Phase Two, a tiny nightclub in Greenwich Village. I sat in a pink spot, wearing my long black dress with the plunging neckline and a yellow silk rose in my bosom. I sang "Two Little Words," a song written by the pianist, which—unfortunately for me as well as for the audience—I performed off-key (my singing teacher had already died, probably of frustration and exhaustion). Bobby Short and Rita Gam came down to see me, and the producer took the spotlight off me and shone it on my famous friends, leaving me singing bravely on in the dark.

Securely installed in the family's lore that obstacles build character, and only a bad sport falls off a horse without getting back on immediately, I did not quit the entertainment world when the stage director took the spotlight off me in midsong. I soldiered on through summers of summer stock and winters of acting school and small parts in off-Broadway shows. "Life in the thea-a-ter," as Aunt Mary called it, never lost its romance for me.

That summer, I joined a summer stock company in Cape May. We interns built sets and occasionally played small roles in the productions. Despite my frantic desire to be part of the group, I was still too insecure to eat with my fellow company members. Instead, I took sandwiches to the woods, where I ate alone, acting out the old habit of stuffing my fear down with food as I had at Foxcroft. The other members of the company probably thought I was a snob—the very opposite of what I most desired—but I really didn't believe that they liked me or wanted me around.

I had a lot of confusion around friendship and acceptance, and perhaps it's never stopped. The feeling of doubt that people really want me around has hounded me since childhood, even when some of the most interesting and evolved people I've met over the course of my life have claimed they do. Some part of me hides from people—who, as a result, think I don't want to see them, whereas it is *I* who think they don't want to see me.

The next summer I was invited to join a company in Phoenicia, New York. It was managed by David Balding, who was friends with two of my childhood friends, Billy and Tommy Hitchcock, who were helping fund the enterprise. Michael Lindsay-Hogg and Peter Bogdanovich directed, and the costumes were designed by Peter's girlfriend, Polly Platt—all of them unknowns at that time. The company performed a repertory of old plays and some new ones, too; the highlight for me was playing the journalist in *The Skin of Our Teeth*. Michael's mother,

Geraldine Fitzgerald, came up for a short stay, and we passed a magical evening around a bonfire, during which she summoned from the flames a spirit she referred to as "the Green Ram." It was a good spirit, she told us, with which she had a strong connection; and she assured us it would leap from the fire in a demonstration of magic. None of us saw the spirit, but it didn't matter. We loved it, and we loved her.

That summer in Phoenicia *was* magical, though, in an important— if not necessarily dramatic—way. I began to feel accepted as a real member of a community and to actually enjoy spending time with the other actors. I realized that I was, in fact, happiest with artists of all kinds. There is an atmosphere of family, albeit often a dysfunctional one, that forms around a theatrical troupe; and I fantasized that from *now on* the theater would be my home.

I did continue to act off and on for the next several years. In 1968 I played the title role of Sarah in a play by Tom Eyen called *Sarah B. Divine*, which was performed at the Spoleto Festival in Italy, and in that same year I carried a spear in one of Gian Carlo Menotti's operas. That was my crowning moment as an actress in other people's plays. I didn't return to the stage for twenty years, and by then I was writing my own lines.

Though I didn't realize it at the time, a pattern was being established. I would find something I loved—or thought I loved—throw myself into it, and then abruptly change course. Sometimes the choice was mine; sometimes it wasn't.

The latter was the case in the summer of 1961, when Mummy announced that she was going to take me on a round-the-world trip—a two-month interlude that would effectively end my first serious romance, with a very attractive, eligible young man from the same world in which I'd been raised. We were having a lot of fun together, and I felt embraced by his family.

I have no doubt that ending that relationship was part of Mummy's plan. For her, everything was a competition, a blood sport that extended even into the realm of my romantic life. If a young man happened to be visiting, she'd invite him for a game of tennis or golf, remarking offhandedly, "Oh, Bo's not very good. She can play later." If she particularly fancied one of my beaus, she would ask him for a weekend of quail shooting at Medway when was I sure to be somewhere else.

Perhaps, too, she was lonely and frustrated, and wanted a companion she could order about. A few years after Daddy died, a Dr. Carnes Weeks had become a frequent visitor at Medway, and in 1952 he and Mummy married. His nickname among the family was Piggy, and it suited him quite well; I've never known anyone who was such a pig about spending someone else's money. No one liked Piggy in our household, despite the radios and other gifts with which he tried to bribe us. He was a *poseur*, drinking expensive wines and listening to Caruso in the big beige chair in the living room at Medway. His valet, Lloyd, looked like a gangster with his black greasy hair. Nobody liked him either.

The marriage began inauspiciously—Piggy developed chicken pox on their honeymoon—and lasted only a few years. It turned out that Piggy was addicted to morphine, and the drugs must have affected his personality considerably. A contemporary of Mummy's later told me that Piggy had tried to poison Mummy by offering her a cocktail one evening at Medway. Mummy had the strong intuition not to drink it and gave it back to him, suggesting he drink it instead. He emptied it into a potted plant. Perhaps the plant wilted on the spot, or more likely, Piggy gave himself away by getting angry. Mummy immediately called a powerful friend, who flew down that night in his private plane and mysteriously whisked Piggy and his ghastly valet away. Did they kidnap him or have policemen in the plane? Naturally I didn't know any of the details at the time … only that he was gone and Mummy took off on an expedition to Nepal.

No one was likely to take me around the world again, but that wasn't really the most important thing to me just then. I felt I was just getting started on my own life. It was pointless to argue with Mummy about the trip, and there was no deterring her and the dates she wanted to go. It turned out Pan Am was about to discontinue their wonderful round-the-world flight plan that allowed one to get on and off anywhere at will and pick it up a day or a month or even a year later. But my life might have gone in another, more stable direction if I hadn't gone with her.

Per Mummy's instructions, I packed ball gowns with matching satin shoes and evening bags; for she firmly believed that "our" ambassadors in every country we visited would throw parties to receive us. However, times had changed since Mummy had toured the world by steamer, and although we left our cards with many an embassy butler, we were never feted and never unpacked the ball gowns. Nevertheless, Mummy was at her best en voyage, unfazed by delays, inedible food, and bathroom showers that drenched our beds in Afghanistan.

Mummy had already bought first-class tickets; however, when we got to the airport the tickets could not be found. As a veteran traveler, Mummy didn't want any fuss and immediately produced a credit card to buy two more! Luckily the indomitable Rose, her lady's maid, produced the tickets in the nick of time.

Our first memorable stop was Bali, where I was captivated by the beautifully carved stone temples where gargoyles huddled in the little stone entrances damp with dark green moss—the carvings making points against the sky, and the whole filled with great charm and mystery.

It seemed to me that the Balinese were constantly eating from small bowls with chopsticks. They ate working and sunning, lying down and standing up, and carrying babies or firewood. And they were all *thin*. I nearly died of envy. The women wore sarongs with various tops ranging from tiny little blouses held with one button to nothing at all but a disreputable-looking bra.

We had been dropped by our driver at a hotel that offered no lunch. After a long period of hot debate, the managers said they would produce a meal for us. It proved inedible, and I was treated to the sight of my venerable mother throwing food out the window! When we noticed the gardener was watching, however, we agreed that Mummy had to continue eating what we'd been served. She had always had a cast-iron stomach, whereas I spent the entire trip with a permanent stomachache from the tension of traveling with her and from meals like that one.

Back on the plane I wrote a soulful letter to my boyfriend about the spirits and gods of Bali. The Balinese have an intimate daily relationship with their gods. At one point during our stay there, we came upon a huge stone pool where women were washing their hair under spouts carved in the shapes of animals, which spit water from their mouths. The pool was actually a sacred spring. According to Balinese legend, many years ago an evil king demanded that the people give up worshipping their gods and worship him, and the people reluctantly obeyed. Angered, the gods sent a great pestilence to punish them; the people all prayed to be forgiven and returned to worshipping their gods again. The evil king responded by poisoning the river so all the people would die. When the gods saw this, they shot an arrow in the air, and the hole it made in the ground became a spring where the people could drink—and here it was.

The Balinese worship the Brahman trinity of earth, fire, and water, but they cover all their bases by making offerings to rice gods, gods of fertility, and gods of wisdom. On the day we left Bali, however, Mount Agung erupted and we flew through a cloud of black ash. Apparently, something had displeased the gods!

On the plane—it is embarrassing to admit—Mummy and I wrote silly postcards to our friends in rhymed couplets.

People think I am sixteen.
At cocktail time, pickings are lean.
At meals we get a lot of rice
And hidden in it dogs and mice.

Mummy I find I must outwit
Or she'll dispose of my medicine kit.
This is my Pandora's box
Next in my heart to my Pan Am sox.

Our next stop was Cambodia, where we were treated to a private tour of the enormous Hindu temple complex of Angkor Wat. Our guide was Bernard-Philippe Groslier, the renowned French-Cambodian archeologist primarily responsible for excavating and restoring the complex. The silence of the vine-covered temple was mysterious and drew me into a world of spirit that I wanted to explore.

From early childhood, I'd been drawn to the idea of other worlds and magical realities. I had hoped that Timmie would speak to me at midnight on Christmas Eve or that I might meet a fairy drinking from the acorns full of dew that I'd left under oak trees. My world at that time was full of imaginary beings more companionable than most of the people around me. I yearned for a spiritual, magical dimension to my own life, and that yearning never really left me.

There was no time on Mummy's busy travel agenda for silence or contemplation, though. I spent much of the time on the flights between different countries worrying about my life. Had I or had I not given up acting? Traveling with my mother—whose motto was "I don't contemplate my life; I live it"—had given me the idea that maybe it was better to actually *do* things rather than spend my days acting out *other people's* lives and adventures. On the other hand, I loved acting and the process of taking real experiences and making them universal and interesting and beautiful, as one can through art. Was I any good at that, I wondered. Was I good at anything?

But this was not a trip that would support such considerations. We were seeing the world as fast and furiously as possible. We zipped through the Philippines, Taiwan, Hong Kong, and Australia, handing out letters and introductions as we went.

In Bangkok, we lunched with James Thompson, an old friend of Mummy's who had also worked for the OSS during World War II. It was rumored that he continued to serve as a freelance intelligence operative even after resigning from the OSS and was engaged in arms trafficking to independence fighters in Vietnam, Laos, Cambodia, and Indonesia. A compassionate businessman of rare insight, he revitalized the Thai silk industry, forming a company that produced the jewel-like tones and dramatic color combinations now associated with Thai silk. In the process, he lifted thousands of Thailand's poorest citizens from poverty, creating a cottage-based based business that enabled the women who formed the bulk of his labor force to work from home, maintaining their household roles while earning money for their starving families.

Trained as an architect, he constructed—using parts of old up-country houses—a sprawling teakwood home on Bangkok's central canal, where he displayed spectacular *objets d'art* he'd collected over the years: Chinese Ming pieces, Belgian glass, Cambodian carvings, Thai stone images, Burmese statues, and even a dining table that was once used by King Rama V of Thailand.

He entertained us royally in his exotic house, took us to restaurants, and even gave us a tour of his factory—where, of course, we ordered lots of silk suits. Naturally, the queen was annoyed by his success, as she wanted *her* business to be the best, and in the end she caused him a lot of trouble.

After a week or so in Bangkok, we flew to Jaipur, the capital and largest city of the Indian state of Rajasthan. The maharaja and his wife, Aisha, were old friends of Mummy's, with whom she'd often gone tiger shooting. The maharaja was also an avid polo player, who had played with Uncle Laddie. We dined with the maharani and watched her bid good-bye to the maharaja as he departed in his Rolls Royce convertible for a trip. She kissed his feet on the steps of the palace. I noticed she wore bracelets of jasmine flowers, prettier and more feminine than any of her fabulous jewels.

Back on Pan Am, we flew to Kenya, where we slept in tents surrounded by game. Always comfortable under canvas, Mummy was in her element. However, I didn't realize the game could come into the camp! One night, I ventured to the bathroom tent and, creeping slowly through the dark, bumped into what I thought was a large wall; it turned out to be the side of an enormous elephant! I rushed back to my tent before trying again.

After Kenya, we headed to Egypt, where we visited the pyramids. Mummy and I rode out on a camel arranging our skirts over our knees. There were so few tourists at that time, we saw nothing but sand and one lone Egyptian visitor astride a lonely camel. We also visited Luxor, and we were the only tourists in the ruins of the temple complexes and monuments on the West Bank Necropolis. In Luxor, our plane to Cairo was delayed twenty-four hours. I'll never forget watching Mummy sitting patiently on a park bench, pricking her finger with the needle with which she was sewing the torn lining of her basket-bag. Only en voyage did she demonstrate that kind of stoicism.

From Egypt, we flew to Kathmandu, where we stayed at the original Yak and Yeti Hotel, which at that time was a crumbling maharaja's palace. By day we toured the city, which at the time was little more than a tiny, dusty Himalayan hamlet, and in the evenings Mummy and I sat with Boris, the old White Russian who had converted the ruin into a rather tumbledown hotel. There we listened to reports on the shortwave radio from James Ullman and his team as they climbed Mt. Everest.

The high point of the entire trip for me was our visit to Lebanon, where we toured the archaeological digs at the ancient Mediterranean port cities of Tyre and Sidon. Each of the various epochs of history was distinguished by a different layer of sandy earth, each a different color. It reminded me at first glance of a multilayered cream cake. But the fact that I was sitting in the middle of the overwhelming presence of antiquity quickly dispelled such frivolous associations, and I found myself intensely moved by the idea of thousands of years of history embedded in the cliff sides, the compressed remnants of entire civilizations that no longer existed. Some creeping feeling of mortality overcame me—of the ease with which my own world would one day become just a colored layer of sand. The image haunts me still.

Our next destination was Ethiopia. I'd begun to suffer from a full-time stomachache—partly from the exotic food we were eating during our trip, but also from the anxiety of traveling with my mother. Although she was definitely at her best en voyage—energetic, uncomplaining, sometimes compassionate—I feared that at any moment I might make some sort of terrible mistake that would set her off.

Mummy assured me that my stomach discomfort would be cured by Ethiopian food. Of course, she had fond memories of her banquet with Haile Selassie almost forty years earlier. No banquets or royal receptions awaited us in Addis, however. One memorable evening we went to a restaurant and sat at a round table covered with a grubby cloth; above my head hung a lamp fashioned from the head of a ferocious-looking animal that I couldn't identify. Our waiter ceremoniously poured an unmentionable looking semiliquid mess right onto the middle of the table, and Mummy said we should tear off bits of the tablecloth—which was actually a large sheet of *injera*, a traditional Ethiopian type of flatbread—to sop it up.

Unfortunately, the food did not improve my stomach, but I dragged myself out the next day to see an exhibition of the crowns of ancient kings, which were displayed on a table in a fenced-in area beside the city jail. The fence itself was decorated with paper flowers. We were only allowed to peer through the links, because, according to Ethiopian lore, many years ago a queen had made a derogatory remark about religion, and from that time forward no women were allowed to approach the crowns.

Though the trip was in many ways stressful, I'm grateful to have had a chance to see the world "BT"—Mummy's acronym for "before tourists." Though she felt that by the 1960s, the world she'd toured decades earlier had already been ruined by sightseers, in my opinion the world hadn't suffered nearly as badly as my digestion.

We ended our trip in Venice, where Mummy rented a house with Ellen Barry. Fortunately for me, my childhood friend Billy Hitchcock happened to be at the Gritti Hotel when Mummy and I arrived, and through him I met a delicious number of rakes and roués from the international jet set—all of whom I invited to my twenty-first birthday party at our house. One of the guests, I recall, was a German prince, Johannes von Thurn und Taxis, who reportedly carried a trunk of German soil everywhere he traveled so he wouldn't be separated from his mother country. There were also a few Austrian barons with "bad reputations."

For some reason, the last straw at that party—from Mummy's point of view—was the arrival of Daisy Fellowes, a grande dame of café society.

"What are you doing here, Gertie?" Daisy inquired.

With some annoyance, Mummy replied, "It's *my daughter's* twenty-first birthday party."

Mummy was clearly shocked that the friends I had been hanging out with, while she was painting pictures of Venice with Ellen, were members of a set that she considered frivolous. She had rejected that lifestyle early-on in favor of hunting and shooting and more "serious" pursuits. Ellen just laughed at her worries; but later I wondered if Mummy's concern might have had a deeper significance. I enjoyed the jokes and banter, which were as much a part of that society as cocktails and champagne. I don't think Mummy ever developed the skill for frivolous banter. That was a pleasant thought.

When we returned to New York in the fall, I moved into an apartment on Fifth Avenue, which Mummy rented and decorated for us both. There was only one bedroom, but Mummy claimed she would stay on a fold-out sofa in the dining room. Luckily, after trying it once, she did not repeat the experiment. During her brief trips to New York she stayed in hotels—a situation that was better for her, and for me.

Shortly after I'd settled in, David Winn, a British friend whose family were old friends with mine, came to visit for a week—and ended up staying on my fold-out couch for four months. He knew one or two people in the New York arts scene, who, in turn, introduced us to many others. His visit gave me an easy connection to what is referred to nowadays as the "swinging sixties," which satisfied my hunger to be part of things and to come to know a world that was vastly different than the one in which I'd grown up. Through David, I met Emile de Antonio who, before announcing he was a Marxist and making political films about Nixon and McCarthy, was an artists' agent. He found Jasper Johns and Bob Raushenberg anonymous side jobs designing the windows at Tiffany's. "De," as he was often called, was just starting his documentary *Painters Painting*, about the abstract expressionists, and somehow I persuaded him to let me be his still photographer.

I accompanied De to the studios of Robert Motherwell, Helen Frankenthaler, Willem de Koonig, Barnett Newman, Robert Rauschenberg, and Larry Rivers, where I photographed them as they worked. At the time Larry was painting in an old bank on Houston Street. Motherwell showed us a Picasso drawing he had just erased, creating a new art form. I watched de Kooning throw paint on the canvas stretched out on the studio floor. During one shoot, Newman announced, "Art is to artists what ornithology is to birds."

De and his wife, Marilyn, had a sparse, Zen-like apartment where a pool table with sawed-off legs served as the centerpiece for a circle of cushions on the floor. There I met even more artists, including Andy Warhol and Frank Stella, as well as a number of De's left-wing philosopher friends. We drank large quantities of inexpensive and very good Beaujolais. I remember a lot of laughter mixed with very serious conversation, all of which I enjoyed.

I knew I loved being with artists. I remember one night I was driving up Central Park West with Frank Stella and a bunch of other artists. We were all smoking pot and laughing hysterically, when suddenly the lights of oncoming cars glared straight into my eyes. "My God," Frank said. "Shouldn't we be on the other side of the street?"

What an apt metaphor for my life at that time.

Andy Warhol picked up on my anxiety, which he noted in his posthumously published *Diaries*: "Went to Tom Armstrong's at 72nd and Park and Leo Castelli was there, and Iris Love and Robert Rosenblum, who said he didn't understand why everybody gave my show at the Whitney a bad review. Bobo Legendre was there, and I was mean to her because she's a phoney baloney. She's a friend of De Antonio's. She's a carpet heiress." Unaware of his opinion of me at the time, I invited him to small dinner that April—just Andy, David, De, Marilyn and me. Andy drew a menu, which we all signed, and it is on my wall today. He had just started making silk-screens, and he made me a gift of a soup can—which I gave to David when he left for England, because I didn't think it was interesting!

Warhol was right, though. I was afraid I was a fraud, a shadow trying to find a form. By the fall of 1962 I'd tried my hand at acting, nightclub singing, producer's assistant, and photography. I'd enjoyed for the first time the camaraderie of friends I felt were on my "wavelength," people I wanted to emulate—artists and writers and others who were considered exotic or slightly unconventional. I wished I could be one of them; but I felt that, although my personality gave me entrée to that world, my creative work was not enough for a passport.

I decided, partly as a result of Mummy's insistence, to try Georgetown, where I had several friends. Washington was surely a place of salty reality and consequence. Through Carter Brown, who was the head of the National Gallery and a cousin of Rhode Island Senator Claiborne Pell, I got a volunteer job in Senator Pell's office. There I soon discovered that, though my family is intensely conservative, I was a progressive liberal. My friends were all Democrats, and I was working for a Democrat. Their ideas were far more genial than those that had been bantered about at Medway!

I settled in a walk-up apartment in Georgetown, walked to the French Market for baguettes and sausages, played tennis in the park, and cooked chicken bourguignonne for friends who strolled over in the soft dusk from nearby houses. They were a pretty diverse lot. Pammy Howard, a Foxcroft classmate, was working for *The Washington Post*. Alice Arlen—who would later write several screenplays, including *Silkwood*—was having babies. Georgetown was a tight little society, so it was easy to meet fascinating people at every turn. Shortly after I arrived there, I was introduced to Walter Pincus and Alfred Friendly, who at that time were at *The Washington Post*, and Cord Meyer, a CIA honcho who tried very hard to convince me that he was in "weather."

While I was busy trying to "be someone," however, many of my friends were busy exploring their consciousness—hanging out with Billy Hitchcock and his twin brother Tommy at their Millbrook mansion. There Timothy Leary and Dick Alpert (later Ram Dass) were holding court and tripping out on LSD with the hippest of the generation. But I was so afraid I'd lose my mind I never went to any of their gatherings. The whole age was about turning on, putting on, and dropping out. I was about joining in and finding out. I didn't catch up until I was in my forties.

However, I did renew my interest in the world of spirit and other dimensions that had captivated me as a child in Aiken. After flitting about the Georgetown party circuit, I'd come home to read

An Experiment with Time, J. W. Dunne's long essay about multiple dimensions, precognition, and consciousness, and Jozef Rulof's *A View into the Hereafter*. I also made friends with Michael Amrine, a journalist who wrote about psychic and spiritual subjects.

At about that time I met Ted Yates, producer of NBC's *The Huntley-Brinkley Report*, and his wife, Mary. I thought working in TV was terribly glamorous and interesting. *This,* I thought, *is something I can really get into.* I quit working for Senator Pell and got a job at the AP as a glorified secretary (at Mummy's insistence I had recently completed typing school).

I was in the bureau office, sitting among the chattering tape machines and hysterical reporters, when the news arrived that President Kennedy had been shot in Dallas. For several days we all wandered around in a daze, never far from the TV. Washington went into mourning. Life there, which had revolved around the young president and the style and intelligence he'd brought to the nation's capital, was over. Many of my friends, despairing, left the city to take other jobs. My own bank account was depleted, and I was at loose ends.

Yet I remained mesmerized by the media.

Mary Yates took me to New York to meet Tex McCrary, a TV and radio host, with whom she and Ted had worked in their early days in broadcasting. Tex hired me as a "producer"—in reality, a booker—for his nightly talk show on WOR radio. I rented a one-room apartment on 63rd Street and gave dinners with a fire blazing in the little fireplace until the guests, asphyxiated by smoke, staggered home.

McCrary's show was about New York, both its seamy side and its glitter, and he taught me how to conduct interviews and book guests. The first guest I was sent to book on my own was a store owner in Harlem who had shot a man during a robbery in his shop. I went to Harlem and persuaded him to appear on Tex's show, saying that after the publicity he would be famous and have a successful career. Having proved myself by booking a guest that Tex wanted, for the next year I dined five nights a week at the Oak Room of the Plaza Hotel with Tex and his guests—movie stars, politicians, murderers, writers, and taxi drivers. Over daiquiris and minute steaks, I learned how to negotiate interviews with senators and chorus girls, entrepreneurs like Billy Rose and stars like Lena Horne. I was twenty-two and thought I had the most exciting job in New York.

To my amazement, I discovered that people *long* to tell their stories and be immortalized on camera or tape. Give them a microphone, and they'll confess intimate details about their lives that they'd never tell a neighbor. Tex called this phenomenon "taxi driver syndrome." When people believe their secrets are being absorbed by an anonymous vacuum, they no longer feel responsible.

After a year of working for Tex, I was landed my own television interview program in Palm Beach. *Bobo in the Celebrity Room* was a twenty-four-year-old's dream of glamour and fun. On Monday nights I dressed up in chiffon evening gowns borrowed from the shops on Worth Avenue. On nights when Cartier lent me diamonds, a security guard stood behind the camera.

I invited all the interesting people who came to town to stop by for a chat after dinner or the theater. And they did. Some guests were easy to book: Bing Crosby, for example, was a friend of Mummy's and Aunt Mary's whom I'd met a few times at Medway. Others—including Joan Fontaine (who laughed when I reminded her that I'd forgotten my only line in a scene with her in a summer stock play), George Abbott, and Bea Lillie—came because they were performing at the Royal Poinciana Playhouse. Writers and politicians also appeared for interviews. When for one reason or another a guest didn't show up, I invited Peter Duchin, who was conducting his dance band in the room next to the studio where I filmed my show, to stop by and fill the time.

To my horror, I occasionally caught myself echoing family prejudices I didn't actually feel—as when I interviewed Sammy Davis, my second guest ever. "Isn't it amazing what you've done," I chattered obsequiously. "And you black, Jewish, and half-blind!"

He didn't seem to care and actually roared with laughter at my *faux pas*, but B'nai B'rith let the station know *they* cared by writing the station angry letters.

During that entire winter in Palm Beach, I lived with Aunt Mary and Uncle Laddie at Los Incas, their enormous Spanish villa by the sea. It was a tropical palace surrounded by palms and guarded by vicious Dobermans. When Aunt Mary and I were not attending parties—a fairly regular occurrence in Palm Beach, where the Tao of dinner parties was practically invented—we dined on trays in Uncle Laddie's bedroom, where he lay partially paralyzed from polo injuries. (Mummy opined that he was just too lazy to get out of bed.) On these evenings, Manola, their Spanish chef, prepared elaborate meals of *foie gras* and quail, and occasionally a dessert called "snowballs": vanilla ice cream rolled in coconut and topped by hot fudge sauce. One evening Rose Kennedy joined us for dinner on trays, and during coffee and liquors, Manola returned in his Spanish dancing costume, complete with castanets, and entertained us with the flamenco in the space between Uncle Laddie's bed and the fireplace. Mrs. Kennedy was in stitches.

I loved Aunt Mary, who was a wholly generous and clever woman. Though my grandparents had initially disapproved of her Hollywood background, she quickly adapted to the Sanford style of life—learning to ride, shoot, and play golf and tennis, and eventually becoming one of the leading fund-raisers on the charity circuit. She would often offer streetwise guidance about men and money. "Don't follow him to South America," she warned me once about a man I briefly dated. "What if he has another girl?" Another time she advised, "Collect jewels; they never lose their value." She had an engagingly flamboyant side as well. She pronounced the word *television* with a French accent, which lent evenings watching some program or other a jaunty flair. She also commissioned an artist to paint the pool house with images of her jewels floating on white clouds, a virtual invitation to burglars (hence the Dobermans).

We often spent afternoons together beneath those floating gems munching on pastrami sandwiches wrapped in deli paper while sipping Bloody Marys from silver goblets. I lay stretched out in my bathing suit, slathered with oil in the hopes of acquiring a tan. Aunt Mary was in tight white pants, three-inch-high espadrilles, and a huge, floppy straw hat with a long turquoise chiffon scarf that matched her turquoise ring, which had a stone the size of a cockroach. "We really must protect our faces," she said, looking pointedly at my gradually bronzing cheeks.

She was also very supportive of my various careers—and quite perceptive, I thought, in her assessment of my mother, whom she once described as "the most selfish woman I ever met."

With Aunt Mary and Uncle Laddie I felt loved and nurtured, a real member, at last, of a real family. I began, tentatively, to sense the emergence of my own identity, a hazy reflection in the mirror of Palm Beach society. The fantasy world of the very rich is not unlike the invented world of the theater. Everything rests on having enough money to keep the production going and enough confidence to maintain the illusion. I enjoyed living in this atmosphere of love and feeling part of things; but, seduced by the tuberose-scented winds of Palm Beach, I let my budding interest in the spiritual dimension slip silently away.

CHAPTER

5

Into the Big World

My experience in Palm Beach gave me the self-confidence to try my hand at interviews in print. In the summer of 1965, I returned to my rented apartment in New York and started writing stories for *The Charleston News and Courier*, which was owned by my sister's husband. I interviewed everyone from Sonny and Cher to political figures in Washington.

I also began dating Jim Fowler, who had recently joined the team of the television show *Wild Kingdom*. I'd met Jim during a brief visit to Medway, where Mummy had persuaded him to bring his hawks for her to see. Jim was about to make a documentary about animals in Rhodesia—now the Republic of Zimbabwe. I wanted to visit him there, but I didn't want to go simply as a tourist or a girlfriend. The Rhodesian Bush War had begun to escalate into a major civil war, and I wanted to cover it as a reporter.

Gathering my courage, I persuaded Mummy to write to her friend Lord Salisbury, requesting an introduction to Prime Minister Ian Smith. The request was granted, and upon arriving in Rhodesia, I hired Jim's film crew to conduct my first television "remote" interviews with Smith and with the Marxist leader of the Zimbabwe African National Union,

Robert Mugabe. Prime Minister Smith, I could see, was quite surprised by my youth.

I gave the tapes to Westinghouse Broadcasting, as had been arranged before the trip, but I never found out if or when they were broadcast. By then I didn't care. I'd had a great adventure, and if they were shown on TV, so much the better.

When I came back, I signed up for a job at the North American Newspaper Alliance, a large syndicate of major newspapers in the United States and Canada, and I eventually parlayed my way into the press corps accompanying Robert Kennedy's campaign. All year there had been protests against the Vietnam War, and finally President Johnson had withdrawn on that issue. In March 1967 was the huge "Be In" in Central Park; in October Allen Ginsberg and Abbie Hoffman tried to levitate the Pentagon; and in December the Yippies dedicated themselves to the end of money and the downfall of "Flower Power." Kennedy was running against Hubert Humphrey and Eugene McCarthy for the Democratic nomination to battle Nixon and Agnew.

I had made friends with respected reporters at *The New York Times* and *Newsweek*, who kindly hustled me aboard Senator Kennedy's planes and buses along with them if I didn't have a press pass. One day in Seattle, I was sitting directly behind the senator on his bus. His window was open as he greeted the crowds surrounding us. Suddenly a woman poked her hand through the window and tossed her wedding ring on his lap. Kennedy shook his head in disbelief and creased his brow in a little frown that made triangles of his blue eyes. His lips were chapped from the wind of endless open-car motorcades, and his hands were small and tough-looking, almost gnarled, as he picked up the ring. The crowd had already closed around the woman as the bus moved on. Perhaps she thought of it as a financial campaign contribution or perhaps an offering of admiration; it was surely a symbol of how much people loved him. The next day at an orphanage, a group of five-year-olds leaned against his knees like puppies waiting to have their heads stroked.

Eventually, we arrived in Los Angeles. I felt happy to be included in this community of journalists, all living more or less together and working on the same thing. I felt I was part of something exciting, of history in the making.

On the evening of June 4, 1968, a party celebrating Kennedy's victory in the California primary was in full swing in a suite on the seventh floor of the Ambassador Hotel. I chatted happily with blond ladies covered with jewels and wearing press badges while reporters in turtlenecks and tweed jackets sat about smoking and drinking. Writer Bud Shulberg, looking wooly and tweedy, chatted with George Plimpton, whose wife, Freddy, sat on the bed in an adjoining room talking to Jean Smith, the senator's sister. Film director John Frankenheimer discussed movies with Dick Silbert, and on the couch Charles Evers—whose brother Medgar had been assassinated five years earlier after returning home from a meeting with NAACP lawyers—told John Glenn, "You're the only people who can do something for us. Kennedy is the only one who can really deal with minority groups."

Finally Senator Kennedy entered the suite, looking tanned and young and glad to see everyone celebrating. He made the rounds accepting congratulations and shaking hands; then, accompanied by his wife, Ethel, he went downstairs to the ballroom to address supporters and congratulate McCarthy for having run a good race.

Everyone was increasingly gay—drinking and laughing. Having knocked McCarthy out of the race, and with only Humphrey to face at the upcoming Chicago convention, Kennedy's success was imminent. Jeff Greenfield, a young speechwriter, stretched out on the floor in front of the television set with his wife, and shortly after midnight we all gathered around to watch Kennedy deliver his speech. We continued to watch the jubilant crowd in the ballroom after the senator left the podium and made his way out of the ballroom through the hotel kitchen.

Suddenly on the TV, the CBS reporter frantically shouted, "Please clear the room," but no one in the suite paid any attention. Then came the terrible words, "We cannot tell if the senator has been shot or not." Immediately, the suite emptied as people tumbled over each other to find out the truth. As I left with them, I heard a woman's voice echoing our collective thought, "My God, my God! Do they have to do this to every decent man?"

I didn't travel east on the funeral train with the other reporters. I felt that was somehow a breach of good manners, as I wasn't formally a part of his press corps and I wasn't really friends with the senator. However, I wrote a story about that evening, which appeared on the front page of *The Washington Post* a day or two later. I expect because of that, Charlotte Curtis, editor of *The New York Times*'s Family/Style section, hired me as a reporter.

But in August of that year, the Russians invaded Czechoslovakia, crushing the Prague Spring. Since I had a journalist's visa—the last before the Soviet government refused to give them out—Charlotte agreed that I could go to Eastern Europe and start working for her in December.

Full of optimism over my burgeoning career as a newspaper and radio "stringer," I took along my twenty-pound reel-to-reel tape recorder, which made a permanent dent in my left shoulder. I'd learned how to plug it into the mouthpiece on a telephone when I was interviewing Mugabe, so now I could file my reports to Westinghouse Radio. I fancied myself as a hotshot war correspondent, and I even bought a trench coat and a fetching felt hat, which I pulled over one eye. I was *sure* this would be an important adventure.

I wasn't actually hired to cover the war, so instead I filed stories about my experiences as I found myself immersed in a world of revolutionary intellectuals, poets, and artists. My first piece of good luck upon arriving in Prague was that Tad Schultz, who I'd known in Washington and was now *The New York Times* bureau chief there, allowed me sleep on the sofa in his office until I found a hotel. After I'd settled in a bit, I met a Resistance leader about my age in a snappy beret, who invited me to join him and his friends in basement restaurants drinking cheap, unmarked bottles of wine. I'd never met anyone like these young revolutionaries, so passionate about everything, planning guerilla strategies against the Soviet invaders in smoky cellars and windowless rooms.

After these clandestine meetings, I would wander alone down the dark, empty streets, their silence shattered by the clanking passage of a Russian tank. Not knowing the language, I couldn't read the street signs; I hoped someone could speak French or English, and I bravely stopped to ask directions of the rare passerby. I can't remember how I ever got home. It was the simple luck visited upon the crazy and the innocent.

Those basement meetings were my first up-close experience of opposition to a government, and they gave me an inspiring view of daring young people up against a palpable and determinedly aggressive government force. I left Czechoslovakia when my visa ran out, but I understood for the first time what real political oppression felt like.

I didn't want to go back to the States, though. Instead, I went to Bucharest, where the wet black trees were hung with golden leaves. The scene reminded me of Shakespeare's sonnet, XXVIII:

Where yellow leaves or none or few do hang
Upon those boughs which shake against the cold,

Though under the Communists Romanian poets and writers kept a low profile, a journalist friend in America had given me a slip of paper with the telephone number of a writer named Joanna Cioranna. I called her from a phone booth, and she immediately invited me for tea later that day. I climbed up several flights of stairs to a tiny apartment dimly lit by a Tiffany lamp and piled with books—so many that there was hardly room for the two ancient mahogany armchairs in which we sat. We drank sweet Romanian wine from tiny gold-rimmed glasses while waiting for the water to boil for tea. She had a talent for drawing people out, and I soon found myself talking more openly than I ever had before.

"Is fall or spring happier?" she asked at one point.

"I don't know," I said. "They both make me cry."

"Me, too. They both make me think of death."

"Why?"

"I'm always thinking about death," she said. "It's so inevitable and mysterious. It makes me sad. But we're most with death when we are most alive, don't you agree?"

I wasn't sure; I hadn't thought about it much, to be honest. So I just said, "Yes, yes, absolutely."

After a half hour or so, we were joined by her friend Nicholae Breban, a writer and essayist with deep-set, dark eyes. We talked and talked about everything—love, death, sadness, the kind of pain that at the same time is paradoxically accompanied by joy … all the things I'd been brought up to believe one *shouldn't* talk about. I had been brought up not to discuss sad things or death: the WASP ethic is to meet grief and challenges with stolidity and a stiff upper lip. When my father died, my mother dealt with it by going for a horseback ride all alone on her favorite mount, Divorcee.

I loved every minute of this deep conversation, in which my new friends revealed themselves. At one point, Nicholae observed, "I don't like an excess of wine or love. I don't like to be out of control."

As he said this, of course, he was sitting on the end of a desk that had been partially cleared of books, drinking tea and eating jam out of a pot with a little silver spoon. "Jam is the only sweet we have," said Joanna wistfully.

Just before I left the apartment, Nicholae handed me a little ink sketch of the three of us sitting around the earth. Our conversation was represented by lines from our mouths that circled the globe.

Later during my stay Joanna took me to a disco, where she introduced me to Camil Petrescu, the disk jockey. He wore a long gray-blue scarf that matched the color of his eyes. It turned out he invited me to dinner with his family on Rue Petrescu. Their spacious, tumbling house was filled with old Christian icons and lamps covered by oriental silk shawls; it felt like a gypsy hideaway. Camil's mother was an actress, his stepfather, an archaeologist. Over delicious meals of Eastern European stew and bottles of wine we engaged in intense conversations about art.

"Art is what is important to us," Camil's mother said at one point. "We can't make money. We can never get anything in this country. So it is the purification of our art that matters."

I asked Mr. Petrescu about archaeology, and he spoke eloquently and at length about the mystery of digging and finding whole worlds we had never known existed, or discovering more about ones that we did know about. He made a story of his life's work, a romantic tale of the endless excavation of knowledge.

I felt with the Petrescus that I had found a niche in a family I wished were mine: artists and historians, generous people who loved each other and respected each other's minds. I wanted to move right in—and not just because of Camil's blue eyes, which might have been enough, but because I tasted the flavor of Bohemian life in those stews and in those conversations. I fell in love with these people and what they were thinking about.

I hated to leave. But my visa ran out, so I headed for Warsaw. A Polish actress I'd met in New York had given me a letter of introduction to Agnieszka Osiecka, a well-known writer and lyricist who would eventually make her mark as a filmmaker. Through her, I met the world of Polish intellectuals at the Writer's Club. We sat in the square-paneled room of what must have been an old palace, eating creamed mushrooms and drinking vodka, and I felt increasing delight in the company of these smart, generous Bohemians. They seemed "skinless" to me, completely free of the social armor worn by most of the people I knew back home. They told the truth about themselves. I realized how comfortable and comforted I could feel talking about sadness, losses, and our yearnings for love or creative satisfaction. It was the first time I truly relaxed emotionally —among strangers who suddenly felt like my new best friends. Instead of thinking I had to *do* the right thing, I felt right about simply *being*.

This is who I am, I thought. *A bohemian!*

The sheer pleasure of talking openly to people who allowed themselves to express their vulnerability was both a revelation and a challenge: dare I be as vulnerable as my friends behind the Iron Curtain? I knew that for the people I'd met there, that boundary imposed terrible fear and hardship; but for me it had served as a kind of protective screen behind which the self I longed to be had finally begun to emerge.

At the Warsaw airport, the customs agent kissed my hand and said he hoped I'd had a good time.

"Yes, wonderful," I replied—and I meant it.

Eastern Europe felt like home.

Unfortunately, it wasn't really mine.

Work at *The New York Times* was less satisfying. I'd imagined I would be sent off to interview people from the theater and politics. Instead, I was sent to the Bride Department to sit behind a gray metal desk and write up endless wedding announcements. Bored, I made spelling mistakes and entertained the News Department by jumping out of a paper cake in my white fur coat at a party for someone's birthday. Eventually, Charlotte did let me write a story or two. But ultimately we agreed—amicably—that the job was not right for me, nor I for it. "Don't waste your time on fashion magazines," she counseled, knowing that some of my contemporaries were working at *Vogue* and *Harper's Bazaar*. She took me seriously as a writer, even though I didn't.

My impatience had gotten the better of me. Having tasted the richness of a life bare of artifice, I wanted to live that way too. I wanted it all, and I wanted it now. No writing humdrum, boring wedding announcements for me. I wanted *meaning*. I wanted *relevance*.

Yet, even then, I had an inkling that behind my impatience lurked an old, familiar fear. I'd lived for so long with the dread of failure, of being exposed as a fraud, not a "real" reporter or artist or actress. I'd been afraid to commit myself to writing, because I might fail.

As I packed up the few belongings from my *Times* desk, it seemed that my star, which had been rising quickly rising, had suddenly crashed.

CHAPTER

6

Interlude in Morocco

Throughout the sixties, I'd been afraid to join my friends on their acid trips and mushroom explorations because I felt our agreed-upon, everyday reality was such a tenuous thing, and my own sense of identity was too filmy to risk such a challenge. However, my time in Eastern Europe had thrust me into an extreme realm full of brave and unconventional people, where I had begun to let go of some of the anxiety that bound me to a very limited way of relating to other people. It was a "trip" without the drugs.

My experience had been specific to that time and place, though, and it hadn't traveled back with me to the States. When I'd returned to New York, I'd found I still hadn't grasped the formula for feeling at peace with myself and others.

As the seventies dawned, I was able to taste some of the flavor of openness and freedom I'd felt among my Slavic friends with Frecky and Betty Vreeland. Frecky was the son of the Diana Vreeland, who lived just down the street from me in her famous all-red apartment. Betty was a fascinating and warm woman who had previously been married to author Peter Tompkins and then had gone on to marry Frecky. They were kind, fun, and original people who made me feel welcome in their world.

They lived part of the time in Morocco, where Frecky worked for the CIA. When they were in New York, they hosted dinner parties where they offered their guests caftans and Moroccan leather slippers. We all sat on banquettes made of *kilims* and dined on Betty's rich, slow-cooked Moroccan *tagines* of lamb and apricots. Those evenings offered the deep conversations and relaxed sense of connection that had characterized my experiences in Eastern Europe.

At about that time, I was reading Lesley Blanch's *The Wilder Shores of Love*, a biographical account of four audacious European women who had left the strictures and conventions of nineteenth-century Europe behind in search of adventure in more exotic places. My favorite was the Swiss explorer and writer Isabelle Eberhardt, the illegitimate daughter of a Russian mother and an Armenian-Russian anarchist, who spent most of her short life in North Africa. She'd converted to Islam and dressed as a man—calling herself Si Mahmoud Essadi—which allowed her to move about in Arab society with a freedom she would otherwise have never enjoyed. I was so inspired by her story that when Betty suggested I go to Morocco with her for a few weeks, I leapt at the chance.

The desert wind bent the palm trees in bows of welcome at the Tangier airport, where fuchsia-colored bougainvillea decorated the terminal walls and a cobalt sky stretched from the city's minarets to the sand dunes of the Sahara. I was instantly enchanted by the flash of color in Moorish courtyards, the old women wrapped in stark black hiding behind their veils, and the men's caftans rustling along the narrow alleyways of the souks. This was the land of the veiled reality and the brief glance. The golden dry desert and the limpid green were reflected in the sharp transitions from shade to sun, where the temperature difference was like changing seasons.

We stayed at a small hotel called Guitta's—which was also the name of a very famous restaurant in Tangier, frequented by ambassadors and royalty. Mercedes Guitta ran the restaurant, which had originally been located in the Grand Hotel Villa de France, where many of the great nineteenth- and early twentieth-century painters—and more recently, the Rolling Stones—had made a temporary home. Each morning while

I had café au lait and croissants, Betty caught me up on the latest installments of Tangier gossip. Much of this revolved around the fact that everyone we met—male or female—seemed to have taken Arab boys as lovers. We'd spend the better part of breakfast trying to figure out *which* famous writers were using varying combinations of *other* famous writers and their Arab lovers as subjects for their novels.

Our first evening in Tangier, we had dinner with Betty's best friends, Joe McPhillips and John Hopkins. Joe was the head of the American School in Tangier, and John was writing a novel called *Tangier Buzzless Flies*, a tragic story about a writer's relationship with a Moroccan he meets while prospecting for oil in the Spanish Sahara. We dined at The Parade Bar, Tangier's version of Elaine's, while Joe and John regaled us with stories of famous people who lived in Tangier: the writer Paul Bowles and his wife, Jane; poet and artist Brion Gysin; and even, for a short time, Mick Jagger. After that, we wrapped ourselves in silk caftans and spent our evenings eating *tagines* with many of the people we'd heard about: Gysin, Bowles, David Herbert (the English aristocrat who reigned over the British expatriate colony in Morocco), and the strikingly beautiful artist Margaret McBey—the "regulars" and the pinnacles of Tangier society. Yves St. Laurent had a house there, too, but I never saw him.

There was something slightly over the top about the whole experience, which I liked. Tangier in the seventies harbored a community that was as exotic and intimate as I could have imagined. Almost from the moment I arrived, I felt as though I belonged there Looking back, I wonder if at that point my mind was in an almost hallucinatory state, a heady feeling evoked by sharing the company of such fascinating people. It was like discovering a new family.

Brion, a close friend of Joe and John's, was one of the main "family" members. The moment I met him at their hilltop house at dinner in their garden under the Japanese lanterns—eating *tagines* served by their kindly old Arab servant—I felt I had made a soul connection. Brian felt the same way it seemed, and he invited me to go on trips about Morocco with him—but there were always complications.

One evening at dinner Brion suggested we take a trip to Fez, about two hundred miles south of Tangier. We hadn't been on the road long when we stopped for gas and three men in caftans jumped out of a big white van and embraced Brian. We had run into a group of Jajouka musicians who lived on a nearby hill, buying gas at the next pump.

Brion was ecstatic. "They'll play for us. You'll see; it will be fantastic!" he cried. He turned the car around, heading toward the mountains in the Rif region of northern Morocco.

He explained as we drove that the Jajouka music was different from the Moroccan music we heard in public squares or in hotels. The Jajouka were Sufi trance musicians whose use of horns, drums, and chanting evoked altered states of consciousness. Brion had been introduced to the music by the Moroccan painter Mohamed Hamri, whose uncle was one of the master musicians of Jajouka, an ancient village in the foothills of the Rif mountains. During a visit there, Brion witnessed a ritual in which a man dressed in goatskins, representing a half-man, half-goat divine figure called Boujeloud, danced around a fire while the musicians played—a ceremony he linked to the ancient rites of the Greek god Pan. In the late sixties, he'd brought the Rolling Stones' lead guitarist, Brian Jones, to the village, where he recorded an album called *Brian Jones Presents The Pipes of Pan at Joujaka.* Jones had died shortly after recording the album, but the Stones released it posthumously in 1971.

Brian also told me an old Moroccan maxim: "You say you are going to Fez. But I know you are not going to Fez. Because, if you say you are going, it means you are not. Why do you lie to me? You, who are my friend?" That proved true, for I tried twice more to visit Fez and each time was thwarted by some more seductive plan.

We arrived at sunset at the Jajouka village of whitewashed huts huddled on a green mountainside. The musicians settled us in a circle on cushions and *kilims* in a clay-floored room lit by a few candles in niches and warmed by a glowing charcoal-filled brazier. They played all night as we lay wrapped in blankets and bolstered by huge kilim-covered cushions, smoking long thin pipes of *kif*—a powdery substance sifted from the buds and leaves of the cannabis plant. The candles flickered in the wall niches, and now and then, in the middle of the room, eleven-year-old boys dressed in silver lamé dresses twirled to the sensual rhythms of the music.

The state to which the music—and the kif—carried me seemed a comfortable, almost familiar one. As a child, I'd often had the feeling of being what I called "dreamy." When Mamie and I came out of a movie, I would have to hang tightly to her hand, because I wasn't sure what town, or street, or even world I was in. Fascinated by the idea of magic and magical worlds, I lost touch with the line between realities easily, and once transported to another place via a film, I had trouble getting back.

That night with the Jajouka musicians I had an experience that has remained central to the way I relate to and understand religion. Energy circled out of my head, into my feet and up my spine. My breathing slowed, and I had a vision in which all the religions of the world passed before me embodied by religious masters, each in the costume of their tradition.

Then, as in a film, the churches, synagogues, mosques, and temples of all the world's spiritual systems unwound before my mind's eye. Next, a great tree unfurled its branches, and each was a different religion, but the trunk was Truth. For me, it was a vision that revealed the essential unity of the spiritual dimension, despite its many different expressions.

I woke from this reverie to the sun slowly rising above the hills and the sounds of goats' bells ringing in the valley. The musicians were already busy frying eggs and flat Arab bread and making coffee over a campfire. I'll never forget the green of the grass, the color of the sky, the incredible comfort, and the lazy, happy feeling of the morning after a night of such total absorption in sound and vision and dream. Walking to the river to wash my face, and thinking of my visions, I realized that it didn't matter which path one took to the Great Mysteries: they all lead to the same Truth of time and the cycles of nature. That realization felt familiar, like something remembered from another time, or perhaps another lifetime. That all religions are fingers pointing at the same moon, all branches of the tree of Truth, has been my essential belief ever since.

That night in Morocco I remembered—or perhaps I just recognized—something I already knew: I wanted this other, wider reality and the familiar, worldly one to meld so that I would never have to rely on psychedelics. Like the reflection of a Japanese moon bridge in water, which forms a circle with itself, I wanted this life to have a spiritual dimension reflected in it directly, so that experience and the meaning might be all of a piece. I had no desire to escape into another reality but instead to make sense of this one.

Back in Tangier, Joe McPhillips, John Hopkins, and I hired the Jajouka musicians to play at a party in their garden. We lit torches around the terrace and served a cumin-scented feast. I danced myself into a trance and floated above the earth. John said he saw me levitate off the floor, and he wrote about it in his book *The Tangier Diaries*.

At first, I had thought the lure of Morocco lay in the red clay fortresses where African palms threw their shadows like gypsy shawls on the sunbaked walls, the brilliant colors of the silk cushions and caftans, and the snake charmers and magic charms sold side by side with barrels of curry and dates. I thought it was the sad donkeys in the souks and the pervasive fragrance of cumin and myrrh; the call to prayer and the sounds of soft leather slippers flapping along a tile hallway; and the blue mosaics and piles of kilims.

But what I fell in love with, in fact, was a country where permission for total abandonment and the freedom to be oneself was inherently part of the culture. What appealed to me was the possibility of throwing off the traces, so to speak, of my WASP upbringing and allowing my huge, soft inner self to bask in the sun and find complete acceptance, at least in my own soul. I liked dancing and singing and feeling part of a deep, sweet culture that was so accepting of everything and everyone. I found that I liked being aware of several levels of reality at once and spending time with people who talked to me about things immaterial.

I discovered that a part of my psyche relaxed in other cultures. I let go of the anxiety that I had to "live up" and "get cracking," as my mother persistently advocated. I felt free. My experience smoking kif with the Jajouka musicians was an important step on a spiritual journey that would evolve slowly, in fits and starts, over the next thirty years.

CHAPTER

California

When I returned from Morocco, New York seemed gray and full of sharp corners after the rounded rust walls and cobalt heavens of Tangier. The door to my spiritual awakening quickly slammed shut as I retreated to the comforts of the material world. I bought an apartment on East 63rd Street and painted the library red and the hallway silver. I started dating an editor at *LIFE* magazine, who urged me to go to California to find out why *Show* magazine hadn't printed a piece I'd written for them about the artists in De's film *Painters Painting*, which was nearing completion. I couldn't decide whether or not to go, because I was dithering about visiting Mamie, who had moved to England a few years earlier. I regularly worried that she would get sick or die without my seeing her or having a chance to say good-bye.

As I dithered, an odd thing happened. I got a call from a friend of Mummy's, a man named Richard Mack. I'd met him a few years earlier, when, fresh from my Eastern European travels, I'd flown down to Medway to impress Mummy with my new adventures. Of course, Mummy dismissed the whole affair with a wave of the hand.

"She's become a Communist," she said to her houseguests.

But Richard, who was among the guests, listened attentively to my stories and flirted with me behind Mummy's back.

Fifteen years older than I, he was a taut, hard, wiry man with curly black hair and a big nose. Sexy. Rough. Mummy obviously liked him. They had become friends on a Smithsonian expedition to Nepal in 1959, just after she divorced Piggy. Richard was an undergraduate at Yale in mammalogy at the time, and he'd been hired on as an animal skinner. He and Mummy had stayed in touch over the intervening years, throughout all three of his subsequent marriages.

I hadn't heard from him since our brief flirtation at Medway, but suddenly he was calling to suggest that I come out and visit him at his ranch outside of Carmel. I would never have even considered it had I not needed to go to California anyway. Still, I vacillated until Richard promised to meet me at the airport with a bunch of roses. For some reason, that persuaded me. I always had a bit of the drama queen at the ready, and roses as I got off the plane sounded nicely dramatic, so I agreed.

What was I thinking? I had a nice boyfriend and a new apartment in New York, and neither Mummy nor her entourage had ever brought me much happiness. I was just caught up in the fantasy that this trip could be a great adventure, and that just *maybe* Richard was *the man* for me—which wasn't really thinking at all. I was ready to leave New York for a little vacation, anyway. Deep down I knew that I should go to England and see Mamie; that was the important trip. But I thought, *Well, I can do that later.*

"Later," of course, is something any wise person knows does not exist. But I was not wise.

Secure in knowing that my boyfriend and I would meet a week later for Easter at Medway, where I had planned a house party, I boarded the plane happy and expectant. I'd dressed carefully in a rust-and-blue St. Laurent skirt and a rust cashmere sweater, with a suede rust St. Laurent bag and matching boots. I felt elegant and gay.

Richard met me at the airport in a jeep, which I thought was vaguely exotic and masculine; but to my astonishment there were no roses. That should have been a tip-off, but I overlooked it. I stayed for a few days at his ranch, and we hiked in the rolling hills and walked along the windy beaches watching whales. We drank martinis, which I'd never had before, and we ate tacos in front of a roaring fire. His rustic, cozy house, made of old railroad ties, was set on a small hill above the redwoods, and it boasted a Japanese wooden tub in the guest bathroom. He seduced me while I was half-drunk in front of the fire. Instead of thinking, *This guy is fast and forward and after something*, I thought, *This is so romantic and so off the charts!*

How blind I was.

The next day, he offered to fly me to Los Angeles for my meeting with the *Show* magazine people in his little Helio Courier airplane. Still caught up in a romantic fantasy, I readily agreed, and he booked a room together for us at the Beverly Wilshire. Although it doesn't sound particularly exciting in retrospect, at the time I kept thinking, *Isn't this amazing? I've never done anything like this before!*

I was easily seduced by the "new" and the unexpected, as well as by the idea of being a little outrageous. Mummy seemed to have had *so* much fun—and for a woman of her era, she had been quite unconventional. It was hard to keep up with her, but I wanted to if I could. I also loved the spur-of-the-moment feeling of the affair. An impulse! *I'm not usually impulsive enough*, I told myself, whereas in fact I was at that time pretty much the world's most impulsive person.

When I got back from my magazine meeting, our bedroom at the Beverly Wilshire was full of flowers and Richard was ready with champagne and caviar and a proposal of marriage. We had known each other a total of five days!

I didn't pause for a moment to reflect that this was the sort of life decision people really take time to contemplate. Instead, in a burst of what I considered superlative independence, I threw caution to the winds, said yes, and flew to Mexico with him and his son Jeff, who was on school vacation for Easter.

I discovered during the flight that Richard wasn't even divorced from his current wife, but I somehow managed to convince myself that it didn't matter! In the ensuing carnival ride—the excitement of being in Mexico and in the throes of a new love affair—I didn't have time to think. I suppose that was just what Richard wanted. All I knew was that, after Morocco, I was hungry for a change in my life. I thought maybe the sense of deep connection I'd discovered with friends abroad could be found in marriage.

I also needed to get away from New York, from the East Coast, and try something new. Perhaps I already felt the pull of my destiny in California. The California part turned out to be true. I did have a destiny there, albeit not the one I anticipated at the time.

As he parked his plane on a dusty strip outside of a tiny village by the sea, Richard said, "Let's elope." It did seem a bit odd that he was in such a great rush to get married. But I brushed off whatever concern I felt, because it seemed oddly *good* for me to do something so unpremeditated.

I bought a pink cotton moo moo that was hanging outside a basket shop, and Richard bought a metal ring. It was too big for my finger, so he cut it with a pair of pliers from the plane. While Richard rushed off in his plane to find a minister, Jeff and I sat on the beach enjoying the sun. I found myself agreeing with him that Richard was making an awful fuss when all *we* wanted to do was lie in the sun and swim.

If I could have seen things a bit more clearly, I would have recognized that I was more in tune with Jeff than with Richard. Despite our shared complaints about a midafternoon wedding cutting into precious beach time, I went ahead with the ceremony—with Jeff as witness—which was held out-of-doors under a pink bougainvillea bower that matched the color of my dress. The minister told us to write our names in a large ledger, and afterward the hotel where we were staying provided us with chicken tacos and a bottle of Gewürztraminer for a wedding picnic on the beach. I ended up getting quite drunk, throwing up behind a sand dune and losing my wedding ring in the surf.

Two days later, I flew to Medway for the Easter house party I'd planned.

"I'm going to marry Richard," I told Mummy. I didn't mention that we'd already eloped.

She looked suitably surprised. As usual, she was more concerned about her plans than mine. "You'd better do it before the fifteenth of May," she said, "because I'm going to London." Then, to my astonishment, she added, "I just want you to know I never went to bed with him."

Since the idea hadn't occurred to me, that remark really set me wondering. Mummy always found a way to put me on edge.

At one point during the weekend, I admitted to a close friend that I was going to get married to someone I hardly knew. There wasn't much time to change my mind, even if I wanted to, and I was vaguely thinking this marriage might not have been my best idea.

"Is there anything you don't like about him?" she queried.

"His nose," I said.

She looked concerned but didn't take a strong stand about it, and I didn't tell her the real problem: that I was already married to him.

It did turn out to be a problem, only too soon. Richard met me at my apartment in New York, and suddenly he seemed very, very different from everyone else I knew, and he didn't fit in. There was something aggressive and defensive about him. A friend gave me an engagement party, during which Richard made an inappropriate toast involving baby girl nightgowns, most of which I have mercifully forgotten. I could tell that none of my friends liked him, but they were discreet enough to refrain from saying so. Much later, a friend told me he made a pass at her.

I tried to swallow my worries. After all, we were already married. To whom could I admit my mistake? To whom could I turn for counsel? What does one do if one marries someone by mistake and then is stuck in it? I desperately needed someone to confess to, someone to advise me. Normally this would be a mother's concern, but I knew Mummy would just get angry or simply brush me off by saying it was my problem. I couldn't think *whom* to talk to about it. So I didn't talk to anyone, and I had to get married, again.

And I knew it was a terrible mistake.

The ceremony took place at Medway on May 11, 1971. William Sloane Coffin, who was a friend of Richard's, performed the service. Mummy kept muttering there was some reason she shouldn't like Reverend Coffin, but she couldn't remember what it was. Coffin was, of course, the Presbyterian minister who had protested the Vietnam War so vociferously that he was jailed. He'd founded SANE, the National Committee for a Sane Nuclear Policy, and he was famous for his left wing, antiwar, and antisegregation policies. Along with Dr. Benjamin Spock and some three hundred others, he'd signed a famous document, "A Call to Resist Illegitimate Authority," which was published in several important newspapers. If Mummy—who had voted for Goldwater and Nixon—had remembered, she would have thrown Reverend Coffin out before the wedding ... which in this case would have been an act of mercy.

A pretty eclectic group of guests came to Medway to witness the catastrophe. An Arab friend brought a caftan from King Faisal's sister; Renata Adler, a writer for *The New Yorker*, came down, but she left before the ceremony because of a literary scrap between Lillian Hellman and Mary McCarthy; a flutist spent most of the weekend in a canoe serenading the people on the terrace by the lake; and a Sicilian princess stunned the servants by coming equipped with enough jewels for a palace celebration. Mother insisted on golf and tennis for everyone all the time, and Richard smoked cigars, which drove everyone mad.

The reception was held in a log cabin on the Medway grounds. There was a band and champagne and I was having fun; but Richard dragged me away almost immediately and took me to a dreary hotel in Charleston for the night. The next day we flew to California and went back to his ranch, which had lost some of its allure after Medway. On my first morning there, I came downstairs to get some coffee and found the housekeeper sunbathing on the dining room floor.

"Well, you snagged the old fart," she said.

I thought, *This is a disaster.*

We spent our honeymoon in Russia, where Richard had been invited to a mammalogy conference in Moscow. I was astonished by the singular honesty of the Russian people. On one occasion, I had left my mink coat in a taxi and it was returned to the hotel by the driver. Another day, I left my camera in the lobby of a hotel we were visiting and it was returned to the "hall guardian"—one of the ancient women in babushkas who guarded the halls of every hotel in those days.

Meanwhile, I began to wonder about Richard. One evening in Moscow I was having dinner with some friends in the diplomatic service; Richard said he couldn't come because he was "busy." It struck me as odd: this was our honeymoon, after all. I'd noticed he was very cozy with the pretty redhead who was our Intourist guide, and I had a feeling that he spent the evening with her.

The conference planners had arranged for a field trip to Lake Baikal for attendees. However, when I told Intourist that my name was Bokara, the agency agreed to let us take our field trip to Bukhara instead of Lake Baikal. We traveled down in a plane that had a round hole for a door; it was crammed with passengers, all of whom had baskets of live chickens stuffed under their seats. We flew over the empty desert—where Tamerlane's armies had marched long ago—to the accompaniment of the chickens' loud and anxious squawking.

I loved Bukhara. It was full of blue mosques, men from the desert in long blue caftans and black boots leading camels, and old men sitting on piles of kilims under trees smoking hookahs and hash pipes. Richard and I ate yogurt soup with mint and mutton kebabs, and we went to the public market. I mentioned that my name was Bokara, and the shopkeepers gave me round loaves of bread with my name stamped on it with some sort of bread mold. They also gifted me with earrings and spun sugar, and velvet pillows embroidered in gold thread with the name Byoxpo (Bukhara in Russian). I still have those frayed pillows on my sofa in California today.

During the next five years of somewhat rocky married life, I called my friends in New York nearly every day, although happily I found a few good friends in California. Meanwhile, I began having fights with Richard about money. Basically, he didn't have any, and he expected me to pay for things. He ordered things for the ranch that I didn't like and for which I had to pay. Instead of viewing him as rough and sexy, I was already beginning to hear how vulgar his speech was. His world was different from mine, and he didn't feel comfortable with my friends. He was a poseur, a man who wasn't what he had seemed. I also discovered that he kept a gun under his pillow. Despite his bellicose attitude, he was a frightened man whose standards were not what I'd thought.

Sometimes we escaped the few ribbons of reality that passed for our marriage for the fabric of semireality extended by travel. The least auspicious of these trips was an expedition with my mother to the South Sea island of Siberut to save the pygmy gibbons from the depredations of loggers. Mummy had rung up a friend at the Smithsonian, and the next thing we knew we were enlisted to go.

En route, at the various cities one necessarily stopped at in those days (Honolulu, Hong Kong, and Singapore), Mummy waited for Richard to pick up the check at every meal—it being her rather old-fashioned view that a man traveling with two women should pay all the bills. Richard waved credit cards around, which I knew I would have to pay. After a week of this, I told Mummy it was her turn. She looked surprised, but I didn't bother to explain. I simply pointed out that times had changed since she had traveled the world.

Eventually we reached the Sumatran port of Padang. We were met with looks of disgust by the natives from whom we tried to rent a boat to reach the island of Siberut, home of the threatened pygmy gibbons we had come to save. How we were to save them did not seem to have occurred to anyone with any real clarity. Mummy had organized an expedition. She liked expeditions, but working out the details wasn't her forte.

"The sea is rough, and the natives there are treacherous," we were informed by a boat captain recommended by the hotel "concierge"—a grandiose title for the guy at the desk in shirtsleeves and khakis.

Finally we rented a twenty-ton diesel copra boat whose somewhat biased captain swore was seaworthy. The trip took a couple of days, during which we sat uncomfortably on deck; the only toilet was a hole in the stern open to the four winds. We disembarked at last on an island of coconut palms, slippery mud, and natives bearing flowers. We were hastily assured that they had very recently given up head-hunting.

In Siberut we were met by a Herr Bucholtz, the island's Protestant missionary. He'd had learned to speak Metawaian as well as Indonesian and had befriended the natives successfully, as a result of which he was expelled from his church in Germany for not sufficiently "converting the natives." Herr Bucholtz immediately arranged for an outboard motor boat to take us around the island to the side where the gibbons lived—under the threat of the Weyerhaeuser Logging Company—and where the native Sakuddei, he said, would receive us warmly.

As we rounded the point of the island, huge swells tossed our little boat up and down between troughs of green water and glimpses of a craggy forbidding coast. Herr Bucholtz announced a gas shortage and abruptly cut our speed in half. He buttoned his shirt over his face to protect it from the sun, and he steered the boat by peeking through a crack between the buttons while he told us about the Sakuddei. They had been famous in the past, it seemed, for shooting arrows at visiting government officials. The officials responded by ceasing their visits, but they showed their mettle by proclaiming that if anyone was purposely or inadvertently beheaded, the compensation to the family must be in goods rather than in the traditional "three heads for one." The murderers' family must pay the deceased's family "a small river for their tears, two hundred chickens for their derisive laughter, and a small coconut grove for his life."

I was so thoroughly rattled by the time we arrived on a bare and windless beach that when our group—which now had been joined by a couple more of Herr Bucholtz's friends—set out upriver in a canoe, I refused to go. Instead, in order to stay on solid ground, I followed an almost naked native with bones around his neck through the jungle. He spoke no English; in fact, I don't know what he spoke. We walked a long, long way.

When eventually we met up again (not without considerable fear and distress on my part that that might not happen), an old man sitting in a hut built on stilts and lined with monkey skulls took my straw hat. Everyone laughed, and Herr Bucholtz said taking a hat was an indication of the intention to marry that person. I retreated to a gaggle of naked women who tried out of curiosity to pull off my fingernails, because they were painted red. That night the pigs ate half my bikini, which I'd hung out to dry on a railing of our hut.

We remarked on the enormous number of gibbon skulls that decorated all the native huts and questioned the inhabitants about killing the gibbons. "Oh, yes," they replied. "Very good eating."

Mummy and Richard wrote all this down, but I didn't see how much would come of it. We were on that island for only two nights before we started our uncomfortable trip back.

We took the motor boat back to the side of the island where we had originally landed, but this time it must have come down too hard on a wave and the lynch pin fell out of the motor. My intrepid mother held it together for the rest of the trip with her Swiss army knife, which she thrust into the offending hole. As night gathered, I felt some concern that this might be our last trip ever.

"Mummy," I said, "I would like to get one thing straight. When I was a little girl and later growing up, was there some reason you didn't—well—include me in your life?"

"I was never around," she said simply but quite accurately.

I returned to the ranch unhappier than ever. Things lit up occasionally when Maggie and Clint Eastwood, Merv Griffin, and a flock of Richard's other friends came over for dinner. I spent my days making Mexican *rellenos* and cakes filled with fresh peaches and whipped cream, and my evenings discovering that Californians talked almost incessantly about ecology and Transcendental Meditation. The whole Big Sur coast, it seemed, was *levitating* on TM. Clint told me that he figured out his movies while doing Transcendental Meditation. It occurred to me as I listened to our guests that I needed not only meditation but another life entirely. For the moment, though, I was stuck, and I didn't seem able to do anything.

On nights when we were alone, Richard and I made roast chicken in the kitchen in our bathrobes. We ate in front of the fire, while Pasha, Richard's black Labrador, and Woozle—a honey-colored Lhasa apso puppy I'd recently adopted and adored as much as I had Timmie—cuddled against us waiting for tidbits.

Richard, sensing a growing emotional gulf between us, decided we needed a second honeymoon in Greece and Turkey. In Turkey we drove southeast from Ankara and reached the town of Göreme in Cappadocia, the Anatolian part of Turkey. In the early Christian era it had been a place of refuge for the religious hermits; they carved caves into the soft stone, which erosion had sculpted into pinnacles like the drip castles children make on the beach. I was utterly captivated by this strange secret spot. It was like stepping into a fairyland of witches' pointy hats made of mottled tan stone. I wanted to settle in one of those magical and reclusive dwellings, but satisfied my longing by sitting for a while in a tiny round room lit only by a small hole set high up on the wall. It was the quietest place I've ever been, and redolent with peace from all the meditation that had been practiced there. Much later I learned that in fact the air in these little dwellings was poisoned by something in the rock or earth, and that was why the hermits eventually abandoned them.

Back at the ranch, being married meant not having peace or any time alone. "Where's Bo?" echoed through the house and through my brain. I decided to start a new life in earnest, for I was desperate for a life of my own, in which I could make my own choices and feel a sense of purpose and even pleasure. I rented an airy apartment in San Francisco, which I decorated with palm trees and cushions. There I quickly became close friends with Angie Thieriot. We had both been to Foxcroft, and Uncle Laddie and his polo team had played with her father and his Argentine polo team. We both led glamorous social lives, yet we longed for deep spiritual experience as well. Angie had studied Transcendental Meditation with the Maharishi Mahesh Yogi, who had empowered her to teach. So one day I went to her house for my initiation; she wore a white dress, and I gave her a traditional offering of marigolds and received my mantra.

I practiced my mantra for a while. I was impressed that Clint Eastwood practiced this type of meditation, but eventually I began to sense that this was not my path. Perhaps taking the initiation from a good friend with whom I partied at night made me less than the perfect *sannyasin*. I was glad, though, to have found someone like me who was interested in spiritual things, and Angie became a lifelong influence on me as a friend and later as a practitioner of other meditation disciplines.

I began spending more and more time in San Francisco, and I thought about finding a job in television again. As luck would have it, I was introduced at a party to the head of San Francisco's PBS station. One day I ran into him at our local Chinese grocery.

"By any chance, are there any jobs available at the station?" I queried.

"As a matter of fact," he replied, "we are looking for an art critic."

"*No!*" I gasped. "Why, I used to *be* an art critic in New York."

I lied, of course. True, I had spent time with a lot of artists in the sixties, and we'd talked an awful lot about art, but that hardly gave me the credentials of an art critic.

A week later, though, I commenced my career as an art commentator on *Newsroom*. I chose to interview artists and discuss their work rather than criticize it. I didn't have enough chutzpah for that. I desperately called friends in the art dealer world to find out how to talk about art. I learned to talk about "the push and pull of sculpture" and various other bits of necessary argot. I did end up talking about art fairly intelligently and began collecting a lot of it. Eventually I discovered that interviewing artists was something that could be an enjoyable occupation.

Meanwhile, I gave dinner parties in my apartment kitchen, which had a fireplace, and I spent time alone dreaming and reading in the garret room under the roof. Slowly, gradually, I found myself again. I began to build a life more like the one I had left, surrounded by people on my wavelength who had normal social lives. It was fun, too, to run around in the "Commune," as we called the building I shared with a dear friend, Frank Bailey, who lived in the lower apartment, and a woman I soon got to know who lived in a nearby apartment. Neighbors on the hill visited for drinks and tea and advice and laughter. And I *met* people: San Francisco was—and still is—full of interesting people, and the more time I spent there, the more my circle of friends widened.

I'd been lonely and isolated at the ranch and needed the stimulation of the city. Richard came to town only when I gave dinner parties, but he wouldn't come just to hang out with me. I, on the other hand, went to the ranch every weekend to spend time with him and his son Jeff, who was growing into a thoroughly alienated teenager. I hadn't the least idea what to do about this, and I often felt closer to the alienated Jeff than to the equally alienated Richard. Agewise, one was fifteen years older and the other fifteen years younger.

The illness that would later partially paralyze my spine started then. It manifested as painful sciatica, which I blamed on the endless drives back and forth from San Francisco to Carmel. It was not just the driving, but the conflict I felt about my marriage and the rest of my life. I was, on the one hand, trying to be a country wife—baking cakes and hiking—and, on the other, a TV career woman and social maven in town. This might have worked if my marriage had felt part of both lives, but it didn't. I was split in two, and my spine bore the stress of that separation. I spent hours at the chiropractor getting cracked and confiding how depressed I was. Finally there came a day when I was going through the checkout counter at the Carmel supermarket, and I couldn't manage to form my face into a smile for the checkout girl. I took that as a crucially important development for the worse.

I went to a shrink and laid out my whole sad story: childhood, Foxcroft, Mummy, marriage. He said, "It's not pills you need. It's your family who need pills." Still, he prescribed antidepressants, which I never took for fear they would screw up my mind. I'd started to meditate with Angie and the sitting groups in San Francisco she organized, and everyone emphasized the need to stay away from drugs that tampered in any way with the mind.

Five years went by, and Richard and I returned by separate routes to Medway. We stayed in a guesthouse called the Honeymoon Cottage. It's easy to surrender to the rituals of plantation life. Even though I don't shoot, Richard did. Duck shooting commenced at five in the morning, followed by huge breakfasts of waffles and eggs. Lunches were often served in the hunting field. Station wagons carried long tables and folding chairs to the woods, and maids in bright plaid uniforms and organdy aprons set out casseroles and salads, Bloody Marys and wine, apple pies, and cheese. At one o'clock, the guests rode on horseback or gathered in mule-drawn buckboards for the trip out to the field. Usually there were five or six "shots"—people who actually intended to hunt—invariably dressed in Miller's green or tan shooting jackets and pants with leather patches on the thighs and shoulders and Gokey boots. They gathered at lunch and chatted about shooting and sports. The rest of the lunch party consisted of husbands and wives of the shots and various guests who didn't intend to shoot, but just came along for a jolly picnic in the woods. After lunch, the hunters mounted ponies or walked carrying their guns through the woods behind the bird dogs.

I walked many of these afternoons, not knowing what else to do, and enjoyed the exercise and the feeling of being part of things. I rarely stayed when it was a dove drive, however, when people settled sleepily around the field on shooting sticks waiting for the beaters in the woods to drive the birds in.

After tea at five, everyone rested before the formal dinners. The men wore velvet smoking jackets and the women tea gowns or velvet pants with dressy tops to these affairs. Guests from Charleston and the neighboring plantations often joined us for dinner and sometimes for shooting, too. Most times no one ever said a deep or serious word. Being entertaining was the trick; and exhaustion, for me, was the result. I've always found being around lots of people exhausting—though I felt so guilty about this that I became inured to the feeling. It took years for me to recognize it. Mummy, who had a different makeup entirely, drew energy from people and chitchat, whereas I gave and lost energy to these kinds of social exchanges. However, I had learned how to give parties from her, and I turned out to be good at it myself; whether it wore me out or not, I enjoyed bringing people together and glowed with happiness when I saw what fun I had created. It was a trait I suppose I inherited that gave me pleasure, even though it was not actually "good" for me, because my inner makeup was different from Mummy's and I needed far more solitude.

At one point during our stay, Richard abruptly informed me that he'd found my precious dog Woozle drowned in the lake at the ranch.

It had happened a couple of weeks earlier while I was visiting friends in New York, and he'd hesitated about how to tell me. It drove me almost mad with grief. Furious and hurt, I thought, *I can't even trust Richard with my dog.* I wondered, too, if that was how he'd really died. I thought there was something odd about it.

Though I was totally distraught, I still had to go on with the dinners and lunches, feeling like a squeezed washcloth. It was Mummy's house, and for her the show must always go on.

Memories of my first dog, Timmie, suddenly vanishing from my life came back to haunt me. I felt that the dog represented my last hope for life with Richard in California. Richard would later say when I brought the subject up, "I knew that would be the end."

It was the end, but the end of a marriage is never short, and I had to take a trip to make sure. I made up my mind to go to the coronation of the king of Nepal—the party that became a pilgrimage.

Many years later, after Richard and Mummy were both dead, an old friend of Mummy's and mine—one of those amazing souls who at ninety-two span the generations—was dining with me at Medway. I mentioned to him how surprised I was, in retrospect, that Mummy had allowed me to marry Richard and how upsetting it was for me that she'd suggested she'd thought of having an affair with him.

"Richard was a disaster," he said. "All her friends knew it. Of course she had an affair with him."

That was a knife in my gut.

"Oh, I know," I replied bravely, as though it was all nothing but a little past history. Then I went upstairs and cried about my being so stupid and my mother being so wicked.

PHOTOS

LUNCH WITH Bokara

Host **Bokara Legendre** leads well-known philosophers, healers, scientists, and spiritual teachers in **provocative conversations**— timeless questions, deep traditions, new frontiers…

13-PART TELEVISION & DVD SERIES

116

CHAPTER

8

An Anchor to Windward

On my way back from Kathmandu, passing through Bangkok, I bought a life-size gold-lacquered Buddha statue. It was emblematic of the change I wanted to make in my life, but one I wasn't quite ready for just then. It took a year for the Buddha to reach California, by which time I was divorced and living in a beach house in Malibu. I stored it in under a blanket in a friend's art studio. My spiritual aspirations would be under wraps until I figured out what to do with my life.

Los Angeles was not the refuge I was looking for—a point that became crystal clear when Mummy's maid called to say that my beloved Mamie had died, alone in a home for the aged in England. Mamie had been such a solid presence throughout my life, the embodiment of love and security. Now there was a hole in the world where she had been, and nothing, I knew, could ever fill it.

We'd kept in touch by letter after she moved back to England, and I had visited her couple of times during the time I was married to Richard. Once, I took the train to Sussex, where she had a tiny service apartment. I'd brought a basket for her from Fortnum and Mason, and as we lunched at a Formica table in her little kitchen she told me a social worker came twice a week to care for her. I cried the whole trip back to

London. I couldn't instantly write a check, hire a helper, or otherwise provide for her, as I was at that time living on a monthly allowance of four hundred dollars and was afraid to ask Mummy for more.

I knew from her letters, written on blue airmail fold-up paper, that Mamie had had to move to a retirement home; she complained that the drugs administered to her made cherubs and angels appear at the foot of her bed. Why hadn't I realized then that she was close to the end and rushed immediately over to see her? My guilt and shame and sadness knew no limit. My mind kept returning to an afternoon when Mummy had rented a house in Sussex. I'd brought Mamie from her little service apartment for dinner, but Mummy wouldn't let her eat at the table with us and sent her off to have bread and cheese with the servants. I didn't dare argue. I didn't dare just take her out to a restaurant for dinner. I never forgot how terrible I felt that night, ever.

Mamie was the only person with whom I had allowed myself to feel totally safe. With her death, I felt orphaned and even more desperate to find a sanctuary, a place that felt like home.

For a solid reality check after the sweet and sour experience of LA, I headed back to the salty atmosphere of Washington. Out went the gypsy gauze dresses and bean sprouts, and in came Yves St. Laurent suits and *saucisson en croute*. I found a place for the gold Buddha in the front hall of my house in Georgetown, under two palm trees, in line with the front door. The rays of the evening sun shone through the front door and glinted on his gold lacquer skin, and the mailman faced him when he brought the morning post. I sat in front of him in the long spring evenings and did my own form of meditation—a combination of prayers and relaxing my mind.

Georgetown was very welcoming. My house, which I'd rented from a newspaper magnate, had a backyard garden with a swimming pool. There were still some friends around from the old days, people who lived permanently in Washington like my friends Mary and Ted Yates. I even found a job producing a daily television talk show called *Nine in the Morning* on the local CBS station. The host was a beautiful black woman who happily shifted from interviewing frazzled school administrators and gloomy sewage experts to chatting with my friends. I invited George Plimpton, a pal from my literary circle in New York, and his friend Muhammad Ali, and they talked about sparring in the ring and out of it. Fashion designer Mary McFadden, with whom I'd been at Foxcroft and had since frequently bought her original clothes, showed her King Tut–inspired collection to the Egyptian ambassador; and when a family of raccoons fell into my bedroom through the attic trapdoor, we did a show about the "wild animals of Georgetown."

I am stunned by my chutzpah in that job. I even wrote a letter to Dick Cavett, telling him to give up his job and come host my show. "There are a million good reasons for you to come to Washington," the letter began. Needless to say he was busy. But I didn't give up writing famous people I had met once or friends of mine I knew might appear on the show.

Several of my criteria for "home" came together in Washington. I had a community, a marvelous place to live and meditate, and an engaging, if frazzling, job. (Worst were the mornings when I arrived at the office at 7 a.m. to find a guest had canceled and I had to find another by nine.) One morning, I woke to the realization that I was actually happy.

Perhaps happiness attracts happiness, for when I went to Fishers Island for a summer weekend in 1978 to visit my mother, I met Arthur Patterson. He was tall and elegant and had blue-gray eyes that changed color like the sea. He liked to dance, golf, play tennis, eat gourmet food, drink fabulous wine, and dress in beautifully cut Savile Row suits. He suited my taste in many ways. As Mummy said, he was an "old shoe," the ultimate WASP compliment. He was everything Richard wasn't. He had charm, manners, and a lovely sense of humor; we moved comfortably in the same social world; and he had a successful career as a venture capitalist.

Arthur was so much taller than I—my head barely reached his chest—that when we danced, I whirled around like a little maenad. Quite unintentionally, I walked several paces behind him on the golf course, for he had the long, muscular legs of a six-foot-four athlete and I was five foot three—a terrier rushing madly to keep up with a greyhound. Our personalities were a bit terrier and greyhound too. I shook life like a bone, while Arthur strode along serenely in charge of his. He had a brilliant mind and a calm way of accomplishing complicated business transactions that made his professional life ultimately more and more successful. I, on the other hand, was constantly rushing in and out of things with little or no contemplation. But the differences didn't matter, because we both had a sense of humor.

About a year after we met we decided to get married. It was so Arthur's style that he asked me to marry him at one of the greatest restaurants in France over a fabulous dinner of Loup de Mer and an unbelievably good wine, which he carefully chose to the sommelier's delight. The wine aficionados of France loved serving Arthur because he knew all about wine, and he had that special ability to "taste" wine knowledgeably.

We married in July 1978 during a hurricane at Fishers Island. Eleven in the morning found me nervously sipping Dubonnet with my cousin Draidy Cochran, who was giving me away, as we watched the storm approach. Our plans for a wedding in a blue tent on our lawn were abruptly canceled when the tent blew away. So instead we walked down the aisle at the local Episcopal church, and the reception was at the golf club. It was a classic summer wedding, complete with foxtrots and gardenias.

Afterward there was a party at Mummy's house, but like my first wedding when my husband didn't want to go to the "after party" at Medway, Arthur didn't want to go to the party at our house. He believed, I think, that a couple should disappear after the wedding— as people traditionally did, with the bride changing into a traveling suit and the newlyweds seen driving away. (Actually, we weren't going anywhere immediately, although after a few days Arthur and I did head out west ... a direction, as it turned out, in which we would continue to travel until we reached the other coast to live.)

We enjoyed being alone together after all the fuss of a wedding with so many people, but we were starving. His parents had lent us their house for the night, but there was no food. I had to sneak into the kitchen at Mummy's house and ask the cook to give me some party food for dinner.

Our honeymoon, backpacking in Colorado, set the tone for our marriage. We set off from Jackson in the morning mists when the woods smelled of balsam, crushed sage, and wet earth. An amazing number of old logs appeared to me as bears, deer, mountain lions, and charging moose. Arthur was very considerate, carrying most of the gear in his pack, but he was always about twenty paces ahead of me on the trail. I trundled along behind worrying about grizzly bears and having little nips of rum to keep my courage up. I think he thought I was fine— which of course I was. I felt happy to be in the woods and surrounded by the leaves and chipmunks and stillness of the hills. Despite the fact that my imagination likes creating scenarios of disaster, I feel most relaxed in nature.

We hiked through fields of yellow daisies and purple lupine and tried to avoid stinging nettles and prickly thistles as the path grew steep. At noon we stopped to put bandages on our blisters and sip ice tea made from the mountain stream. At dusk we made camp, and Arthur fished while I read Graham Greene's *Journey Without Maps*. I discovered to my delight that Greene was afraid of large moths. What a relief to find someone so intelligent who shared my own weird paranoia. Though I loved all other animals, for some reason I was repelled by the thin dusty wings of moths and butterflies. A psychic had told me that they represented death to me in some way.

Since neither Arthur nor I was an accomplished fisherman, we drank lots of rum and canned pineapple juice toasts to his successes as we sat happily blinking in the shifting smoke and grilling trout over our campfire. Hiking with Arthur was a pilgrimage of sorts, and the fact we both loved nature created a deep intimacy between us. For a long time 6-12—the insect repellent with which we slathered ourselves—was for us, redolent of romance.

When we got back to Jackson after our ten-day hiking trip, we had steaks and baked potatoes at The Pickle Barrel. We had been there once before and loved the name and the steaks. "Eating steak together is always a bonding experience," said Arthur. I thought so, too.

In September, we settled into an apartment overlooking the reservoir on Fifth Avenue. It had once been part of Mrs. Merriweather Post's apartment. It had huge plate-glass windows overlooking Central Park. I filled the giant living room with white sofas and red Moroccan carpets and the red velvet pillows embroidered with the word *Byoxpa* that I'd bought in Russia. It was just right for me, and—as long as he wanted to be in New York—just right for Arthur, too. It was glamorous without being ostentatious and managed to be intimate despite the high ceilings and big living room.

I found a place for my gold Buddha in the living room between two palm trees where the setting sun gilded him anew each afternoon. I thought it was perfect that it faced the same way as it had in Georgetown, and that I had recreated my little oasis of spiritual life in the middle of our New York apartment. Sometimes in the evening when I was alone, I lit candles and incense and meditated on a pillow in front of the statue. As usual, I thought I needed a costume to suit the occasion, so I dressed in a long Turkish maroon velvet robe embroidered with gold.

On those evenings I felt peaceful and happy, transported to an exotic and peaceful place. The candles flickered, throwing shadows of the palm trees on the Buddha, which animated his expression. I sensed a presence that the Hindus call *jiva*, the divine fragment of the universe in each of us. Basho, a new Lhasa apso puppy I'd bought when I'd moved back to Washington, sat next to me and occasionally howled at the flickering light—or perhaps at some presence invisible to me that only he could detect.

As I sat, I connected to another reality. A voice whispered in my mind, telling me that I would now be taught by a circle of elders and that I must pay attention to what they said. Suddenly I had a vision of a circle of men and women in long white robes. They told me to come regularly to meditate, to listen and write down what they said—and, oddly enough, to smoke grass or hash in order to relax into this reality. I felt as if I was being carried back toward the revelation given me in Morocco, but now the teachings would continue. I understood now why I had not taken psychedelics in the sixties; I needed to dive into this new dimension in a very safe and sacred setting—alone with my mind.

I "saw"—or did I "hear"?—that the secret was to let go, to stop grasping at life, at the people and the parties, at my idea of nirvana. Relax—let life happen instead of forcing myself to happen to life. I couldn't anyway. It wasn't in changing my locales—which was my wont—but in changing *my mind*, my point of view that would bring peace. Looking at life one way, the mind can settle and view time as a still pasture; looking at it another way, for me, it felt jagged and unstable.

However, I didn't give up my "Society Bobo" persona, as a playwright friend named one of his characters. I was good at giving parties, so I gave a lot of them. I would spend exhausting days shopping for food and flowers, cooking, and setting the pink silk tablecloths with cloisonné elephant candlesticks, silver crabs for salt and pepper, bowls of exotic flowers, and thousands of place cards.

Why didn't I listen to my circle of teachers? In retrospect, I have had these spirit teachers and real ones who suggested simplifying—watching the breath, spending time calming the mind—and although I understand and think about what they say, I don't practice it enough. The great challenge in my life has been the endless distractions that I am privileged to have, but that stymie the simple life of spiritual practice.

By seven in the evening, painted to the floor by my preparations, I faced my closets. What to wear? The more clothes, the worse the dilemma! I finished off by crying with exhaustion in the leftover chocolate mousse at three in the morning.

"Everyone loved you," Arthur would say encouragingly at these times. But when he came home in the afternoon to find me in hysterics over cooking pots and table linens, he might say somewhat plaintively, "Why can't we just stay home and play backgammon or read?"

Unfortunately, I hadn't quite taken in that now I was married, I could just stay home and relax. We were in town; I thought one did that only in the country. Where did I get that idea? I think it has to do with hanging out in nature. Nature frees me into relaxation—somewhat.

The evenings were full and exciting. Wallace Shawn performed a one-man play he'd written about an impoverished South American country. We celebrated the publication of countless books; movies were planned; and my guests and I exchanged ideas for philanthropic projects.

One evening the Hindu teacher Mother Mira, who never speaks, laid her hands on guests' heads and then stayed for dinner. Sogyal Rinpoche, a Tibetan meditation master, came and gave a teaching. Sometimes political writers and spiritual historians offered up their insights.

"Bobo is keeping a salon for the radical left wing," said a journalist friend; but really, that wasn't my intention. As I found people who revealed some new slant on life, I invited them in so that my friends could hear what they were thinking about. Secretly, I hoped that, in the way that some trees take on the perfume of a nearby sandalwood tree, the talent of my literary and spiritual friends would rub off on me.

Those evenings wore me out more often than not. They fed my ego but not my soul—which was better served by my being alone with the "unincarnated" teachers who whispered in my head.

One night as I sat before my Buddha, energy circled out of my head, into my feet and up my spine. My breathing slowed to half its normal pace. I had a vision in which a circle of elders appeared above me and said, "You will know what to do because we will teach you. You are one of us."

For me, these elders really existed, though not in any conventional sense. It occurred to me that there were vast, uncountable folds in space and time and that my personal reality or identity was merely a molecule of an instrument in an immense cosmic orchestra. I knew I should take this initiation seriously, even if it was imaginary. "Death," they said, "comes sooner than you imagine. In this life, the more we practice kindness and love, the more we think of others, the more ready for death we will be."

So commenced a rather eccentric spiritual practice, through which I began to give my inner spiritual life as much attention as my outer social life. A Jungian therapist I'd started seeing urged me to recognize that the former might be more attuned to my true nature than the latter. Arthur understood my spiritual calling more easily than my social one, despite his own upbringing. Like my father, he found the endless parties tiresome. Looking back now, I realize that I gave some evenings over to social life and parties, and others to spiritual life and solitude, but not many to just being married and relaxed. This inattention wasn't very kind or thoughtful of me and, in the end, meant that I didn't enjoy some aspects of marriage that I needed to learn about. I could vaguely sense the uneasiness this situation created, but I didn't quite "get it."

Was I running away from the person who loved me and with whom I could find a home?

One glittering fall evening, Harold Talbott, the friend who'd arranged for some of the details of my trip to Nepal in 1975, came by for a drink. I'd known Harold for years. His parents had gone on an expedition to Africa with mine back in the twenties; and in the fifties, when Harold was studying Buddhism at Harvard, he and I went to debutante parties together. He became a student of the Dalai Lama long before there were Tibetan Buddhists in the West, and he spent all of his money building monasteries for Tibetans in India. Eventually he became Thomas Merton's traveling companion in Asia.

My Buddha statue shone like copper in the setting sun that evening, and the living room was perfumed by vases of white lilies. Basho lay curled in the corner of the white sofa. Obsessed with costumes as ever, I had donned Mary McFadden pink silk harem pants with a black cashmere sweater and a big gold necklace.

Harold was at his best with a chilled silver martini shaker, so we had one or two, while he chatted about one of his favorite subjects—royal lineages—about which I knew absolutely nothing. I listened distractedly for a while, but then I surprised myself by confiding that although I was married to a wonderful man and giving these wonderful parties, I was still feeling unsettled.

"I'm so depressed," I concluded.

"Buddhism teaches you how to deal with suffering," Harold replied a bit primly but with a friendly smile.

"But I don't suffer," I assured him, looking around my splendid apartment, thinking of my kind and gentle husband—and feeling guilty. WASPs don't talk about suffering. We are taught from earliest childhood not to complain and fuss. So Harold knew the only level to which I could admit suffering was a trivial one.

"Suffering could be not finding an extra man for your dinner party," he observed.

After a moment, he added, "I'd like to take you to see Tulku Thinley Norbu Rinpoche. He's a wild Tibetan yogi. Would you like that?"

I imagined a half-naked *saddhu*—his hair in knots, a bone in his nose, standing on one leg and spouting wisdom. "Oh, Harold! How divine! Let's go tomorrow!"

"We'll see," Harold replied. "Maybe he's in town. He sometimes borrows the apartment of a friend of mine in the village."

The next day we climbed the stairs of a brownstone in the East Twenties. The door was opened by a sturdy young man with darkish skin wearing khaki pants and a Lacoste T-shirt. He invited us to sit around a low table adorned with blue china tea cups and a blue bowl of grapes. I waited politely for the yogi to enter. The silence was interrupted occasionally by guests noisily sipping tea.

Harold appeared to be in a state of bliss, and the man in the T-shirt appeared unconcerned about my mounting impatience. Finally, it dawned on me that he *was* the wild yogi. Lamas, I've since learned, confront us with the silliness and insecurity of our Western minds without us ever having to do a thing.

Eventually, when he did begin to speak, all I heard was a senseless drone. My hands went numb, and I felt as though I were flying around the ceiling. The rest of the visit passed in a flash of incomprehension.

As we left, Rinpoche said, "Bobo should take refuge with Dodrupchen Rinpoche in Sikkim."

Refuge, Harold explained as we left, was a Buddhist vow of commitment. Dodrupchen was Harold's teacher and lived a reclusive life in a monastery in Gangtok, the capital of the Indian state of Sikkim. As we hurried down the stairs, I confided to Harold that perhaps Rinpoche had put LSD in our tea, because I'd had an out-of-body experience and went temporarily deaf.

Harold roared with laughter. "It's not uncommon," he said, "to have that kind of reaction to a lama with whom you have a deep karmic connection."

"But I can't remember anything he said," I complained.

"That's okay; I took notes."

I went home and copied down his notes in a special blue-and-red brocade book:

> For the practice of Buddhism, it is necessary to have a very clear understanding and belief in karma. If you do not believe in the next life and past lives then the only thing you believe that is real are the phenomena which your senses can perceive. Relax in the natural mind for as long as possible and do not be surprised by the many thoughts which come up. Just bring the mind gently back to the Buddha awareness.

There was much more, and only much later did I really begin to understand those teachings. One thing he said, which I'd completely overlooked, was

> When you get old and the body is deteriorating, nobody wants you, and you are dying. Then, if you have done the meditation you will have inner awareness to rely on. Without it you will go around trying to have it all back again.

"Those were very high teachings," said Harold with respect. "Not the sort of thing one usually gives to a beginner."

I immediately wanted to act on Rinpoche's advice, even though I had only just gotten married and was supposedly settled. I persuaded Arthur it was absolutely *vital* that I leave for Gangtok as soon as possible; and indeed a few months later I did. It was March 1979. Harold was delighted to have the excuse of escorting me to his teacher.

Arthur and I gave a party for Harold's birthday before I left. Arthur raised his glass and said, "Here's to my new wife going off with a man I've only just met to find a religion of which I've only just heard, in a country I can't find on the map."

That was one of the reasons I loved Arthur. He had a delicious sense of humor. We loved cracking each other up.

My trip to Sikkim was about exploring my desire for a spiritual life, but in retrospect, it was also about satisfying my craving for adventure. I could have studied Buddhism in New York and been more "in the marriage." I'd found a home and a wonderful man; but, like my mother, I thought I could really find myself only in another culture—in my case, a spiritual one.

Fortunately, with Arthur it was unusually clear where home actually was. In sailing terms, he was an anchor to windward. I felt tethered to someone, even if I roamed a bit.

CHAPTER

Sikkim

That trip marked the true beginning of a lifetime of spiritual pilgrimages—journeys to find out who I was, and my place and purpose in life.

My longing for a profound spiritual connection had actually begun while I was still a child in Aiken. Later, in Charleston, I read magazine stories about women who manifested the sufferings of Christ, and I was fascinated, frightened, and a little envious. I yearned to experience a transcendent dimension to life in a different but parallel reality, and I saw dramatic possibilities in Christianity. I dreamed that I saw Jesus's face in the moon—but somehow it was Mamie's face, too. I became convinced that I would develop stigmata, that my side would open and spurt blood and that my hands would develop nail holes. "Oh, darling," Mamie would counsel, "you mustn't scratch your mosquito bites."

My experiments with Transcendental Meditation and my pilgrimage in Nepal after the coronation debacle had whetted my appetite for more, as had my experiences while meditating at the feet of the gold Buddha and the meeting with Tulku Thinley Norbu. But I couldn't shake the feeling that, so far, my life had been lacking something that neither travel, relationships, parties, nor work had satisfied. I was always in a state of longing. I wondered throughout the flight to India whether I would find the spiritually centered "home" I'd been seeking among people who believed in karma, in a devotional life, and in the impermanence and emptiness of everything I had been brought up to believe was important.

Our plane touched down in torrid Calcutta on Shivratri Day, which, according to the *Lonely Planet* guidebook, was a Hindu festival of purification, new beginnings, and fertility. When we stepped out of the airport terminal, we were assailed by a potpourri of pungent scents: spices, burning dung, wood smoke, incense, unwashed humanity, and damp earth. As we drove through town, our first glimpses of rickety huts, brilliant saris, and tangling rickshaws were blurred by an auspicious drizzle. Rain, said the *Lonely Planet*, was considered a good omen for Lord Shiva, the Hindu god whose holy day it was.

Immediately after settling into the Grand Hotel, Harold and I ordered samosas and lassis, while Harold answered my questions about Buddhism. He told me that not only does Buddhism acknowledge that life is full of suffering, but we can end it by letting go of our attachments. He added that in Tibetan Buddhist tradition, which was what we were about to study, visualization of deities and mandalas is considered important. I was worried about this, as I wasn't sure if I believed in the existence of deities and mandalas.

"Where are they?" I asked. "In the sky?"

Harold chuckled and told me not to worry. "We're going to be studying Dzogchen."

"Dog what?"

"*Dzog-chen*," he replied, enunciating a bit more clearly. "It's a Tibetan term meaning 'great perfection.' It's a specific discipline that teaches how to see reality and the nature of the mind with intense precision and clarity. But it takes a master like Dodrupchen Rinpoche to provide the necessary instructions."

My childhood friend Carola Kittredge had come along on the trip just for fun, and she brought her camera to record everything in the hopes of selling the photos to a magazine. While Harold and I were discussing the spiritual import of our journey, she ran into a group of British jet-setters in the lobby of our Calcutta hotel, who invited us to a dinner party. I have to admit that even though I had set my mind to making a spiritual pilgrimage, it was fun to run into a little social life purely by accident.

That night at dinner I sat next to a TV reporter, Naresh Kumar. "The political situation in India is terrible," he told me. "India has no leader, and Indira Gandhi is finished."

I told him about a poster I had seen. "It had the cartoon of a lady in an oxcart giving away jewelry to bandits."

"That represents the Congress," he replied. "And Indira is the lady."

From that first night, we decided to rely on Carola to arrange the social side of things. I was quite relieved not to have to do that anymore, and I noticed I could take it or leave it on this trip. It turned out that that dinner party was the only social event of that kind, though; from then on it was the lamas whom we met who invited us for lunch. They sat on their high brocade thrones while their attendants, bent double, passed us course after course of curried vegetables as we sat on pillows on the floor.

Sitting by the hotel pool the next day, Harold and I reflected on the way the three of us saw life and the warmth of the goodwill toward each other that we shared.

"Carola sees things with an old worldview," said Harold, "and would like a select group of familiar friends in a known environment. A little bit last century. *You* see things in the present reality, and you engage with various careers and love meeting new people."

However, he confessed to being a bit torn. "I do love the same sort of Henry James–Noel Coward milieu that Carola enjoys."

"Yes," I countered, "but you're also a spiritual seeker. You're fascinated by the question of what reality really is. Isn't that why you've taken up with Buddhist teachers and practices?"

"Yes," he replied.

"Do you think we can be in both worlds?"

"I think perhaps not for the long term."

"I think we can," I said

But at that moment, Carola came by to say that everyone else fun had left the hotel.

We stayed in Calcutta three days before heading to Gangtok, a nearly four-hundred-mile journey. The first step was a plane to Bagdogra, which turned out to be filled with members of the Bhutanese royal family dressed in long black coats with huge white cuffs on their sleeves, red sashes, and high suede boots. They were met by an impossibly elegant servant in a costume as splendid as their own.

We were met by a wiry, dark Indian named Basnet, who drove a robin's egg–blue jalopy and would serve as our chauffeur to and from Gangtok. We planned to stop over in Darjeeling, traveling precariously along a switchback road that zipped up seven thousand feet from the thick rain forests of the plains to the foothills of the Himalayas. Dusk was falling as we arrived in what was once the summer resort of British colonials, rajas, rakes, and robbers, and was now a flourishing outpost of Tibetan Buddhism. Tiny ponies clattered along the cobbled track, where shapeless human bundles of colored blankets gathered around spicy-smelling fires on which kettles sizzled. The faded blue door of the Oxford Bookstore stood open to reveal a closet-sized room of shelves filled with dusty books in various languages.

We settled at the Windemere Hotel, a somewhat down-at-the-heel remnant of the British Raj. There was no heat, but huge fires burned in our bedrooms.

Delicious!

Harold, Carola, and I dragged our blankets from room to room visiting each other as though it were at a children's sleepover. Harold and I exchanged views on Basnet, who Harold believed was an Indian government spy sent to watch what we were doing with the Tibetans. Harold saw everyone as spies and later confessed that he thought I was in the CIA. I told him a friend in the CIA had told me he'd actually considered recommending me to the agency, but he decided I talked too much. I never knew I missed my calling as a sleuth because of being chatty, but I truly didn't mind.

After breakfast the next morning, we strolled out of town to visit Harold's friend Tragawa Rinpoche, a Tibetan doctor, and his patroness, a woman called Ama-la Dorje. They greeted us on a little jutting balcony hanging in a blue haze over a cliff, which looked out over mountain slopes terraced with tiny cultivated fields. Their parlor also served as a shrine room; it was lined with tiny tables in front of mattresses covered with bright Tibetan rugs. The walls were hung with Tibetan Buddhist religious paintings called *tangkas*. Tragawa Rinpoche filled our palms with a sticky liqueur, like Calvados brandy, to rub on our hair so that the blessing he would confer on us would really stick, and then he sat down on a tiger-skin pillow to talk.

"As you look at everything in your life, you are seeing the Buddha," he began. "The point is to give up searching and grasping for happiness. The beginning of our need for Buddhism is the realization of life's unsatisfactoriness."

Those words struck a deep chord in me. For years I'd felt faintly guilty that while maintaining a façade of having a good time, behind the mask I felt as though life was rubbing me like a rough blanket on soft skin. While listening to Tragawa Rinpoche, I finally began to understand that one of the first lessons of Buddhism is the recognition that all people are troubled by that same unease. Paradoxically, I found great comfort in this lesson. I was becoming a part of a great lineage of people who recognized and were willing to admit to the profound emotional discomfort of ordinary life.

I rose early the next morning to watch Mount Everest flush rose in the sunrise and then turn dazzling white. A donkey brayed in the distance, and on a nearby hill the aged gray gauze of huge Tibetan prayer flags flapped in the chill dawn breeze. I prayed silently that this trip would lead me to a deeper discovery of the essence of myself and a deeper, truer connection with the Divine. So many of the journeys I'd taken up till then had been motivated by the urge to run away from things. This time, I wanted to move toward something.

Later that morning, we clambered into Basnet's blue jalopy for the sixty-mile trek up a winding road to Gangtok. Towering tree ferns, bougainvillea, and banana plants gave way to desiccated leaves, military trucks, and dust as we reached the town of Gangtok. We drove straight to Dodrupchen Rinpoche's hermitage, where he and his wife, Khadra-la, welcomed us in the garden by wrapping our necks with katas.

Afterward we entered a low-ceilinged, oblong room down the center of which stood a long, narrow table lined with polished metal cauldrons the size of bass drums. They turned out to be butter lamps—traditional offerings to the Buddha—but these were the largest I'd ever seen: great brass pots filled with clarified butter in which wicks of inch-thick ropes floated. Piles of red-and-blue Tibetan rugs were scattered about the floor, and at one side stood a low wooden throne piled with pillows for Rinpoche.

An attendant brought tea, which I'd now come to expect as part of the ritual of meeting a lama. We sat for a while quietly enjoying the light sweeping across the oriental carpet spread around the shrine room. But eventually I couldn't resist the impulse of ingrained social habit of chatting over tea.

"Oh, Rinpoche, you must tell us about the lovely butter lamps!" I gushed.

Silence.

"I am dying to hear all about Buddhism," I continued, undeterred.

Silence.

Slurp. Slurp.

I glanced at Harold for help, but he was sitting with his eyes closed, apparently in some rapturous state. I looked at Carola, who responded by tentatively remarking, "What a lovely dress Kadre-la has!"

Silence.

I began to wonder if Tulku Thondrup, the young lama who was serving as translator during our stay, was, in fact, translating what we said. I clung nervously to a wadded-up Kleenex as I waited for some response. Finally I gave up any attempt at conversation.

Shadows of the trees outside waved on the carpets, and gradually I sank into the sleepy, warm atmosphere created by incense smoke and the singsong drone of the Tibetan language conversation among Harold, Tulku Thondrup, and Rinpoche. I wondered if they were sharing important mystical insights; but when I asked Harold later, it turned out they were talking about Khadra-la's toothache and the problems of getting copper pipes for the plumbing.

In the evening, Carola and I headed to the bar of our hotel for generous helpings of Red Star vodka and Black Cat rum with lemon squash. Harold had stayed on at the monastery.

"I thought I was going to go mad in the silence," I said. "These people don't talk!"

"I know," Carola replied. "It makes me gushy and say I'm more enthusiastic than I am. We're like two schoolteachers on holiday carrying on about the wonders of our trip and being boring about it."

After a few more drinks, I started feeling a bit gushy myself. "I'm getting drunk," I observed. "We'd better eat."

The waiter said that the only food available was Chinese.

"I thought these people hated the Chinese," Carola whispered.

"Well, they hate the Indians, too," I replied. "They're grateful for a place to live, and they're annoyed it's not their own country. I'd feel the same way."

The next morning, Tulku Thondrup lit the butter lamps in Rinpoche's bedroom, where I was to be formally initiated into Tibetan Buddhism through the ceremony of taking refuge. As Harold had earlier explained, taking refuge meant accepting the Buddha, his teachings—collectively referred to as the Dharma—and the community of realized masters and practitioners, known as the *Sangha*, as guides and protectors against the temptations and challenges of samsara, the crazy, troublesome wheel of worldly life. Rinpoche sat on his brass bed playing with the new movie camera we had brought him. Harold nudged me to join him in doing three full-body prostrations before Rinpoche. I didn't know enough then to disarm myself of my shoulder bag, and the camera and tape recorder I'd brought along, so I clanked and crashed up and down with considerable difficulty.

We sat on the floor while Rinpoche performed the long chant that made up the refuge ceremony. Afterward, he gave me a Tibetan name: Pema Yangchuk Drolkar, also known as White Tara, the female emanation of the Buddha's wisdom and compassion. Then Harold and I recited the Buddhist vows: *I go for refuge to the Buddha, the Dharma, and the Sangha.*

Afterward, Rinpoche gave a short teaching, explaining that in meditation we must practice objectively and nonjudgmentally observing our minds. We must simply look at the thoughts and dreams that arise as nothing more than the continuous, creative expression of the mind's energy—and just let them go. My waking mind was full of the detritus of daily life, whereas my dreams were like going to a good movie, which I really enjoyed. Buddhist meditation, I thought, might prove a bit difficult on that front.

Rinpoche then suggested that I stay the night in his monastery—in a room I later discovered belonged to one of the resident lamas, Lama Sangye (*sangye* is the Tibetan word for Buddha). Lama Sangye, kindly enough, spent the night on a bench in the hall.

As I lay under a pile of blankets looking out the window at a glittering new moon, the night wind smelled of burning leaves and incense and farm animals. A profound peace swept over me, a sense of oneness with everything. Loneliness, which had for so long resided in the marrow of my bones, vanished into a sense of rightness in being here in this monastery on this trip with these people. It was very reassuring.

In the morning, Carola and I climbed to a temple up the hill and sat listening to a group of lamas blowing long curved Tibetan horns. The sound is said to evoke a vibration in the spinal column that raises *kundalini*, the mythical snake of energy dwelling in the lower back. And indeed, as I listened, I felt as though someone was gently tickling my back with a blade of grass. The feeling of peace and belonging was so strong I thought I might want to spend the rest of my life right there in that temple.

Carola interrupted my reverie by whispering that there was no light and she couldn't take pictures. After that, half of my mind was drifting with the sound and the other half, in response to Carola wanting to move on, was saying, *Don't just sit there; do something.* I didn't want to move on, though; I was happy. In fact, I was feeling quite blissful. Why should we "move on"? This urgency to keep moving, I thought, was a perfect example of the delusion of samsara, which Tragawa Rinpoche had alluded to a few days earlier: the belief that we can find contentment by grasping at external things or arranging situations to satisfy the cravings or aversions of the moment.

I resolved not to give in to temptation and stayed where I was, while Carola went off in search of better light.

The following afternoon was given over to meetings of a more social nature: two lunch engagements. I pulled out of my bag a crumpled wool skirt, which looked reasonably presentable.

Our first lunch was with Dzongsar Khyentse Rinpoche, a young lama who would eventually become a prolific author, a major sponsor of Buddhist monasteries and schools in India, Nepal, and Tibet, and a notable filmmaker—whose two major films are *The Cup* and *Travellers and Magicians*. At the time, Rinpoche was in his early twenties. He sat on a high brocade throne while we sat on the floor, eating course after course of sumptuous, spicy curries. The event was so lavish, we were all reduced to silence.

Dzongsar Khyentse was also a teacher of Chogyal Namgyal, the host of our second lunch that afternoon. The Chogyals—a term that means "religious king"—were absolute rulers of the former kingdoms of Sikkim and Ladakh for more than three hundred years, until a public vote in 1975 transformed Sikkim into an Indian state. Our host was a *tulku*, a reincarnate lama, and had wanted to spend his days in a monastery. However, after his elder brother was killed in a car accident, he was forced to assume the royal mantle, which carried no official authority. He had helped many teachers escape from Tibet when the Chinese invaded.

The Chogyal was, as Mummy would say "old shoe." Suntanned and fit, he emerged from his faded yellow English-style country house dressed in gray flannel pants and a sweater. We followed him down a flower-lined garden path to a white tent, under which was an assortment of aged aluminum garden furniture. An elegant servant offered us sherry and Dubonnet from bottles dusty with disuse.

A ragged Tibetan terrier came in to be petted as we dug into the chicken pot pies, following our ten-course meal of curry, and everyone relaxed. I asked the Chogyal about the Buddhist teachings. He replied with a story about a legendary Buddhist king.

"The king was famous for his generosity," he explained, "and gave everything away, even his children. Finally when he was old and had nothing left to give, he was stopped on the road by a stranger who asked him for his eyes. As he was about to give this last gift, the stranger turned into the god Indra and revealed that he was testing the king's generosity and compassion."

As I listened to this tale, I remembered a story I'd heard a while earlier from a Buddhist scholar. In another early incarnation, the Buddha was born as a rabbit; but even in that form he emanated extraordinary virtue and generosity and was considered a king among other animals. On a particularly holy day, when it was customary to offer alms to anyone passing through the forest, the rabbit realized that he had nothing to give but his own flesh and blood. When a starving traveler passed by, the rabbit offered himself unreservedly, and with no expectation of thanks or reward he jumped into a fire the traveler had built. However, the traveler was actually the god Indra, Lord of the Universe, and seeing the rabbit's generosity, lifted him out of the fire and placed his image on the face of the moon. It's said that when the moon is full, the discerning viewer can see this image.

The Chogyal, I thought, seemed to have the same tragic karma as the mythical king and the fluffy rabbit, without the reward of Indra's intervention. He hadn't been able to fulfill his dream of living in a monastery; he had a title that was worthless; and he was pretty much a prisoner in his own house.

That evening, I asked Dodrupchen Rinpoche about the Chogyal's karma. "From the Buddhist point of view," he replied, "the Chogyal is purifying bad karma from a previous lifetime in this difficult incarnation. So he could view it as a good life because it clears his path to enlightenment."

This perspective—understanding unhappiness and misfortune as necessary pain on the road to joy—cast a different light on my childhood. Perhaps I was burning bad karma from some past life. I nudged Harold and tried to make eye contact to see if he "got it" from the same point of view, but as usual, he was sitting with his eyes closed, blissed out while listening to his teacher.

Dodrupchen, who seemed to be speaking from some inner place that broached questions, went on to explain that, according to Tibetan predictions, we are in the throes of Kali Yuga, the age of the demon Kali, sometimes known as the age of evil—a morally and materially degenerate era. The Tibetans believe that the world will eventually burn up when five suns come together; but it will ultimately reappear and will be blessed by the emergence of Maitreya, the future Buddha. This would happen very soon, Rinpoche said, unless we quickly moved to improve our collective spiritual integrity.

At the time I couldn't tell whether he was speaking in terms of years or eons, but things did appear to be unraveling.

"Now is not the moment to search for personal answers," he said, "but for universal ones."

I felt a pang of guilt on hearing that, since I was constantly worrying about myself and my own personal situation. I resolved to try to keep the universal and the personal in some kind of balance.

We left Gangtok in a shower of katas and presents in the bright morning sun. I had a cold, which Khadra-la said was a "gift of the Chorten," an outward sign of purifying old ideas and goals. Giddy from the experiences of the past few days, we drove down the twisting road in a state of glorious relaxation and laughter.

"We're driving out of the crags of serenity into the slough of hilarity," I said.

As we descended to the plains, we passed a herd of rhinos, placidly roaming with birds perched on their backs. "Are those egrets on the rhinos' backs?" I asked Harold.

"Yes, rhinos vinaigrette," he replied.

We laughed uproariously because we were still in the blissful influence of our spiritually high time at the monastery.

Back in India, there was red powder on the shrines and the dust of the Raj on our bureaus. In Calcutta we met a couple of friends who'd just arrived from America. Together we took the train to New Delhi, drinking gin and tonics. I was already light-headed from my experiences in Sikkim, and somehow my inner discoveries all came together. As I leaned against the compartment door, I announced, "I have to admit I have lived my whole life in great discomfort."

Everyone laughed, not only because we were drunk but also because everyone knew how spoiled and privileged I was. Still, it came as a relief to finally admit out loud that even as I was laughing and carrying on as "Society Bobo" I was deeply unhappy. The life I'd been living was spiritually bereft and familially barren. As I looked at my friends laughing and drinking, I knew we were all kidding ourselves about who and what we were. But what was there to do? This was, I realized in that moment, the ghastly paradox of being spiritual beings stuck in physical bodies.

The next day Harold and I drove for several hours from Delhi to Dehra Dun to hear Dilgo Khyentse Rinpoche, a very great Nyingma lama, give teachings on White Tara, the embodiment of compassion whose name I'd been given when I'd taken refuge a few days earlier. I fell into a sleepy trance at the sound of Tibetan chanting, the smell of the incense, and the peace of the atmosphere. Although I didn't understand a word Rinpoche was saying—the teaching was all in Tibetan—I saw an image of Tara slowly emerge from Rinpoche's plump upper arm. Transfixed, I whispered to Harold I was seeing Tara. I don't know if he quite understood what I was saying, but a few minutes later he said we had to leave in order to get back in time for cocktails at the hotel where we were staying.

This seemed ridiculous to me in the middle of my spiritual experience, but I gave in—which pretty much characterized the challenges I faced in my spiritual search. It's constantly interrupted by the distractions of my social life and other people's desires.

Back at the hotel, we had drinks by the pool with friends. "Haven't I changed?" I asked Harold hopefully.

"Well," he replied, "you do look a bit thinner."

"But my *mind* has changed," I wailed. "I'm a different person because my perspective changed up there with Dodrupchen."

He just shrugged.

"Everyone changes, and we all stay the same."

The conversation about sightseeing and train schedules spun around me as I tried to put into words what felt different. Slowly, I was able to identify that the change I'd undergone was an acceptance of the existence of suffering and the willingness to let it just be, without running away or chasing after some distraction or escape. Admitting suffering, it turned out, was okay.

Finally I said, "I'm not unscathed, you know. I'm terribly scathed—by some sad things that I didn't think mattered at the time."

Harold looked vastly cheered up.

"Now you're a Buddhist," he said—by which I think he meant that I'd finally accepted that suffering is an inevitable part of life, pretty much what I came to India to learn.

If only I could have held on to that realization.

But then, part of being a Buddhist, as I would learn, is being willing to let go of everything—even those stunning moments of insight.

Life with Arthur

Despite the insights I'd gained in Sikkim, I was still under the sway of old social habits of profound insecurity. I thought that the more people I invited over, the more friends I had. This was a long-term error in my thinking, which went back to my life in New York and Washington, where I entertained many fascinating people but got to know few of them.

Nicholas Soames, an English friend who came to one of these gatherings (and who would eventually serve as defense minister under John Major), once painfully summed it up for me. Looking around the room, he said, "You have a lot of interesting guests, but do you have any close friends?"

I surveyed the many well-known faces who enjoyed my dinner parties, but with whom I had never had an intimate lunch. I was shocked, but he was right. I was a hostess, not a pal, a whirling dervish who brought other people together, never believing they would want to get to know me. Sometimes I did ask a small group of six or eight people for dinner, but after they left I still felt depressed and empty. Even then, I was bringing them together for their sake, not mine.

Arthur said, "They are—or think they are—stars, and that for us, their presence is enough. That's why they don't ask us back and you feel depressed when they leave."

I realized I staged productions so that other people would meet and have fun, assuming that was the only reason they would come over. Who, I thought, would want to meet or talk to me? I realized this idea came from my childhood, when I was not considered interesting enough to have around; and later, when I was grown and married, I still felt I was, to use Mummy's term, "a second-class citizen." I was living in a conundrum between my desire to surround myself with smart, glamorous people and my new realization that happiness lay in living in nature and perhaps in allowing my marriage to take first place.

That winter, Harold stayed with us a lot because we'd decided to write an article together called, "Experiments with Lamas." We planned to sell it to *Harper's*, which, not surprisingly, had no interest at all.

In 1979 I gave a big dinner party, after which I felt the usual letdown. The next day Harold, who had thoroughly enjoyed the evening, took me to see Dudjom Rinpoche, the teacher to whom I'd delivered *tsampa* in Kathmandu back in 1975. On the way we chatted about the evening, which had been attended by writers vying with each other under the pretext of talking about their books, and an artist who had boasted about her art show. As usual, I felt I never did anything but cook for successful people, not seeing that if I would just stay home instead of shopping for rabbit stew and great wines, I would have time to do something of which I might be proud.

During the interview, Dudjom Rinpoche said that children come in with their own karma, which is frequently not what their parents want. All souls are born with their own destiny, despite their taking on the characteristics of their parents and environment. In my case, perhaps I did have a destiny, but I'd never lived it out. Could it be that the little seedling of what could have been shriveled through a lack of nourishment?

I'd been thinking about that very subject before he began to speak, wondering why I was so attached to my mother's very conventional habits and mores. In my heart I had already discovered I was most attracted to bohemians—artists, writers, and people in the theater—who often lived very unconventional lives, to which I was afraid of committing completely.

After relating Dudjom Rinpoche's insight to the counsel of the shrink I'd been seeing, I announced that I now understood myself and would like to "graduate from any more appointments." He got furious and said I wasn't at all well or I wouldn't be stuffing myself with food and alcohol and hating my mother. Eventually, I confessed that although I was now happily married, I was sad that I was still behaving so badly and was so spoiled. We both cried when I described this.

He said, "You should come here more."

I went back to my old habit of giving parties—a perfect example of which was a hilarious dinner I gave for Phillipe de MacMahon, the duke of Naganthe, wherever that is. I've no idea how such an odd person came briefly into my life. He launched the conversation by saying that he had just had lunch with the queen of England at Windsor Castle, along with ten members of her family and five of his.

"Then the queen and queen mother dropped by"—his words, not mine—"for lunch in my sixteenth-century castle in Burgundy. We talked about something and nothing," he said, and he expressed the hope that the queen would have stayed more than two hours "just to chat." He claimed to also have entertained Jean-Bédel Bokassa, the self-crowned emperor of the Central African Empire, for a weekend at his castle (on another night, indeed another month, I presumed).

"How did you get your staff to wait on that terrible Bokassa?" I asked.

"I know everyone in the village," he replied. "It was no problem."

Harold and Arthur could barely keep straight faces. Harold kept coughing in his napkin and turning purple in the face.

"What's more," my illustrious guest continued, "my wife left me because she didn't like castles."

We all shook our heads in sympathy for such bad taste.

As he left, he said, "Maybe I am a terrible person."

"Oh, no," I replied, ever the charming hostess.

It's truly no wonder that Arthur often chose to play backgammon on some evenings when these little get-togethers were taking place. My shrink said, wisely, that when I discovered the real creative flow, when I worked at something because I loved it, I would no longer have such compulsive habits.

As it turned out, he was right.

When Arthur started a venture capital firm in Silicon Valley, I found myself back in California, almost ten years since I'd moved there to be with Richard. It seemed my destiny was on the West Coast—since, whoever I married, I ended up living in San Francisco and Big Sur. It turned out to be a very good thing too, for in California my life changed.

I arrived at the San Francisco Airport with nine suitcases and my Lhasa apso, Basho. (Much later, a friend would say about those years in California, "Bo went from debutante to shamanette.")

In one of my suitcases was a copy of the *Upanishads*. One line in particular struck a chord in me: "You are what your deep driving desire is." I had to admit that social acceptance, sex, and real estate had been my driving desires, but I was ready for a change. All of my life I'd equated finding a physical place with finding home. Unfortunately, when I did find such a place, I had a tendency to leave it; so naturally, the desire for real estate remained strong. In California, though, I found a place to call home.

Or had I?

Arthur and I rented an apartment in San Francisco, which had a moose head hanging over the fireplace, and I renewed some acquaintances from the old days when I was married to Richard. Still in dinner party mode, I invited leaders of what was referred to as "the human potential movement"—Fritjof Capra, author of *The Tao of Physics*; Michael Murphy, who owned the Esalen Institute; Richard Baker Roshi, head of the San Francisco Zen center; and the Taoist Tai Chi master Chungliang Huang—and mixed them with my old social friends. The conversation was very different from the discussions of art and politics in New York. In California, my guests considered questions about the meeting place of science and religion, the potential of the human brain, and whether or not human beings were evolving to a higher state of consciousness.

For the summer, I found a shack—a friend's pool house—in sunny Woodside, at the foot of some golden hills on the edge of a grove of eucalyptus trees. It was near Silicon Valley and convenient for Arthur.

"You've found a sylvan wood," he said appreciatively.

I thought I had, too. That cottage emanated a kind of magical and creative energy. We had use of the owner's pool and the tennis court. In the evenings, after a game of tennis and a swim, we ate salads at a card table by the pool while Basho sat on Arthur's lap eating tidbits. The wind smelled of damp earth and celery.

"This is my family," Arthur said.

I felt the same way. I found I was happy in a small house, where my life was simple and for the most part not very social, because I had found something I really wanted to do.

One night, I dreamed of painting birds on window shades that I pulled down, and the next morning I set out to find some. The man in the art store pointed out that artists generally use rolls of paper, not window shades, so that's what I bought. Since I didn't consider myself a "real" artist, I bought acrylic paints, which were inexpensive and somehow seemed less "serious." I wanted to avoid falling into my usual habit of believing that if I wasn't the best at something, it wasn't worth doing.

When I returned home, I turned one wall of our bedroom into an art studio by tacking up plastic sheets. I had to dip the rolls of paper in the swimming pool to make them uncurl. At my first try, I painted a six-foot-tall parrot at which Basho growled.

"You must have been uncomfortable with those huge birds inside you," Arthur said.

I hadn't thought of that. I loved the idea that I'd had huge birds wanting to burst out of my head!

"When will they fly?" asked a tennis pal.

"Never," I replied. "These birds sit and think. They don't fly. I'm grounding myself."

I felt I was making up for a lifetime of extroversion. I hiked and stayed alone by the pool, painting. Over the years, painting has been the one creative act I've succeeded in keeping just for me. I didn't feel I had to have a show or put any other burden on myself. It felt wonderful, and I didn't miss a social life at all.

In the middle of this peaceful existence in Woodside, I developed the most horrific back pain and odd lumps here and there. I went to a doctor, who diagnosed it as valley fever, which archaeologists and construction workers get from working perpetually in dry, dusty environments. Since I was living in a damp, green sort of place, I couldn't understand how I'd contracted it. However, every day I was in the habit of phoning my friend Indiana Nelson, a painter and writer who lived in Arizona, during which we had long talks about our need to transform our consciousness. She had had valley fever for some time.

"Maybe you caught it over the phone," Arthur suggested.

While seeking an explanation—and, I hoped, a cure—I found a book called *The Way of the Shaman*, by Michael Harner, which explained how to take a shamanic journey. As he recommended, I lay down on a mat with a scarf over my eyes and visualized myself descending through the earth until I came out on a beach where I lay on my stomach in the sun. A scaly, copper-colored insect, about six inches long with many legs and long chin feathers, walked slowly up my bare back. Afterward, I felt no pain for the next few hours.

I immediately signed up for Harner's workshop at the Esalen Institute on the wild Big Sur coast—a decision that proved to be one of those quirks of fate that would change my life. At dinner, the other participants wore wool hats and striped tights under their shorts. I felt a bit out of place in my Pucci slacks and ballet slippers. What would I talk about to the wooly-haired men and their girlfriends in floppy pants and turbans?

I needn't have worried. We lay in the dark for the next week taking shamanic journeys, which were vibrant with activity and color. We usually descended through a familiar tree stump or cave to a channel that led downward to another reality, where we met a spirit animal who showed us some answer to our questions or some revelation we needed.

One night during the workshop I had a vision in which a dappled horse, brown with white spots on his rough coat, transformed into girl in a pink leotard who I realized was me. She split in two: one-half of her, dressed in a black-and-white moo moo, died; the other half, still wearing the pink leotard, danced happily with a burro in a cowrie shell halter. The vision seemed crucially important for some reason—which became clear a few days later.

Arthur came to Esalen for the weekend. We hiked in the golden hills full of the scents of sage and bay. As we walked along a ridge where hawks roosted, Arthur said, "Let's live here."

"Really?" I said. "I adore this country. I'd love that."

There had been a huge landslide earlier that year that blocked the coast road below Carmel, so nothing was selling. A new friend at Esalen told us about Santa Lucia Ranch, the "ranch of sacred light," just down the road from Esalen. Arthur and I walked along Route 1 to the site, and there in the field in front of the house stood the dappled brown horse from my vision. I had a strong feeling that we had to live there.

The gray redwood house huddled like a beautiful swan against the green cliff, which dropped away abruptly to the ocean hundreds of feet below. The living room walls were glass, through which we could see, on one side, a lake full of lily pads, and on the other, the roaring Pacific.

The next day I used the shamanic journey technique to ask about the property we had seen. In my vision a crow brought me a piece of a fence. When Arthur discovered that the lawyer for the estate that owned the house lived across the fence from our little shack in Woodside, we knew we had to buy it.

I'd been traveling to faraway sacred places, but now I found one in Big Sur. I let the sky and the sea and the perfume of the hills ooze into my being. In the afternoon light, the mountain range behind the house took on the curves and crevices of a woman's form. Just to be sure, we spent one night in the house under a red-and-white checked tablecloth. A friend visited, too, and we all agreed that it was perfect.

In 1984, we bought the house and started spending weekends there. Arthur suggested I buy some furniture, but instead I spent all the money for it on a stone Buddha, which we put on a rock jutting into the lake. We agreed it was an appropriate blessing to our place before we bothered with furniture.

I was at the edge of the continent and at the edge of some old way of being. Flakes of my personality were crumbling away like sand. I wished I had a psychological Rolaid to digest all these wonderful changes to our lives.

We turned the barn into my art studio, and my dogs, Basho and his new wife, Tashi, curled up on the studio step like two fur commas. My paintings started taking on a clairvoyant aspect. Flaubert had said that "Art is a discovery as much as a recognition." For me, it was also precognition. I painted a woman in an iron collar years before I got an illness that fused my neck. I painted mountains with armies of the dead marching through a pass that a Tibetan lama, Gelek Rinpoche, later told me was the exact place where he'd escaped from Tibet. I painted a huge monarch butterfly with teeth. In Greek the word for butterfly is *psyche*. I had been a social butterfly, and it was killing me. Big Sur, home of the actual monarch butterflies, offered me an alternative.

Painting gave me a way to discover what I really thought about things, and what was happening to me on a deeper level. I pushed myself just a little beyond what is easy to endure, and success came. I painted my best paintings sometimes when I was exhausted after working on them all day. Inspiration at last!

However, nothing lasts, and no sooner did I fall into a regular rhythm of painting, hiking, and meditating than Arthur and I went to Fishers Island to visit our parents. We stayed at Mummy's house. The day we arrived, she gave us a wing of the house to ourselves, but the following day she took it back and offered it to friends of hers who had just arrived. We were dispatched to a regular guest room.

Her friends were at breakfast the next day. The wife had a tiny transistor radio droning away by her plate. Her husband turned to

Arthur and said, "This country is being ruined by environmentalists. We haven't built an oil refinery in twenty years."

We were horrified.

I confided to Mummy that I was working on an article about my experience in Sikkim and Tibetan Buddhism.

"Why do you do it at all?" she said, looking annoyed.

"Well," I replied, "I think people will be interested in spiritual exploration, and this trip was really interesting."

She scowled at such an idea.

Later, when she discovered Arthur and I had made plans to go fishing in the evening, she changed her dinner party so that we would have to stay. I wondered why we had left Big Sur, and I think Arthur did too. We were, however, good little WASPs with family obligations and the unrealistic view that it might be fun to visit.

The only way to cope was to drink. Everyone drank all the time, and I kept pace with them. Maybe it's generational, but Mummy was able to have a daiquiri before dinner, wine with dinner, and liqueurs afterward. By the end of the evening she was not only upright but not at all drunk! I discovered that I could also put away quite a lot of liquor, although nothing like that. At first, I drank so that no one would know I felt shy, and later so that I wouldn't have to feel what was really going on around me. But over the years, it took more and more to get to that numb place.

With relief, Arthur and I boarded our flight to California. Sitting next to us was a little girl, perhaps ten years old, in floods of tears. Arthur, with his special wry humor, said, "A little girl enjoying her flight." She was so surprised she stopped crying and smiled at him.

There was always something both humorous and healing in Arthur's funny comments. I think he had my father's wry sense of humor.

After Arthur and I returned to California, we spent a weekend in the country with friends who loved to entertain. It struck me there were too many people around, too much housekeeping and cooking. I went and sat on a hill by a lake with the hostess's dog curled up on my foot and listened to the birds. There were rolling green hills in the distance and dry yellow grass all around me.

I wondered why I seemed to spend my life giving dinner parties, when even attending someone else's party seemed exhausting. At one such dinner, the hostess had been brought up very much the same way as I had. Parties were in our genes. I remembered that when I was about eighteen, and my mother and I came back from Tahiti with lots of hula skirts and coconut hats and paper leis, she threw a party at which she wanted me to do the hula. I was embarrassed and didn't want to do it. She got furious and said, "You have to *give-give-give!*" I was furious, too. I didn't want to be a puppet to entertain like a hired musician or a belly dancer. But that's how important entertaining was to her, and I was too afraid to disobey.

After our country weekend, I had lunch with an old friend and we agreed we were less interested in having dinner parties than we used to be. She said if she didn't like her seat at dinner she left. I was stunned with envy at such courage in the face of being rude. The truth was that I thought if I had a place at someone's table for dinner, I had to show up. I was always annoyed when a guest called to say she had a magazine piece due or when people rang and just said they couldn't come after all. What would it be like to consider one's own life more important than someone else's?

It took me years to actually integrate that concept. It had been drummed into me from childhood that it was more important to please everyone else rather than myself, and despite my protests at lunch, I kept up the party scene. I organized dinners for eight. At one we talked about teleportation and aliens; at another, about the gas crisis and friendships. The third night I dressed up in my velvet costume and stayed at home. I meditated, and in my mind's eye I saw the circle of elders dressed in white. This time, they sent me messages about what foods to eat: figs, honey, and yogurt would be best for now. Later, as I mixed a bowl of this delectable combination, it occurred to me that it was something I wanted to eat anyway.

I loved those nights at home more than anything. Alone with the gold Buddha and engaged in my thoughts and visions, I wondered whether it would have any effect on my behavior as "Society Bobo."

We still went back and forth from New York occasionally when Arthur had business meetings, and I dragged him to parties. But something had changed, and my spiritual life traveled with me. I learned that my life was best when I totally trusted my hunches and intuitions, and that I must keep plugged in to the unconscious in order to live my life in the happiest and most relaxed way. Revelations are only real if they create a change permanently.

About this time, Tulku Pema Wangyal, a lama to whom Harold had introduced me, came for tea at my apartment in New York. I told him about my journeys in meditation.

"Don't worry about those experiences," he said. "It's just like flying over the country and passing Colorado. Not our destination."

About this time, I found a new "destination." A friend, Gigi Coyle, whom I'd met on a trip to Santa Fe, invited me to a "Donut Meeting." The "Donuts," as members of the Threshold Foundation were called, were a large group of people—now so large it has split into several groups—who do philanthropy, both together and separately.

The group was started by Josh Mailman, who felt that many of his friends should learn about philanthropy, as he himself was learning. He gathered together his friends, whom he amusingly called "the nuts with dough." It is a fabulous organization, as it does inspire people to do philanthropy and gives them a model for doing so, as well as congenial people to work with. Groups called "Social Justice" and "Ecology," etc., meet and talk about work in the world they will do together or independently. Since then, the Threshold Foundation has expanded into specialized donor groups, such as Business for Social Responsibility, for businesspeople who desire to have socially responsible businesses, and the Social Ventures Network, which promotes new ventures.

At this meeting I met Josh, who became a friend and continues to inspire me and others around the world to acts of greater generosity.

Back in Big Sur, the workmen banging hammers as they built the dining room in the house drove me mad. When Arthur was silent, thinking his own thoughts, I felt lonely. *Maybe I need another shot of foreign spiritual input*, I thought.

Was I wanting to run away again—and from what?

During one of our trips to New York I had met Winn and Sally Chamberlain, who invited me to their house in Goa. They promised we would go to an important Indian temple, where the goddess was supposed to practically incarnate before our eyes. Naturally I imagined an airy beach house, filled with colorful Indian fabrics and a sacred temple where finally I would feel confident of my connection to the world of spirit.

So, as the winter fog rolled into Big Sur, I bid Arthur and the puppies good-bye and headed for India. When I'd last seen the Chamberlains in New York, they were living in a nice apartment and wearing ordinary clothes. In Goa, I found that Winn had grown a beard and that they'd both donned *dhoti* pants and sprouted yards of beads. I elected to move into the Fort Aguada hotel, rather than stay in their concrete hut with only a hose and a bucket for plumbing.

I wanted to leave instantly, but the travel agent I spoke with said that, due to an ongoing boat captains' strike, all the planes out of Goa were booked for months. My back constricted, and my heart raced. I wasn't accepting these—very minor—troubles lightly, and meditation eluded me. Since Buddha didn't immediately answer my prayers for escape, I asked God to send me some dreams that would explain what was happening.

I dreamed that a butterfly was caught in a jar, destroying its wings by beating them against the walls. The neck of the jar was too small for it to fly out; but the top was actually open, and if it stayed still someone might tip the jar and it could escape. I knew the butterfly was me and stillness was my only hope. It was a clear message that I needed to stay still.

My beaded and dhoti-ed friends urged me to embark with them on an eight-hour trip to Kollur, where there was an especially holy Hindu temple honoring a goddess of whom I had never heard. I was expected to rent a Land Rover and hire a driver—who took us hundreds of years back in time along a dusty red clay road that wound through jungle villages. Old bullock carts driven by hollow-eyed men in ragged turbans clattered beside women in brilliant saris, with bangles and nose rings, carrying huge baskets on their heads. Tiny thatched huts huddled in the midst of miles of green rice paddies. When we finally reached Kollur, we saw that in lieu of bathrooms, the guesthouse had pits and pails, and very little paint. It cost three dollars a night. Nearby a baby elephant was having a bath in a rice field.

As soon as we settled in, we walked to Mookambika temple, one of the holiest places in India. It was a dark and slippery place. Wet black rocks and crushed marigolds lay under our bare feet, and a huge lingam with a gold tip towered in the back. The statue of the goddess was wheeled around the temple in a tumbrel, led by eight-year-old boys dancing in elaborate silver dresses, jewels, and makeup. It seemed to me more of a theatrical spectacle than a deep spiritual experience, but I enjoyed it anyway.

That night I lay on my lumpy palette at the guesthouse, reading *Autobiography of a Yogi*, about Paramahansa Yogananda's search for enlightenment. I was amazed when I reached a passage in the book that seemed to be a response to the dream I'd had in Goa. In it, Yogananda described this earthly reality as a jar and the butterfly of omnipresence as a free soul. According to this interpretation, my dream was telling me that I wanted my soul freed of this earthly reality. I felt blessed but wondered what to do next.

The next day, the Chamberlains and I had lunch at the home of a friend of theirs, who was a Brahmin priest. There was no furniture, save for a TV in the middle of the room on a stand; it had a blue cover that said, "Showtime." We sat on the floor and ate with our fingers from banana leaves.

Our host's son, Ravendra, had also read Yogananda's book, and he told me that he was studying with a yogi in the woods nearby. He showed me a picture of his teacher, Lakshmi Narayan, a peaceful-looking saint with a long white beard. I instantly wanted to meet him. His picture radiated something; he seemed to be the embodiment of peace.

After lunch, I asked if he would take me to meet his teacher, and he led me through the jungle on a narrow path crisscrossed by a stream to

Lakshmi Narayan's little concrete hut. It sat by a brook, and only the sound of water and the twittering of birds broke the warm tranquil air. We entered the hut, where the yogi sat on a deerskin mat, dressed in a pink silk shirt over yellow silk pants—the perfect Bobo guru. MGM couldn't have done better.

His eyes sparkled as he said in heavily accented English, "What do you want to ask?"

"I saw your picture, and I wanted to come," I replied.

He said, "Trust your intuition. You are already where you want to be; you already have what you are looking for."

He held my gaze for a long time, piercing my soul with his shining dark eyes.

"You are already home," he said. "What we are looking for is in us. Our faith. Our intuition. God. It is already in us. Just practice and meditate."

I felt myself relax completely.

I loved Swami Narayan; he was my idea of the perfect guru … from his peaceful face and long white beard right down to his divine pink and yellow costume, and he delivered the perfect message. Walking back to the village behind Ravendra, I thought about my dream of the butterfly in the jar and finding the exact answers in the Yogananda book; and now I'd met this marvelous yogi. *These are signs*, I thought, *that the cosmos confirms I am on the path.*

The next day as we rattled our way back to Goa in the dusty Land Rover, I worried about whether I should have stayed with the lovely swami in pink, or whether my "practice" should be staying home with my husband and really being in my marriage. I decided it was going home. I flew back to New York, where I found Arthur busy with meetings, glad to have me back, and somewhat mystified by my need to go on these endless searches for enlightenment … or new shores … or whatever they were.

The insignificance of my own little worries became clear when one of my dearest friends in New York, at forty-two, contracted a fast-spreading cancer. Terry Clifford was a "dharma sister" whom I'd met through other Tibetan Buddhist friends. A vibrant, small-boned brunette with ivory white skin and huge blue eyes, she lived alone in a walk-up flat. It was Arthur, not me, who kindly suggested that she move into the guest room of our Fifth Avenue apartment, and shortly thereafter she did. That was very generous of him, as she would share his dressing room bathroom.

In July, I accompanied her to Massachusetts for a retreat with our teacher from Sikkim, Dodrupchen Rinpoche. As we drove, we ate bags of carrot chips, because they were supposed to be good for fighting cancer. Poised on a low hill, the temple in Hawley was an exact replica of a red-and-yellow Tibetan monastery. It was surrounded by fields of tangled, dry yellow grass, and its multicolored prayer flags hung limp in the summer heat.

We left our shoes on the porch and filed into the meditation room, where people had staked out their places with bags and mats and cushions. Room for us was made near the altar, since Terry was known to Rinpoche as a longtime student. All afternoon we sat listening to the monotonous Tibetan chanting, trying to keep our eyes open in the buzzing summer heat, while mosquitoes circled our heads.

Afterward, Terry and I had an interview with Rinpoche. We met in what was really his bedroom. Rinpoche sat on the bed, and we sat on the floor; but there was a formality to it all that made me feel as though we were in a temple.

"Try to let each thought go the moment it arises," he said. "The gap between the thoughts is like a sneeze. The mind stops."

He said a great deal more, of course, but that was what I remembered most clearly.

In the evening, some of Terry's friends joined us in the little shack next to the temple where she was staying. We lay on pillows on the floor, drinking beer by candlelight.

"I feel so relaxed," I said. "There's a wonderful spirit of camaraderie in this room."

"It's because you have found spiritual friends," Terry replied. "You've seen samsara, but most people still want the things you already know aren't worth anything."

I remembered how I'd felt in Kathmandu and in Sikkim—the same close camaraderie of spiritual friends. It felt so special. Yet despite knowing how happy I felt on retreat, each time I left I embraced worldly life again. So much of my life outside the temples was like carrot chips—not bad, but not all that nourishing.

Back at the Olde Willow Inn, where I was staying, I dreamed that I was in a temple of threads, eating healthy food with my dharma friends. My mother and sister arrived with a mass of desserts and said, "If you'll eat these we will too, and we're dying to have some." So to please them, I started eating chocolate and meringues.

When I woke up, I saw the connection between the dream and my childhood, when I was starved by the lack of emotional nourishment from my family. More importantly, I did things that made me unhappy—like riding—or things I didn't enjoy, just to please others. Real nourishment was being curled up with dharma buddies in a shack with no electricity and a dear sick friend. As I did so often on spiritual retreats, I received insights into aspects of my life I hadn't even been consciously aware of.

One of the pleasures I found in Hawley was the small-town atmosphere. It occurred to me that in days gone by people must have collected at their village church after the service and had a meal together—just as we did after the teachings. This community of dharma practitioners was a kind of family based on common interest instead of common blood, a tribe. Staying with this type of community, though, was always a problem for me. On these spiritual retreats we were automatically a family, and I was hungry for that feeling of belonging.

One night toward the end of my stay, Terry and I took a walk in the tepid twilight. Where the yellow sandy road ran close to the brook, she stopped and unwound the mala of wooden prayer beads from her wrist.

"Dilgo Khyentse Rinpoche's wife gave me this, and it's been with me a long time," she said. "I want you to have it."

I couldn't speak for the tears in my throat. This gift was the tangible tool of her many years of practice.

"Practice hard," she said. "You have a gift for this path."

I wrapped it around my wrist and hugged her in thanks. She felt so thin and frail. She held my hot suntanned hand in her cool white one. We were both fighting back tears, facing the reality of death.

"Sometimes I don't trust the teachings," I said. "And a part of me is skeptical."

She put the tips of her fingers together and looked over the tent they formed with big luminous blue eyes.

"You have a meditator's mind. Be humble and listen, and study with everyone. Don't get caught in sectarianism. Follow what feels right for you."

My head ached and felt congested with sadness. Maybe Terry's did too, for she said she wanted to walk on alone for a little while. The light was translucent, and there were halos in the leaves.

I went back to New York the next day, but Terry stayed on to be with Rinpoche for a while before going to live with her mother in Brooklyn.

One morning a few months later, I was working in my art studio in a rented house in East Hampton. On an impulse, I set down my brushes, put up a clean sheet of heavy watercolor paper, and dipped a sponge in water and India ink. In a few quick strokes, I painted a woman sitting in meditation with a veil over part of her face. As I finished, Arthur came out to the studio to say Harold was on the phone.

I went into the house and picked up the phone.

"Terry died fifteen minutes ago," Harold said.

"Was there anything over her face?" I asked.

"Yes," he replied. "The sheet was over one side."

I gasped.

"I just painted a picture of her like that. Maybe Terry visited me as she left this earthly realm and appeared on my paper."

"That could be," Harold said.

I woke in the night and sat on the deck, holding Terry's mala and watching the clouds scud across the moon. The sky looked like a painting I'd done recently of a pass between two golden mountains, through which marched the spirits of the dead.

As the following year passed in Big Sur, I sank into the peace of the enormous silence and the vast sky. Everything felt right there. I didn't need to travel. I needed, like my painted birds, to stay in one place and see what emerged on the canvas. In my paintings, I began to see a new dimension to my spiritual life. I began to understand that painting was my way of physically expressing spiritual revelations.

With Arthur, I was anchored but I had solitude: a perfect combination for an artist. I knew, if only for the moment, that having one foot in Big Sur and one in New York offered a wonderful combination of resources. I loved Arthur, and he was endlessly kind. Knowing that I could see my friends in the East, yet enjoy the peace to pursue my painting and spiritual life in the beautiful hills along the Pacific, suited me and made me happy—until the monster of restlessness captured me again.

CHAPTER

On the Rocks

Big Sur isn't particularly known for its rocks, although it has a few nice ones. In 1988, I became obsessed with rocks. There were huge, craggy ones on the hillsides, which from a distance looked like dogs and whales; one, like the head of an Indian; and another, like a being from outer space. There were rocks on the beach, too: big, rounded boulders I climbed on to sit and watch the waves, and smooth pink and gray stones I could put in my pockets. I painted the rocks leaning out of the mountains and the small crazy ones in the garden. I gathered rocks and made archways, which in my mind's eye I saw as gateways, passages through which I could travel between the phenomenal world and the spiritual one. I painted them incessantly. There were no rock archways on the hills or the beach: they were all in my mind, like a dream that feels really real.

"These are portals to another world," I told my friend Joan Halifax—a certified Zen Roshi, a shaman, and an anthropologist. She knew from rocks.

"Bobo is getting stoned." She laughed, watching me furiously painting away.

I found some deep satisfaction in painting my rock archways. I was bringing spiritual and material realities together for myself in my studio. While I painted, I felt completely connected to my wisest and most serene self.

But after a while, a shadow overtook me and led me away from this creative peace: a side of my nature that needed more—that needed to be famous, to be known for my wisdom and therefore be assured that it was real. I was not acknowledging that I was *finding* my wisdom right there, and my lack of confidence in myself drove me to destroy the happiness that could have been mine, and to destroy Arthur's happiness too. This restless monster in my soul drove us apart. It also ultimately broke down my body, for I had a chronic back pain, which was always aggravated by travel—sitting on airplanes for hours on end.

The voice that wanted more was afraid that somehow the life I was leading wasn't valid, was not recognized as worthwhile by the Great Judging Mind I imagined. That was why, whenever I was given a chance to go where there would be teachings from an acknowledged guru, or to a party with brilliant or famous people, I wanted to go. Arthur couldn't understand it—and I didn't understand it at the time, so I couldn't explain why I felt compelled to go. I expect he thought it had to do with him, because that is the way our minds work.

So, in the middle of "getting stoned" on my portals, I rushed off to Los Angeles to hear the Dalai Lama teach about wisdom, instead of accepting the fact there was a certain wisdom in what I was already doing. While I was in Los Angeles, my friend Angie Thieriot, who had initiated me into Transcendental Meditation years earlier, took me to dinner with Carlos Castaneda, author of a series of books about his work with Yaqui shaman Don Juan. In these books he told stories of how he moved easily from one reality to the next, jumping off cliffs and flying about.

I asked him about rocks, and he said, "Rocks live in time so slow that we cannot perceive it."

This thought animated my rocks in a new way. Now they really "lived," and, it appeared, in slow time. Before, I'd believed they were imbued by magic; now, a famous shaman had agreed there was living magic in them. He validated my experience, which made me realize that that was what I wanted: a fellow believer in magic to understand my realizations, too.

"What do you practice?" I asked, rather hoping he would teach me to fly through my stone arches or something equally exotic.

"Recapitulation," he replied. "If you look at your life from the present backward, you'll notice that you make the same mistakes over and over again in a variety of situations. Eventually you'll become so bored with old patterns of behavior that you'll give them up in disgust. I do it by losing my persona, my image. To make this shift I use the method of recapitulation— slowly going over my experiences from the present to the past."

I thought about my repetitive patterns of behavior with alcohol, food, and men—and the fact that I was still caught up in them—and I felt that I'd just rather forget about them. I knew if I allowed myself to be honest and look at how I behaved, I would get terribly depressed. As it was, since I didn't consciously acknowledge how bad this to-ing and fro-ing was for me, my body pointed it out with endless bouts of back pain and exhaustion, during which I felt as though my energy bled away.

I couldn't just sit still in my marriage, though, because of the voice that said, *You aren't doing enough. You aren't good enough. If you want to be really evolved and different, you must keep trying new things.* This was the voice of my darkest shadow, which I had picked up from Mummy— and perhaps the challenge I came into this life to conquer.

"Think how much energy you use just presenting yourself, creating an image for people," Castaneda said.

I knew how much of my energy had been devoted to creating a "fun" image of myself for people so they would like me. I was beginning to think perhaps it was time to give it up. I didn't need to do it anymore.

"Being impeccable is being your absolute, ultimate best," Carlos continued. "It's being completely authentic and losing your attachment to the self."

It was as though he'd answered my thought. This insight was a part of almost every spiritual practice I'd been exposed to—being present and real and caring for others. I remembered Dodrupchen Rinpoche in Sikkim saying, "This is not a time to search for personal answers but for universal ones." But I wasn't ready to let go of my attachment to the self.

I thought I needed to *find* myself, to be rooted in myself, before I could let go into the spirit of caring for others. In retrospect, I think that what was crazy about this was that caring for others was the exact practice the Dalai Lama had suggested in his wisdom and compassion teachings.

Florinda Donner-Grau, Castaneda's chief "witch"—that's how his female companions actually described themselves—had been at the dinner, as well, and she called me a few nights later to urge me to join her and the other "witches" working with Carlos. I asked her what the arrangements were between them and Carlos. She said that if one of them died, the others would be willing to as well.

"If any of our number dies, all our lives are in jeopardy," she explained. "Wait and see. There is no love among us, but in a way there is great love, but only as magical beings."

"No, thanks," I said. "I don't want to be a witch."

What had attracted me to Castaneda was his ability to move between the worlds of spirit and material phenomena. I didn't want to be one of his witches and die—or indeed, do anything—at his behest. I wanted to belong comfortably in both worlds the same way he did, and I wanted him to teach me right now (of course) how he did it.

A few weeks after I came back back from Los Angeles, I went on a hike along the Tanbark Trail with Brother David Steindl Rast, a friend who lived up the mountain at the Camaldolese Monastery. At one point he said, "The longing for belonging is longing to belong to God, not desire for something we imagine would make us happy on this earth."

As we hiked past the old hunting retreat known as the Tin House, I told Brother David that my longing for God was being satisfied a bit by my slow realization that God was manifested in nature. I told him about my rock arch paintings and about the images of holes in mountains that I'd recently started painting, which led to the "other" reality, which I understood as heaven or a spiritual reality. I also confessed that I was having trouble making this other reality a part of my everyday life. Where was this spiritual sense and wisdom when I got annoyed with Arthur?

We sat down to have egg salad sandwiches and iced tea and watched the turquoise sea crashing against the rocks way below. Brother David, who knew I'd been to the Dalai Lama's teaching in Los Angeles, reminded me that thinking of others was part of the practice the Dalai Lama had described, and part of spiritual practice in general.

"It's also part of common sense," he said, "the senses that we share in common."

Several months later, Brother David came for dinner in Big Sur, along with my Taoist friend Al Huang and Joseph Campbell, both of whom I'd met at Esalen. In fact, over the years almost *everyone* in the spiritual, consciousness, and philosophical worlds who was open-minded came to Esalen. This was due to Michael Murphy and Richard Price, who founded it; both of them have always been considered integral and creative forces in promoting these ideas.

At one point, Campbell said, "Women are initiated by nature and men by society," which I loved because it felt true. He said a lot of other interesting things I've forgotten, but Brother David and I had a conversation about God. I told him that, walking down the beach, I'd picked up a handful of different-colored pebbles and realized that it was like looking at the infinite expressions of God's face.

I do remember Campbell thought Brother David's outfit very chic. The Benedictine uniform is white pants and blouse with a black jerkin and brown leather belt. It is what fashion people called "timelessly chic."

Arthur was rarely present for my dinner parties, as he came down from San Francisco mostly on the weekends. We hiked and grilled steaks by the lake and tried to catch up on each other's lives. But our days apart were so different that it was easier to just enjoy together what we both loved about Big Sur—the land, the hiking, the peace, and the happiness—than to try to discuss our separate pursuits.

Despite my happiness in Big Sur, I had terrible pains in my back and a serious eating disorder. The pain drove me to drink, which of course made it better for a short time and much worse in the long run. I also stuffed myself with food to fill the emptiness, which was still there despite my efforts at spiritual life. There's nothing like a chocolate cake to push down feelings of fear, and I discovered that Campari and sodas gave the world a lovely pink glow.

I tried to tell Arthur that something was wrong, but he only suggested that I relax and be happy. My shrink in New York, to whom I spoke regularly by phone, told me, "The forces of good and evil are at war for your soul. You have to decide at every moment what the right thing to do is—and when you don't have any backbone to say no, or to do the right thing, you get sick."

How could I be suffering while living in paradise? I couldn't be present for my days because I was eaten by fears that I was wasting my life. I was so anxious I woke up in the mornings in a panic of indecision about whether to go to San Francisco for a cocktail party or to watch the sunset from a hilltop I called Sacred Mountain, which towered behind our house. I usually chose the mountain.

My friend Angie invited me to go with her to a Vipassana meditation retreat in Yucca Valley near Palm Springs. Of course I accepted, because this was something new, a possible route to healing my life. Silence reigned for ten days as we examined the true nature of our minds.

"No one can speak except in interviews with the teachers," said Jack Kornfield, our teacher. "Sit and watch your mind."

I watched my recollections of childhood, my dog disappearing, Mamie dying.

"Feel your body," he said.

I felt my heart breaking over all that had happened and all that might happen.

"Be mindful of your walking," he continued.

I seemed to have forgotten how to walk; my feet wouldn't move in front of each other.

Then on about day nine, something happened. I tried really hard to watch my breath and stay in the moment; suddenly everything got very calm as the world of everyday stuff seemed to melt away.

"You went quite deep," said Jack when I told him about my experience.

I went back to Big Sur, my puppies, my rock paintings, my hikes, and dinners with Arthur, though the peace I found there was sometimes shattered by anxiety, like summer lightning bursting through a calm sky.

One day, Josh Mailman called and said I must—absolutely *must*—come to a Threshold Foundation meeting at a hotel in Southern California. The members gathered in a circle and passed a talking stick modeled on Native American meetings. Individuals got up in the middle of the circle and spoke about their lives, their hopes, their families—whatever was holding them back or helping them move forward. A man in a toupee sang Wagner; a woman spoke about her mother dying; and others spoke of spiritual transformation or their business.

For the most part people were expected and encouraged to be vulnerable and real in their conversations and dealings with other members. I came away transformed, not only with the discovery of a liberated way of being, but also with a new view of what to do with money. I realized that, in a sense, giving away money is one of the most satisfying things one can do.

It changed my life.

Soon after that meeting, my aunt Janie died and left my sister and me the contents of her apartment. We kept some things, but much of it was very ornate furniture, inappropriate for our houses. There were also paintings. We tossed a coin for each major object, and I got a Matisse. I created the Tara Foundation with the million dollars it brought at Christie's. I was so excited when the auctioneer said, "Now this Matisse is sold by the Tara Foundation," I practically cried.

Mummy was furious when I told her. "I could have used that money," she said. "Why would you give it away?"

However, the next day my friends Mike Murphy, the creator of Esalen, and Steve Donovan, the president, were going to see Laurance Rockefeller to ask for money for the institute, and they took me along. Rockefeller complimented me on my decision and made me feel as though a million dollars was a fortune and that I was embarking on an important and worthwhile project. I was so happy; that affirmation was just what I needed to restore my confidence in myself.

Soon, adventure beckoned again. I might have been a budding philanthropist, and perhaps I'd gone "quite deep" at the meditation retreat in Yucca Valley, but I *had* to rush off and find another teacher in an exotic costume. This time, it was in a jungle monastery in Thailand, where my fiend Nina Wise, who led an improvisational acting class I'd briefly tried out, was going to see a great Buddhist teacher.

Nina suggested that we go first to see the abbot of Wat Thamkrabok, a few hours north of Bangkok. When we arrived, he was nowhere to be seen. While waiting for him, I watched some men in red sarongs drink a purgative and then throw up while a gaily dressed band played a tuneful melody. Afterward, they filed into a steam bath to the same perky music.

"This regimen cures them of heroin in three weeks," said the abbot, who suddenly appeared beside us.

Our chauffeur threw himself at the abbot's feet and said he had been here ten years ago.

As we were driving back to Bangkok, I thought, *If only I was an addict, I could benefit from the abbot's cure.* What if peace and enlightenment eluded me because I couldn't participate in his regimen?

Nina assured me that our next stop, Suan Mokkh, a forest monastery in southern Thailand, would be more attuned to our needs. To get there, we traveled for two days—by plane, boat, car, and on foot. When we arrived, we found the abbot, Buddhadasa, dressed in a dark rust robe, sitting cross-legged on a bamboo bench, while a black chicken nibbled his toe. The heat and the mosquitoes were beyond anything I'd ever known.

Not wasting a minute, I asked him, "What is the most important thing to know?"

He replied, "There is no self. Get rid of self. Practice is the bicycle, not the teacher. One must ride to learn to ride. One must practice to be enlightened."

He knew I wouldn't practice and closed his eyes and laughed and laughed, like a jolly Santa Claus wrapped in a gold brown cloth—or like one of those wooden statues of a fat, laughing Buddha.

"Beyond sad and glad is peace," he said as another chicken perched on his arm and a dog crawled under his bench.

As we walked around the monastery, waiting for someone to agree that we could stay there, I found a picture of a Buddha with a quotation affixed: "Oh boundless joy to find at last there is no happiness in this world." Our mosquito-ridden cell, with two concrete platforms for beds, confirmed this point of view for me. Since we weren't allowed to eat at the monastery, we ate from the meager wares of a food stand in the road where the bicycle rickshaw drivers ate.

That there is no happiness in this world is why I'm looking for another reality, I thought, entirely forgetting that only a week earlier I'd been quite happy in Big Sur and had received actual teachings in meditation, which I was not getting here. *What peace*, I thought, *to let go of trying to change things and make them better.* It was the same lesson about learning to accept suffering that I'd learned in Sikkim.

As I lay in a hammock strung between two palm trees, thinking how wonderfully evolved this trip was making me, I noticed that my hands were clenched into tight little fists, my nails digging into my palms. Was traveling to the ends of the earth for enlightenment the way to evolve?

When I got home after two weeks in Thailand, I was exhausted and convinced my life was a disaster. Arthur pointed out that these kinds of trips can get you down.

"Why not just stay home and go hiking and paint?" he suggested.

I did that for a while and tried settling in, but I was still obsessed with my feelings of not being good enough—for love, for anything. I wanted to talk about this incessantly, which can be tiring for others, especially if they share the same sentiment about themselves and don't much want to keep reconsidering it. Arthur excelled at his career as a venture capitalist, but he'd also had parents who weren't particularly supportive or admiring; yet he didn't obsess over it or let it get in his way. I couldn't let go of the idea that I was insufficient, no matter what I tried.

A couple of months later, we went to New York. Despite the pain in my back, I was determined to go to a party and hobbled out of my bedroom in New York one night, a crooked witch in white sequins, barely able to straighten up. However, as Arthur and I walked down the curving staircase at the River Club to dance, my cheeks flushed, my back straightened, and we danced the tango.

"You're a maenad," said Arthur. "What happens to you when we go to parties?"

I didn't know myself, only that my need to perform was so great I could ignore my body to the point I didn't feel it. When we got home, I was almost paralyzed, exhausted, and hungry for my new favorite orange pain pills. Why did I do that? Some inner need to perform, which I demanded of myself, drove me—the same one that drove me to stuff myself with food and throw up, and to get on airplanes when I could barely walk due to the pain.

Looking back, I'm horrified at my total lack of appreciation for my life. It seems I had an almost suicidal tendency to destroy what was, in reality, a blessed existence. I was destroying myself physically, but I had a lot of nervous energy, and I used most of it to keep going.

I heard about a woman called Thelma Moss, who I thought taught qi gong, but it turned out she led guided meditations—which was lucky, because when I visited her I had a vision of who I thought I was, deep down, at that time. In it was a little girl, who, through a series of adventures with a magical frog, eventually turned into an artist made of rainbows and grokked the mysterious secrets of the universe.

When I described what I'd seen to Thelma, she said, "This vision is clearly about the conflict in your life between earthly things and desires and the spiritual path. It's not every day someone comes in here wanting to be a shaman."

This vision haunted me. In my art studio at Santa Lucia, I turned the vision into a book with illustrations. But was what Thelma told me true? Did I want to be a shaman? I thought about it as I climbed the dry mountains in the summer, when day after day the sky was an arc of deep blue, until the fog rolled in and clung to everything like wet cotton wool. I thought about the "longing to belong" of which Brother David had spoken. Could I be married and be a shaman? Arthur didn't mind what I wanted to be. The conflict, the restlessness of heart and mind, was mine alone.

In 1989, wanderlust once again got the upper hand in the form of an urge to set out on another spiritual pilgrimage. I still wasn't ready to accept that my home was with Arthur and my puppies. I was always searching for the ephemeral Shangri-la where I would finally feel complete.

I'd read somewhere that "We are what is done to us." I was convinced I was an unwelcome, untalented, and generally disappointing child, and I never lost that belief, no matter what I did. I saw a movie about a woman who was tattooed by the Nazis when she was their prisoner. No matter what operations she had, she could not get rid of the tattoo, because it covered her whole back. Eventually, she died of her attempts to get rid of it, and she had never made peace that it was not "hers."

The pain in my own back was a constant reminder that I was splitting my life; but I couldn't seem to acknowledge that I was changing and that I was no longer the disappointing person I thought I was. I kept looking for some way to be not only fulfilled, but also helpful to other people. Why couldn't I see that I could be helpful if I would just pay attention to other people—among them my long-suffering husband?

But off I went on another search. This time I headed to Kathmandu for the funeral of Dudjom Rinpoche, to whom I had delivered tsampa from the mountain monastery back in 1975, and whom I later saw again, briefly in New York in 1979. He had remained in a meditation position for thirteen days after he stopped breathing, still exuding warmth from his heart chakra—which in Tibetan Buddhism is considered a sign of profound realization.

The taxi driver at the Kathmandu airport suggested Dwarika's Hotel near the temple complex at Boudhanath. The hotel consisted of three traditional carved Nepali houses set in a garden, with old-fashioned wicker furniture under the jacaranda trees. When I arrived at Dwarika's, my anxiety lifted. As I stepped into the atmosphere of the surrounding temples, one of calm and satiety completeness, a wave of peace swept over me.

Everything suddenly seemed easy. An old dharma buddy, Vivian Kurz, whom I'd met through Terry, was staying at a monastery nearby, and she agreed to accompany me to the funeral of her teacher the next day. Together, we walked to Rinpoche's monastery and watched two lamas lift, from the back of a pickup truck, what looked like a brocade hatbox.

"Rinpoche is salted in that box, and he's covered with gold," Vivian said.

We filed into the stupa and sat on cushions while the monks chanted and Dilgo Khyentse Rinpoche, who had become the head of the Nyingma lineage of Tibetan Buddhism after Dudjom Rinpoche's death, performed a long ceremony. A sleepy peace floated on the clouds of incense rising from the braziers.

In the afternoon a monk, bent double with humility, ushered me in to see Dilgo Khyentse Rinpoche, whom I had met back in 1979 during my trip to India with Harold. Seated on a yellow silk throne, Rinpoche was a mountain of a man who, that day, wore a strapless pink silk petticoat held above his chest by an elastic band. He had very long fingernails, like the Chinese Mandarins, and hidden in rolls of tanned skin were two glittering brown eyes that squinted out at the world, like slits of light from eternity. Most of the time, they were at half-mast or actually closed—probably, I imagined, because his inner vistas were more interesting than the more mundane ones shared by the rest of us.

He spoke to me about Dzogchen, the main discipline of the Nyingma lineage—to which I'd been introduced during my trip to Sikkim—a specialized training in seeing the nature of reality.

"It is comprehension of our awareness," Rinpoche explained, "in which everything is contained. Awareness has two aspects: emptiness and appearances." Another way to describe these two aspects might be the recognition of the essential transience of everything that lives and dies and the appearance of a permanent reality. At one point, he tapped me on the head with his long fingernails, and I told him that I wanted to change my life but didn't know how to start.

"Think that other people's happiness is more important than your own, and try to make them happy," he said. "Happiness will also come to you."

I put five hundred rupees on the altar, but it kept falling off, which made me wonder if it was enough. The exchange of money for spiritual teachings is a touchy thing. What is worth what? Theoretically, the teachings are priceless, but the lamas expect donations for their monasteries and, I suppose, themselves.

The next day, I hiked up to Nagi Gompa, a hermitage above Kathmandu, with Andrew Harvey and Lavinia Currier. Like me, they'd come to Kathmandu for Dudjom Rinpoche's funeral; when we met there, we discovered that we had many mutual friends in America and we were all students of Dudjom Rinpoche and Sogyal Rinpoche. At Nagi Gompa, the great Nyingma master Tulku Urgyen Rinpoche gave us an experience of "spacious mind" by suddenly clapping his hands. It was as though the whole world went silent and the top of the universe opened into a vast space, like the huge snow peaks around us, silent in the blue sky. This was my experience of *rigpa*, which, in Dzogchen, is "seeing" the nature of reality as your own mind.

That evening, we walked along the *ghats* of Kathmandu, the long flights of stairs leading down to the riverbank. The sky was pink, the same color as the faded temples. As we walked by the river, peering into the little fires and trying to see inside the hovels along the bank, an *aghori*—a man who collects the wood, lights the funeral pyres, and beats the drums for death—beckoned to us from his dark little hovel.

So packed was the tiny room with pictures and statues of Hindu deities, that there was hardly space for us to sit around the fire in its center. The aghori was a pretzel of limber bones in his ragged dhoti. His long hair and curly beard were matted to dirty brown cotton, and he looked at us with disturbingly huge, brilliant eyes. He lit a strange little pipe without a stem and passed it to us. It looked like a baked potato with a hole in it. As I puffed on it, I could feel the world reel.

"Here was my father," he said, passing around a skull for each of us to hold. It was smooth and soft like polished leather, tanned by years of fire smoke. "All people, all countries are the same," he continued. "Sweet, sour, hot, cold—all the same all over the earth. All religion is the same. We come. We go."

Abruptly, he turned to me and said, "You are Kali."

Then he turned to Andrew and said, "You are Saraswati."

Looking at Lavinia, he pronounced, "You are Mira."

Kali is the Hindu goddess of death, portrayed with skulls around her neck; Saraswati is the goddess of music and writing; and Mira was a Rajasthani saint known for her love of God. After leaving the aghori's hovel, we walked along the ghats in the moonlight feeling spaced-out and laughing. It was as if we had flown into another time warp. This sense of euphoria lasted through the next day, during which everything had a magic synchronicity. *This must be a taste of awareness*, I thought.

A few days later, I took the night train from Delhi to Dharamsala, where the Tibetan Government in Exile is headquartered and the Dalai Lama resides. I immediately went to bed at the hilltop Hotel Bhagsu with a terrible cold and a blinding headache. The Tibetan hotelier said, "This is the blessing of the dharma, the purification after the teaching."

Not that broken record, I thought. *I practically have to schedule sick time on these pilgrimages!*

Nevertheless, I went to the afternoon teaching that His Holiness was giving in his lovely, airy shrine room, awash in the yellow-and-maroon robes of lamas. Happily, I found myself sitting on the floor next to Nicky Vreeland, an old friend from New York, who had become a lama. He lent me the gadget on which one could hear a simultaneous translation of His Holiness's teaching in Tibetan.

"Give up all desire and hope of worldly gain," His Holiness was saying. "Compassion is the root and preparation for wisdom. The best thing would be to move into a forest cave where the animals would neither praise nor blame you."

The next morning as I was lying in bed feeling depressed by my cold and wishing I lived in a forest cave surrounded by friendly and nonjudgmental animals, a friend brought two visitors: Vikram Seth, author of *A Suitable Boy* and several other novels, and Maura Moynihan, the daughter of Senator Daniel Patrick Moynihan and a force of nature in her own right. Maura, dressed in flowing Indian pants and a little vest, curled up on the bed, and Vikram lay on a bench by the window with his head on a papaya, as we giggled and gossiped about everything from American politics to Indian music. In the late afternoon, the Dalai

Lama's private secretary sent word that I would have an appointment with His Holiness the next morning. I had come to Dharamsala to discuss my spiritual life with His Holiness, but I felt so comfortable with Maura and Vikram that I invited them to come with me to my audience.

His Holiness received us in his private visiting room of his monastery. It was painted pale yellow and sparsely furnished with a few tables and chairs and silk Tibetan *thangkas*. Vikram presented him with a pile of books with two statues of the Buddha on top. His Holiness laughed and said the scripture goes above the Buddha, and put the books on his head. Vikram and Maura talked about Indian politics. I could see His Holiness was having a wonderful time, so I let go of thinking I was going to talk to him about my practice. I realized that for me the feeling of friendship with Maura and Vikram, and seeing the Dalai Lama laughing and enjoying himself, felt more wonderful than trying to figure out my spiritual life.

Afterward, Maura, Vikram, and I danced down the street like Gene Kelly in *Singin' in the Rain*. That's the effect hanging out with highly evolved people can have. We ran into Nicky Vreeland in his maroon-and-yellow robes, and the four of us sat at the Rising Horizon Cafe eating banana cake and drinking ginger tea. We wrote postcards to Nicky's grandmother, Diana Vreeland, and Maura's father, Senator Daniel Patrick Moynihan.

It occurred to me—for what seemed like the millionth time—that when I went on spiritual pilgrimages, I found a community of people who made me happy. Was I traveling only for adventure and teaching, or to find my "home" with fellow students?

As the sun set the next day, Maura, Vikram, and I boarded the chaotic train for Delhi. After a sleepless night of laughter, Vikram served us coffee in his garden full of peacocks, while Maura read my palm. "You'll have great success and much spiritual accomplishment," she advised encouragingly.

The end of a pilgrimage is rather like New Year's, I thought. *One truly believes one will do better.*

When I returned, exhausted as usual from a trip, Arthur said, "If we don't spend more than half our time together, what are we doing married?" He suggested we look at our calendars, and at the end of six months, take note of how much time we had spent together. We actually spent the next two years trying to figure it out.

What was I thinking? I was running away from the one man I knew loved me and whom I loved. And yet I felt abandoned by him—though in truth I was abandoning him. While I was I was happy in Big Sur, I was still seeking community through my spiritual pilgrimages. Or was I using my search as a way of escaping my marriage? Despite all my studies in consciousness, I remained unconscious of what I was actually doing. I could hear my mother's voice: "All you think about is yourself." (Which was true but not much help; and the same thing could easily have been said about her.)

How was it that Arthur and I decided to part? I'm not exactly sure I can say. We were different sizes, and we lived at different speeds. It was not only that he was a good foot taller, but also that he saw the world from a vertical point of view, whereas I saw it more or less horizontally. I was a jack of all trades, constantly trying new things and dropping most of them, while he was a master of one. As for our speeds, Arthur thought carefully about things before he did them, while I rushed into everything without much consideration. As Brother David had said to me, "Bo, you're intuitive, but you need to think more."

I was drawn to the East—India, Nepal, Thailand—and embraced a spiritual path that was grounded in Eastern wisdom. Arthur preferred the West—France and England—and thought religion was a sort of addiction, like smoking. True, I went to France and ate gourmet food and drank fabulous wines with Arthur, and he had hiked through Ladakh with me. But I wanted to discuss our relationship constantly, and after ten minutes Arthur would say, "It's been ten minutes." In retrospect, ten minutes was probably enough; those kinds of conversations can be pretty wearing. Unfortunately, the chattier I got, the more silent he grew. Once he said I was like a piece of antimatter. I knew what he meant: it was as though we were from two different species. My painter friend Indiana, who had become a close confidante, said, "No Harvard WASP wants to discuss relationship for even ten minutes."

Of course, he came from the same social background as I did: a family of blue bloods, a class of people who, by and large, feel completely entitled and don't need to discuss their feelings. Most don't even know how. Certainly, my own family didn't. Shrinks came into fashion, I think, with my generation.

I could see many of the same characteristics in myself, in the way I thought things should be done immediately and correctly for me. Spiritual practice and lots of therapy had made me a little more tolerant and a little more accessible; but a certain WASP-y sense of privilege clung to me like a spiderweb.

I wanted to be on the same wavelength with my husband and talk about the deep, important things in our lives. I wanted him to be interested in my spiritual pursuits; yet I didn't take an interest in his business and his business colleagues. Why, in retrospect, should he put up with lamas and gurus if I wouldn't put up with some brilliant venture capitalists?

Sometimes I tried to tell Arthur about my insights and visions, and he would just look blank, not listening at all. *Okay*, I'd think. *That's it. It's over. We'll get divorced.* Then he would do something so sweet I could hardly bear it—like bringing me a Buddha statue for Valentine's Day—and I knew what a brat I'd been. *He understands me*, I'd realize suddenly and gratefully.

But I'd changed during the eleven years we'd been in Big Sur. I was more aware of my feelings. I'd learned that it was normal to suffer and that my "longing to belong" was the desire for God. And I'd come to see that God, or the Great Spirit, or whatever you want to call it, for me manifested in the natural world.

Arthur was kind and thoughtful, but he was much more connected to his mind than his body. He'd freeze rather than put on a sweater when he thought he shouldn't be cold. I had been the same way growing up, so I understood that part of him; it was the legacy of our shared upbringing.

Still, we couldn't really jibe, in the sense of being in accord, so we were in for another kind of jibe. In sailing terms, "jibing" refers to a sudden change in course. The sailboat is running before the wind—boom way out, sail way over—and then the sailor abruptly changes course, the boom swings over with a crash, and the wind catches the sail from the other side. It can be a violent maneuver.

I felt I had to get on another course, and there was no easy way.

I had to jibe.

I told Arthur that he should find someone better. I actually urged him to find a beautiful blond wife who would treat him well. I loved Arthur, and I felt there was nothing else I would regret in dying except leaving him and his feeling sad. So why did I want to split up? I was caught in the insane delusion that my life was an unhappy mess. Looking back, I can see it was the life of a very lucky and totally unaware person. My spiritual explorations were not sinking in at all.

It occurred to me that maybe my chronic back pain was caused by the struggle between wanting to hold on to him and to push him away. Was I withholding my best self from Arthur in an effort to control our marriage?

On some level I knew that choosing to stay in my marriage didn't mean rejecting the life of a seeker. It meant committing to the reality of my life as it was. I wouldn't learn any more on a desert vision quest or in a mountain monastery than I would right here in Big Sur. The real lesson was to open my heart and "be here now," as Ram Dass, who had become a new friend, urged. This was the message of every spiritual master I had ever met. It was certainly what Arthur suggested, and it was the path of least resistance.

In September, I began painting a series of pictures to explore my feelings. In the first, a woman was on a boat with other people. But she dove into the sea and the boat left her behind, and as the tide carried her away, I painted her grabbing a dock piling. She lost her grip, though, and in the next picture she floated dead in the sea. She landed on an island, however, and I painted her, alive again, on a long voyage through many lands filled with different-colored foliage. In the final picture, she'd reached a far country where she entered a temple with a butterfly painted on it. In new robes, she was initiated and transformed into a priestess.

As I was painting, I thought about the possibility of divorce. But while he was driving down from San Francisco, Arthur was in a car accident. He was almost home when it happened; the highway patrol called me, and I rushed to the scene. The car was destroyed. The balloons he'd bought for my birthday the next day were hanging out of the shattered windows, but Arthur emerged almost unscathed. I took him to the hospital, but after receiving a couple of stitches in his forehead, he said he wanted to go home. I loved him and took care of him. It was such a shock for both of us that we didn't mention anything unhappy for quite a while.

Around that time I went to a psychic who told me, "You'll have a happy life and a terrific career if you let go of negative thoughts and stay with Arthur."

Why didn't I listen and remember that? I think impatience and lack of discipline got the better of me. I was always moving too fast. I was blind to the truth of my life, blind to my mind's delusion. I imagined that religion—some teacher in a long robe—could tell me what life was about. In fact, being present with Arthur and the beauty of Big Sur was true and happy-making enough.

My shrink had a different take. "There's a hole in your personality that can't put a correct value on things," she said. "Look at your vision of goodness and truth as the fox in *The Little Prince* wanting to be tamed—and your mother *kills* animals."

It was yet another dichotomy I didn't know how to handle. How could I still have this confusion?

Eventually, Arthur and I fell back into our separate universes. Sometimes he would read a book during dinner while I got drunk. We both hated what the other person was doing. This went on for about a year, until we finally ended up seeing a lawyer—who was perplexed by the decision we'd come to.

"You are both such nice people," he said, "and you seem to get on so well. Why are you getting divorced? I know I'll lose money, but I think you should stay together."

Nevertheless, we thought the marriage was over. Yet even after we separated and I got my own flat on Telegraph Hill, we occasionally had lunch and dinner. We missed each other.

The divorce was finalized just after my fiftieth birthday. A friend who gave me a party didn't invite Arthur. Weren't we divorced? she wondered. Well, we were; but we were still friends and I wanted him to come to my birthday party. It was strange, as though destiny had taken over: Arthur did end up marrying a nice blond wife, as I'd suggested, with whom he had four children; and I went right on seeing the possibility of abandonment in anyone I met.

Arthur let me use the house in Big Sur for a while after we divorced. One day, I made a prayer arrow out of a crooked stick, wrapping it with colored yarn as I prayed that I would remain friends with Arthur, even as we parted. I planted it by the stream in our garden in Big Sur, hoping that, like the Tibetan waterwheels, which send prayers through the mountains, my prayers and friendship would flow into his lake.

CHAPTER

12

Home Is Where Your Pain Is

My life did not snap into place after my divorce. Far from it: I gave in to my desire for youth, sex, and shiny boyfriends to trot around. At fifty, I felt a new vulnerability to add to the pile I already had. Sex was a great generator of creative energy for me, but I lost any sense of peace.

While I'd suffered from chronic back pain for years, I plummeted into a health crisis. My neck felt as if it was in a metal vise, and my whole body ached. Sometimes, I was so weak I could hardly carry the heavy bags from the grocery store, or pick up the dogs when they were recalcitrant about going out. I needed to lie down a lot.

The pain in my body wasn't new; I'd suffered through years of chiropractors and pain pills. But the emotional wounds from my divorce and from leaving my life in Big Sur were hardening in my psyche and in my heart, and they were bringing me to a standstill physically. I felt as though I had both arms up—clenched, shielding myself from a blow—and the pain in my heart was echoing all over my body.

This was my personal diagnosis of the problem, not a medical one. But how different could they be? Very different, as it turned out. When I finally went to see a specialist, I was diagnosed with ankylosing spondylitis, a rheumatoid illness in which joints slowly fuse together of their own volition. It appears to be caused by an inherited gene that is activated by stress. There is no cure presently, though anti-inflammatory drugs help the pain. Now I see that my body was translating the confusion of my mind into bodily pain.

I became so ill and weak that I needed both hands to lift my hairbrush. My doctor prescribed cortisone, but I wouldn't take it. I was convinced that it was my broken heart echoing over my whole body. The pain of leaving Arthur, the pain of childhood, the pain of wrong choices and wrong actions—everything seemed suddenly to pile itself up and cascade through my being. I painted pictures of hearts smoking with rocks falling through them and women whose arms were branches wildly tearing a black sky.

I moved to a big house on Russian Hill, where I could have my own art studio and a live-in caretaker. Brother David provided a novice monk, who dressed in one-piece denim costumes he made himself. He was happy to serve as my hairdresser and cook, as well as to clean the house and take care of my dogs. I was the envy of my friends in San Francisco for having, in one assistant, such a combination of talents.

When I started to lose the vision in my left eye, I went to yet another doctor. "You have an autoimmune illness that is fusing your spine," she said. "And you have iritis, an inflammation of the eye. You may have premature aging disease as well as ankylosing spondylitis. Start by taking sixty milligrams of prednisone a day."

I was terrified and determined not to be sick—certainly not to age prematurely. *Am I not aging fast enough?* I thought. Denial descended, and I refused to accept the diagnosis or take the medicine.

I thought practicing Buddhism might make it go away. Whenever things go wrong, I return to Buddhism. I decided that a Buddhist pilgrimage in the middle of winter in Bhutan would cure me—just what I needed! It was to be with a group of people led by Bob Thurman, professor of Indo-Tibetan Buddhist studies at Columbia University. We'd become friends in New York, where he and his wife, Nena, had created Tibet House. Surely prayer and a pilgrimage would pacify the demons of illness.

Bhutan is a cold place but steeped in Buddhist practice. Our plane, operated by the nation's only airline, Druk Air, careened over the Himalayas and down a narrow pass that is accessible only when the wind is right. Against the cobalt sky, clumps of old gray prayer flags blowing in the wind looked like flexible gravestones.

I clutched Sogyal Rinpoche's book *The Tibetan Book of Living and Dying*, which described a special practice of compassion known as *tonglen*, a Tibetan term that means "taking and sending." The practice involves using the breath to take in others' suffering along with one's own and then send out peace, joy, and well-being, thus making the experience of pain a gift to humanity. Inhale suffering; exhale healing. I hoped everyone else on the plane was exhaling healing, too.

Bob met our group of fifteen pilgrims at the Thimphu airport. He was accompanied by the writer and philosopher Sam Keen, author of *Fire in the Belly*, who would be filming our experiences. They were both dressed in cowboy boots and hats, and leather string ties. I wondered if this was a spiritual pilgrimage or a roundup.

I was so tired I slept through dinner and woke in the middle of the night with the sensible thought that I wasn't strong enough to do a trip in Bhutan in winter. A little book called *The Teachings of the Buddha*, which I found in the night table drawer, said, "The disturbances and defilements of the human mind are aroused by greed as well as by its reaction to changing circumstances." Both were true. Nevertheless, I was now committed: "The show must go on."

The next day, we traveled south by bus to Kyichu, one of the oldest and most sacred temples in the country. According to legend, it was built to subdue a giant demoness who lay across the whole area of the Himalayas. Bob showed us the demoness on a map. We were sitting on her left foot. I considered what relevance this had to my left side being in permanent spasm. Would it make it better or worse?

Then he told us the story of a woman who had great reverence for this temple. She asked her son to bring her a relic back from his trip there, but he forgot until the last minute. As he neared home, he saw a dead dog by the road and extracted one of its teeth. He presented the tooth to his mother in a precious little box and said it was a tooth belonging to the Buddha, which he had brought from Kyichu. For years she worshipped it. Finally he decided to tell her the truth. Just then, a deity appeared and told him to let her alone. He saw that the tooth was radiating rainbows—for, because of his mother's devotion, it had become a sacred relic.

A stream flowed by the temple, turning a prayer wheel of mantras that supposedly flowed into the stream and thus sent the mantras into the world. "When we say mantras," Bob explained, "the purpose is to keep worries at bay and give the mind something to do. Mantras released into the air and water bring blessings to the earth and its inhabitants." Bhutan, where colored prayer flags swathed the trees and fluttered from thousands of hillside poles, was a forest of whispered blessings. I was happy that I'd put my prayer arrow in the Big Sur stream to flow into Arthur's lake.

In the distance was a storybook white house with painted red trim, tidy as a Swiss chalet. Painted on its side was an enormous, lifelike pink phallus decorated with a blue ribbon. The Bhutanese are very taken with fertility, and they honor it with especially dedicated temples. Later that day we visited one of them, but not before we had passed countless neat dwellings decorated with huge male organs decorated with ribbons and bows. We were all somewhat stunned.

We stayed in little houses, whose owners rented very basic rooms. That night, the wind whistled through one wall of my room, which was made of black plastic garbage bags. I shook with cold and the frightening conviction that this trip would make me sicker. My roommate, Leslie, an editor at Bantam, had brought with her a copy of Eric Leed's *The Mind of the Traveler*, a history of travel that included insights from many travelers throughout history. She suggested the book was the perfect companion for such a journey. As I sat shivering, she read a quote from Albert Camus: "What gives value to travel is fear. We are seized by a vague fear and the instinctive desire to go back to the protections of old habits … At that moment we are feverish but also porous, so that the slightest touch makes us quiver to the depths of our beings."

It sounded true to me. I was dying to be home in my cozy bed.

At our next stop there was a Bhutanese-style hot tub, a wood-lined pit of water into which boys shoveled burning rocks from a bonfire nearby. A wire mesh separated us from the rocks. A few candles burned around the edge. Hot water, cold night: heaven!

In the morning, Bob led a meditation on precious human birth. Tears rolled down my cheeks as I vowed to serve humanity, forgive everyone, and spend the rest of my life in prayer. It turned out the meditation was really about something else. I later found out that "precious human birth" is one of the essential contemplations in the Tibetan Buddhist tradition: it is difficult to be born as a human, but it gives us the ability to change our karma and help other people.

We made our way slowly south toward Bumthang, in the Paro District, the last stop on the trip before we turned around. On the way, I drove in the jeep with our Bhutanese guide, who said that American tourists gave bad ideas to his country and that he agreed with the king that the culture of Bhutan should be kept pure of outside influences. But here we were with our American tape recorders, magazines, and videos. I wondered what he thought of us.

Thank God, in Bumthang there was a woodstove in our bungalow. To light it, Leslie and I immediately used everything we had that was flammable—including pages torn from our journals—we were so desperate to be warm.

"This trip is a metaphor for my life," I said gloomily, crawling into bed as Leslie prepared for dinner.

Leslie pulled out her copy of *The Mind of the Traveler*. "'Often I go to some distant region of the world to be reminded of who I really am,'" she read. "'That is not always comfortable, but it is always invigorating.' That's from Michael Crichton."

I took a handful of Advil instead of dinner, as a special treat.

The next day I climbed the hills alone while everyone else was visiting a monastery. I sat down on a stone by the road and thought, *My life is shit*. I looked down. Next to the stone was a pile of manure. I moved to another stone. My heart felt like a raw piece of meat ripped from my body and exposed to the cold wind. On the ground I spied a small golden stone shaped like a heart. I put it in my pocket.

Back on the bus, I discovered that I wasn't the only one who was hideously depressed. We were freezing and rattling our bones through the Himalayas trying to be good pilgrims, but we were all falling apart. For the most part, I realized, other people's lives weren't going much better than my own.

At our next stop, several hours later, I hiked up to a high plateau where I felt that, like a hawk in the wind, I could rise from the craggy rocks and fly. Maybe Bhutan would turn out to be the charnel ground from which I could rise to a new life. *Perhaps it is the end in which is my beginning,* I thought. I'm always imagining that on pilgrimages, just like on diets: *This time I've done it.*

The next day Bob and I went to a temple where there was a coat of heavy chain mail. The temple keeper said that if we wore it walking around the chapel, it would clear away our sins. So we did. I prayed fervently that all my errors would be erased and my new life would start as soon as I shed the heavy metal jacket. I definitely felt lighter when I took it off. I'd worn fuzzy, white fur après-ski boots to give myself a psychological lift, and a crowd of children gathered in the temple yard and petted my feet as though they were puppies.

That evening over dinner, I confided to Sam, Bob, and Leslie, "I'm at the end of the road and the turning point of my life. I've always felt homeless, so a voyage is a perfect metaphor."

"You need to stay home with your pain," Sam replied mercilessly. "Home is where your pain is."

"Being homeless is a good practice for seeing how little you need," Bob added.

"Change your life, and live the way you want," Leslie advised. "Hang out with people who represent who you want to be."

"That's what a sangha of 'virtuous friends' is," Bob agreed.

When I thought about this, I realized that I wanted to be with artists and spiritual people. That would be my sangha.

The last day, we staggered up a rock wall to Taktsang Monastery, also known as the Tiger's Nest Monastery, a temple complex perched on the cliff side of the upper Paro Valley. One of our party suddenly produced from her knapsack a container of funeral ashes to deposit in the rocks. We performed a small ceremony with her, admired the various paintings and the amazing views from the mountain fast, and then made our way back down. The trail seemed even steeper on the descent. When I finally arrived at the bottom, Bob was standing with his arms outstretched. "Here's Bo," he said. My heart rose with happiness. *I have friends*, I thought. *I know that now.*

But in the town of Paro, at the end of the trip, when my new friends rushed to the pay phones to tell their families they were coming home, I had no one to call.

I returned home in midwinter to find that my dog, Basho, had gnawed away the fur on his chest, perhaps from loneliness. I was lonely enough to eat a hole in my own chest if I could have reached it, but my spine was so rigid I couldn't bend my neck at all. The boiler had broken, and the house was freezing. The day after my arrival, the maid quit because I asked her to help carry in some firewood, and the secretary quit when I asked where the second half of my address book was.

"The pages blew away," she said unapologetically. "Anyway, you are twice my age and much thinner than I am."

Then she burst into tears.

I spent the next several days in bed. Friends persuaded me to go to a doctor, who told me I might have any of several terrible illnesses. "You could die," he said. "You should have an exploratory operation for bowel cancer."

"I won't," I replied. "It's my neck that's killing me."

"You'll come in here with cancer in five years," he predicted angrily.

I shriveled with fear and fury. How dare a doctor try to scare me like that? I refused to do his tests.

He flew into a rage. "No patient has ever treated me like that!" he shouted.

I hated him, and I never went back. That day, when I was so vulnerable and so roughly treated, taught me something about doctors. I learned to stand up for myself and not be pushed around by authoritarian white coats, ever. I got a prescription for a dose of eighty milligrams of cortisone a day from another doctor. As the cortisone made the pain ebb, I got strung taut and hyped into overdrive. Manic energy kicked in, and my artistic life suddenly blossomed.

I rejoined my friend Nina's improvisational acting class and wrote a monologue called *Monkey Bones*, about my life growing up. Joanna Miles, president of the Women's Project, offered me a production in New York.

Simultaneously, I began a love affair with a thirty-two-year-old named Skye, who had long hair, crumpled clothes, and a lot of sex appeal. Soon we were thinking of moving in together. He came from a world of free-loving, drug-taking hippies in a commune. I had been feeling lonely, old, stiff, and sick; but mercifully, the cortisone gave me a new life and two passions: the theater and Skye—a star-crossed love affair from the start. Living with a hippie didn't fit with anything else I was doing. Anyone who knew us could see it, but I was careful not to let too many people see. I knew for sure my romance with Skye was a big mistake when, one night, I painted a huge brown dinosaur weeping as it eked its way out of primeval slime.

Susanne, my director, said, "Bo, you have to commit not only to doing the play in New York but to staying there and working in the theater."

I knew she was right, but I also was aware that Skye would neither join me nor stay in a relationship with me if I did. I was torn between two creative forces born from the same energy—sex and making art.

I tore back and forth across the country, once again living a split life. In New York I had dinner with writers at Cafe Luxembourg and lunches with social friends at Mortimer's. I knew Skye would hate it, and I would hate him in this setting. I had lunch with my friend Nelson, who was soothingly dressed in a well-cut tweed jacket with gold cuff links and highly polished loafers. What a relief to be with someone so civilized!

"We've discovered who we are late in life," he said, "and finally found our core as creative people. That is the only secure thing."

It felt so good to talk to someone from the same background, that I couldn't bring myself to mention the extremely alternative lifestyle I felt compelled to lead in California. It was so comfy to be there, and it was so difficult to be split in two.

It seemed as though everything in my life was pulling me first one way and then another. I was in New York for the theater and in California for romance. Then my mother called to say that if I didn't come for Christmas at Medway, she was throwing me off her newly formed "Plantation Board," which would be making decisions about the future of the place. I had already made some suggestions, which she didn't like; clearly she expected me now to go down and toe the line.

"Mummy, I'd love to come and see you," I told her. "But I just can't come then."

Taking this as a lack of interest in her foundation, and therefore in her plantation, she screamed at me, "You only want to see *me* and care nothing about the place!"

Her response gave me an insight into where I'd gotten the idea of putting material things before my own self-worth. She actually thought her land was more important than she was. Her possessions defined her.

I suggested I would come for her birthday in March.

"All booked up," she replied. "No room for you; people are lined up for beds."

I heard Doris, her secretary, in the background say, "Mrs. Legendre, we'll find a bed for her someplace."

"Okay, you can come. But leave before my birthday dinner," she said cruelly. This last, I thought, was just a way to win the argument for the moment.

In an effort to make my life more stable and cozy, I decided to move to "the country": Mill Valley, about twenty miles north of San Francisco. I found a cottage by the sea with a lovely garden, a dock, and lots of sun. I rented it and moved in. Immediately, Skye wanted to move his family in, but I drew the line. In fact, I drew more and more lines until Skye was outside all of them—and out of my life. I loved my cottage; I loved my friends who were nearby. I set up a painting studio looking at the sea. It felt like home. It still does.

A year later I bought it. There's a deck off the bedroom with a hot tub and jasmine and flower beds full of roses and pink gardenias. The art studio has a sofa where I can flop and critique my painting. The living room has a red sofa and a yellow one, green chairs, and a red rug all covered with designs. The walls are plastered with pictures—by friends, by well-known painters, by me. I cook in the kitchen, which is open to the dining room and the living room. Everyone loves it, and I happily share the furniture with my two white Shih Tzus.

Oh! And the stone Ganesh I bought to guard the doorway and welcome guests is covered with moss. One day, a little stone rabbit showed up from nowhere and now sits next to him. Both covered with a fur of green moss, they sit peacefully among the roses.

Buying the house was not about giving up New York—of course I didn't—or traveling. It's just a cozy base that's about the right size for me. Neither the house nor I are very big at all.

Nonetheless I was sick, and the illness was only masked by cortisone. I wanted to be in a relationship, which was in California; to continue in the theater, which was in New York; and to be part of family decisions about Medway, which was in South Carolina. I felt like the subject of those old engravings of horses pulling criminals apart.

I spent Christmas Day with Skye's family in Big Sur, as I'd promised to do. Everything felt strange and wrong … from the food (we had salmon) to the kinds of presents they exchanged (his mother gave us some sort of cream for sex). Skye wanted to talk about our relationship; I didn't. I wanted to say, as Arthur had said to me years earlier, "We've talked about it for ten minutes." I curled up on a sofa and went to sleep for the afternoon.

Back home in my studio, I painted a picture of a woman with masks falling off her face. I felt the social mask and the mask of "Everything is just fine" were dropping from me. I wasn't going to play other people's games—something strong and "mine" was growing in me.

By the end of January, my neck was stiff as a ramrod. I was rigidly trying to hold all the pieces of my life together, and I couldn't. My chiropractor said, "Bo, it's not the play that's driving you mad. It's Skye with his projects and problems."

It was true. Instead of my encouraging his life to become more sophisticated and luxurious, Skye was forcing mine to be more banal. I kept struggling to follow the advice of Mayumi Oda, a painter friend who said, "You have to be ruthless about your work. That's the way artists have to be." But I had trouble with this, as I'd always been taught to respond to what other people wanted.

When *Monkey Bones* first opened in San Francisco, my friends gathered with advice and applause. Jack Kornfield telephoned just before I left for the theater and said, "Think of yourself as part of a lineage of shamans telling their stories, and how people love it and shamans love to tell it."

Ram Dass, who came to the opening, threw yellow roses on the stage at the curtain call.

Skye was jealous and sour. "You just say the same lines every night," he complained. "Why not do it in your living room?"

All *he* wanted to talk about was making clay tiles for a roof from the mud in the driveway. Did I see it—yellow roses or mud? It can sometimes take a while to get things through my skull.

In March, I shifted from actress and harassed lover to prodigal daughter and flew down to Medway for Mummy's ninety-third birthday, to which she had unwillingly invited me. She had been sick for the past year after having a small stroke, but she'd since rallied. So I was surprised to find her still in bed an hour before her birthday party for fifty guests at the log cabin. Her doctor thought she had pneumonia. She was lying flat on her back among unopened presents, and there was a sickly, airless smell of rubbing alcohol and unwashed skin in the room.

"Now, what shall I wear?" Mummy said, examining a lineup of matching orange, red, or green Pucci pants and shirts hanging on the screen with matching suede shoes lined up underneath.

"Let's just stay here," I said. "We'll hang out awhile."

As I lay on the bed next to her, holding her hand, I noticed how torn I felt. I wanted to be kind to my mother, and at the same time I was repulsed by this old, smelly woman who had been so dismissive of me for as long as I could remember. But I stayed there. We didn't say anything; I just stroked her hair, which could have used a wash. I felt how much she needed this attention—an old woman missing her birthday party—and how foreign it was for either of us to give or accept it.

"The best place to be when you are feeling sick is in bed," she said appreciatively.

I agreed. I began to feel better about myself and about her. I felt empathy and sorrow that she could not allow herself to see what was happening to her and her plantation, because she was stubbornly holding on to her fossilized ideas about how she'd run it and the life she'd lived there.

She asked me to go to lunch and tell everyone to have fun. I went down to the log cabin, drank a toast to her saying she was amazing, and conveyed her request for everyone to have a fun lunch. Then I went back to the sickroom. The rest of the family stayed.

But Mummy had taken a turn for the worse, and her nurse had called an ambulance, which arrived just as I returned to the house.

"I won't go," Mummy said like a petulant child.

"Now, Mummy dear, why not wear this lovely pick wrapper?" I coaxed.

"Will you come too?" she asked like a child. "You came last time."

I'd gone with her to the hospital several months earlier when she'd had the first of several little TIAs—small strokes—over the last year; and I had helped her through the dreary administrative red tape.

"Can I sit in the back with my mother?" I asked the ambulance driver.

"If we have an accident, we don't want you to be in the back," he replied darkly, and he turned on his siren full blast.

I hopped into the front. I couldn't figure out where I'd be more likely to be killed. The front, I would have thought.

"You know, there is a five-mile driveway and nothing here but us,"

I said. "Do you mind turning that off and not scaring the wild animals here?"

He did.

At the hospital, the receptionist asked perkily, "How do you feel today, Mrs. Le-gen-dre?"

Mummy looked at her and said, "A bit off today."

Then she was rolled into the horror that is the daily routine of hospitals, with huge syringes and hurried nurses in green and the ghastly smell that's both dirty and antiseptic.

"I'm thirsty," she said. So I gave her a paper cup of water.

I remembered Dilgo Khyentse Rinpoche saying to me in Nepal, "When you think of the other person, it makes you feel better." Yet I also remembered a visit to Medway while I was at the lowest point of suffering with my fused neck. I was bent over like an old woman, I weighed about ninety pounds, and my friends in California were afraid I was dying. Mummy and I had been having lunch with her friends, and one had said, "Gertie, you must do something to help Bo. She looks terrible. Take her to the Mayo Clinic."

Mummy's reply was, "She could just have her neck broken."

Now I found that, despite that remark, something surfaced from the spiritual teachings I'd received, and I was able to behave kindly.

I got her settled in a private room and went back to the plantation to find the family arriving by dribs and drabs, sure of her imminent death and raring for a fight. I didn't think this was to be the end, and indeed it wasn't. I spent the next three days dashing between the hospital and Medway, where Mummy had invited a group of "coachers" from Millbrook, New York, to bring their old-fashioned coaches and horses for a party. The men wore morning suits with top hats, and the women wore long, old-fashioned dresses and huge lace hats. Matched pairs of horses with braided manes and tails pulled the coaches around the plantation, while the coachers drank martinis and scotch from monogrammed bar utensils. It was surreal: my mother at the hospital on an antibiotic drip and the house full of merrymakers, with my nephew Sandy in the lead, all having too much fun to worry about their hostess.

Often, I lay in bed in a guest room. I never really had my own room after childhood, when I was on the top floor with Mamie and Mummy's lady's maid, Rose. Though I left some of my clothes in my father's old dressing room, they were usually moved for guests when I was away. This time I was in the blue guest room—the "ghost room," as it was known, where a woman supposedly sat by the window waiting for her husband to come home from deer hunting. But he had been killed and was carried back on a gate.

I thought about how furious Mummy got when I even mentioned my spiritual life or my creative life. She screamed at me when I mentioned either. I lay half-awake unable to sleep thinking, *I must fill two purposes in the spirit world: dying and offering up my body and as a live entity in some way having to do with my voice.* But here, in this house, unrest and lethargy prevailed.

Mummy had always mixed up love and money with her children. She gave us money or took things away from us to control us. When I had needed to borrow money for a ticket to Africa to interview Prime Minister Ian Smith, for example, she took the car she'd given me the year before. She sold it and kept the money.

Now that she was old, she dangled the plantation in front of her children and grandchildren in an effort to control us. Some people wanted the actual real estate, others the proof of her love. I was blessed with wanting neither.

She proceeded to alienate the whole family—from herself and from each other. "Blood is thicker than water" was one of her favorite mottoes, but she couldn't bring herself to honor it. When blood equaled her relatives and water her land, then the Medway lakes took precedence over family bloodlines. In the end she wanted to be like British royalty, having a place that was passed down through the family. She wanted to be the "matriarch" of an elephant herd—or, more precisely, like the elderly countess or duchess of a long line of landholders. All I could think was, *What rubbish!*

I lay staring at the molding on the guest room ceiling, thinking
The South has time to wait for its prey.
The black water drips from the lake to the spillway, waiting.
Someone dies and quiet mud sloughs off the tragedy.

The light is African on the gray road.
Time slides by like an alligator sliding off the riverbank.

After a couple of days on the drip, Mummy wanted to talk about Medway. Clearly, while lying there she had been contemplating death and what would happen to the place after she was gone.

"It's good this happened, isn't it, Bo?" she said. "We'll have to get the Plantation Board better organized."

"I'm glad you see it that way," I replied. Pneumonia had been a knell of awakening for her. When I'd mentioned the need to do this before she had screamed, "You know nothing and don't appreciate the place!"

"We'll have a meeting," she said now.

I noticed the sky hadn't fallen when I'd disagreed with my mother. Originally, she'd said I couldn't come to her birthday at all if I wouldn't come for Christmas and the Plantation Board meeting. Over the last three days, she'd come a long way toward facing her worries about the future of the plantation.

It was ironic that family members were arriving like vultures around a kill, thinking that Mummy was at death's door, while I left her happily eating pancakes in the hospital and getting back to her fighting ways.

A few days later, I left the troubles of Medway and family behind and went to New York, where I did several more performances of *Monkey Bones*. After one performance, at a theater at Columbia University, literary agent Lynn Nesbitt threw a party for me. It felt wonderful to be celebrated, for the first time in my life, for something I'd done. I did a few more performances at a little theater on 42nd Street, after which the producer, Julia Miles, urged me to stay in New York and write a play. I wanted to, but what was I to do about Skye?

How could I have made such a mistake—a lifetime opportunity of participating in a world I wanted to be in versus another month or two of clinging to a momentary fixation? I didn't even stop to think that I was throwing away the life I most wanted.

CHAPTER

End of an Era

Back in California, I had dinner with Ram Dass, who had become my main spiritual friend. He was always so right in his observations of me it made me laugh.

"I've been in love with Skye, and now he's turned into such a horror and I'm vacillating," I wailed. "And I have another life that makes me happier. I can act and write and paint. Oh, dear. What to do?"

"If you stay with Skye, you'll learn and grow, but the relationship won't get better, because he's a narcissist and things will continue to go wrong," he replied. "If you don't stay with him, you'll agonize over 'Where is he tonight?' 'I'm lonely'—that kind of thing. Either way, you'll suffer and deal with your stuff. Take your pick."

I chose that latter, and in doing so I had some more practice in letting go.

Illness closed around me when I cut the cortisone dosage. My back felt like a black, creaky piece of machinery that sent electrical currents of pain through my body. I was tortured with depressing insights about my misspent life. A winter thunderstorm raged outside the window and in my mind. I'd just read a book called *Planet Medicine*, which said,

"Disease is the primary weapon of the spiritual world so man's first power is medicine." I knew that this illness was a physical expression of my mental torment. But instead of appreciating the fact that I had been loved by someone twenty years younger than I, and by a very nice and devoted husband, I felt desperate, lonely, and abandoned. I dismissed as unimportant the fact I'd left them—not the reverse—and wallowed in despair and self-pity.

Day after day I watched my mind change like the weather. As the rain cleared, the days stayed white, like worn-out sheets of sky. The cotton sky entangled my brain in its weave. Even my thoughts had a bleached sameness. It took me five minutes to get from lying to standing, so I didn't do it very much. I could neither roll over nor turn my head. Friends came by occasionally to visit. Sometimes I pulled myself up to get groceries and take care of the dogs.

I felt like a plant that is being repotted, its roots in the air. Plants have to wilt and almost die in order to survive repotting. If a plant doesn't have a moment of rest while it wilts, it dies. I intended to paint a plant, but when I went to the canvas, I found myself painting a picture of a hawk flying away from a green mountain and looking back over its shoulder. I knew a part of my life was over: the part on my mountain in Big Sur.

I went to a rheumatologist in Berkeley who said, "You definitely have anklyosing spondylitis, which is very uncommon in women. Your body is acting against itself, your antibodies turning on your own body instead of against invading organisms. Why don't you call the Arthritis Association? You'll enjoy their course."

Enjoy? I thought—and I sought other advice.

I did think about what the rheumatologist had said. My body was turning against itself. It was an apt metaphor. I was turning against my own possibility for happiness as my body turned against the possibility of health. I was falling into a world of cures for an illness—physical and emotional—that I had created, or at least opened the door to admit.

Ram Dass visited with sushi and plum wine and suggested, as I lay on the sofa, "It's okay not to move. Stay and suffer these feelings. Allow them to transform you. My teacher Maharaj-ji said, 'You get wisdom

198

from suffering.' You're lucky to be doing a retreat in a nice house with friends to visit occasionally."

A supremely health-conscious friend advised me to try Panchakarma—an Ayurvedic cleansing program—with Dr. Gabriel Cousins, a fanatic health food enthusiast living in the dry, barren hills of Arizona. So I dragged myself off to Arizona, where it was pouring rain for the first time in months.

"Never saw anything like it," said the man at the gas station. "Never rains here this time of year."

At 5:30 a.m. I was led by a tired-looking man dressed like a gypsy to a tiny stucco hut where a large Buddha statue appeared to be covered with sheets. An alarm went off, and Dr. Cousins emerged from underneath the cloth and said, "Choose your oil for Panchakarma"

He lined up some jars of various colored oils and asked which one smelled good to me. I chose a red-colored oil, which he said was the most expensive one. I was scrubbed vigorously by two people: a nurse and a musician. Then I had a steam bath, lying in a red wood box like a coffin while hot oil dripped on my head. Afterward, I did an extremely limited yoga routine in a tent—the canvas sides of which flapped like a schooner in full sail while the floor tipped as though the boat was heeled over.

After a sunset fire ceremony involving dung, ghee, and a crystal, the other Panchakarma patient, Ken—a doctor with a heart problem—and I were given lettuce leaves without dressing for supper. We had been promised soup. The rain had brought an unexpected cold snap to the normally baking desert. Like soldiers in a foxhole, we became allies in discomfort. We insisted on soup the next day; instead, we got ground-up seeds.

The cold snap continued.

Everything ached.

After the rain, the desert smelled of herbs and grass and earth. Clouds and lightning hung over the mountains. A family of warthogs grunted along. The baby warthog made purring sounds.

The hungrier and weaker I became on Gabriel's diet, the more I worried that I wasn't doing enough for humanity. Ken and I sat in the dining hut in bathrobes with our heads wrapped in towels, crying with hunger, exhaustion, and the plight of the world … and waiting for our next oil treatment.

My health did not improve during the week I was there.

After I returned from Arizona, I kept trying things, sure that something would work. An expert on cutting-edge therapies I met through a friend urged me to see a vitamin and diet doctor in New York. So I booked a flight and went to see him. He was in a hurry and impatiently rattled off my new diet: "No more wheat, milk products, alcohol, sugar, meat, or spices."

"For how long?" I asked.

"For the rest of your life," he snapped.

He gave me some supplements and vitamins. "Extract of green mussels is good, he said. "A happy emotional life is important, too."

Both things were hard to achieve.

"Do you treat other people with anklyosing spondylitis?"

"Everyone in the waiting room."

I peeked out into the waiting room. It was full of people with wheelchairs and walkers: crumpled people, patiently waiting. *Cripples,* I thought. *Am I a cripple, too?*

I walked down Lexington Avenue blind to the stores and the traffic. *Will I be in a wheelchair? Will people call me a cripple? Is my life over?* I tried to watch my mind watching myself in the reflection of store windows. I couldn't really turn my neck to see. How had this happened? I felt as if the elevator had hit the basement floor—a kind of empty blankness.

Then denial kicked in. It wasn't happening. The doctor was wrong. I would find a doctor who would know how to fix this. I would be a kinder and better person. Someone could make it go away. I'd take a vacation; that would heal me. I just needed rest, I decided. The distress of my heart and mind was destroying my body. This was more than a metaphor; it was a terrifying fact.

I rented a house in St. Barts, where, amazingly enough, they had green mussels—fresh! I invited two male friends, hoping to have a restful vacation writing, swimming, and meeting new people. They'd squire me around, I thought; it would cheer me up. *Life isn't over,* I told myself. I might even find someone with whom to have a new relationship. I was sure that depression over Skye, loneliness, and being in foggy California were all contributing to my ill health.

"Don't worry about being stiff," a friend counseled. "You're still very attractive." But I knew I wasn't.

To my surprise, as I had assumed that my friends would at least be loyal and supportive, they invited their girlfriends. I ended up being housemother for two vacationing couples! This was on top of having anklyosing spondylitis and feeling ugly and in pain. The vacation was now horribly stressful. After one of the women clinched an argument with me by saying, "Well, at least I don't have an old face like yours," I suggested they leave.

Alone again, I had the ghastly realization that I'd missed my chance at finding a real partner in life. While I was rushing about with young men, I overlooked the fact that I was getting older and sicker.

Ram Dass arrived shortly after my "guests" left. I told him about the debacle with my houseguests and complained about how awful they were. His response, as usual, was totally realistic. "You have to get used to aging," he said. "That's the lesson of this trip."

I turned the whole ghastly experience of being a sick, reluctant hostess and bill payer into a monologue called *Tornado,* a two-word pun: tournedos, a filet mignon (my glamorous life), and tornado (what my life felt like—a storm!). I performed it under the temporary influence of cortisone at the Solo Mio Festival when I returned to San Francisco.

It was around that time that I made a new friend, who would become a dear, close companion. I'd heard about writers who had get-togethers to read from their work and ask other writers for comments. I thought it sounded like a good idea. So I called my friend Susan Griffin—a wonderful playwright and author of several books, including *Chorus of Stones*—who lived nearby in Berkeley, and asked her if she'd be interested in such a gathering. She said she would be and suggested that we ask Daidie Donneley, who was writing a book about a Tibetan nun.

When she arrived at my house, Daidie—a dark-haired, pale woman dressed in loose, Berkeley-type clothes—noticed an old photo of Mummy, Uncle Laddie, and Aunt Janie, all dressed in 1920s-style costumes. Mummy was a gypsy; Uncle Laddie was a maharaja; and Aunt Janie was herself, as a flapper with a band around her head.

"That's just like my parents!" Daidie exclaimed. "They were in costume all the time!"

"Mine too!" I replied. "In that era, a certain 'world' of people loved costume parties. There were never too many pirates, maharajas, or Mata Haris."

"I *know*," Daidie said.

We looked at each other in astonishment. We knew without another word that we'd both come from the same social background: one in which people believed they were put here to have fun. They enjoyed a carefree, playful attitude toward life that soon faded in the face of the increasing problems of the world. Our generation takes life more seriously, perhaps because the world is in worse shape.

There were other synchronicities, too. It turned out that Daidie and I were both interested in shamanism, spiritual practice, and the wilderness. From that night, she has been among my very best friends. It's nice to have a friend to whom you don't have to explain anything.

Meanwhile, none of the "cures" I'd pursued had been successful, and in February 1997, just as I was trying to reevaluate the situation, Ram Dass was felled by a severe stroke. We all take two steps forward and one step back. He had been holding my hand; now I went to the hospital to hold his. Ram Dass accepted the illness as fierce grace, and I had a chance to see how a spiritual teacher behaved in the face of a terrible illness. Perhaps more than the others, *that* could be regarded as a cure.

"I was stroked by my guru," he said. "I realize I didn't take pain seriously enough. I thought I knew what pain and physical suffering were, but I trivialized it. Now I see the error of my ways. The pain was more than the pain pills could take care of. As my body got paralyzed, it was the pain of the body tightening, terrible at night. Morphine can help a bit."

The following year he was up and in his wheelchair but still having trouble writing and reading. He was living near Tiburon, not far from my house in Mill Valley.

"Aren't you threatened by your pain?" I asked.

"I think I am awareness, and awareness isn't a thing," he replied. "If the 'I' is not a thing, what can threaten you?"

His reply reminded me of a dream I'd just had. "Ram Dass," I said, "last night I dreamed that I was on an endless hike, rappelling my way up a mountain face with a rope, but the place I was trying to reach was always a bit farther. Finally I reached the sea. The sea was death. The trip was my life. I'm hurrying to nowhere."

Instead of rushing to do, or cure, or fix, I saw what was happening to me: it was illness and pain, which would surely end only in my death. Ram Dass was teaching me to be aware of the "hike," which was also the lesson of the dream.

"A-a-h-h," Ram Dass murmured appreciatively, closing his eyes as I related this.

I put dessert on the table.

"In this life I have plum wine and chocolate cake, and I am close to God," he said.

We toasted each other with the plum wine and ate some chocolate cake.

"In my last incarnation," he said, "just the wine and cake. In my next one, no wine or cake, and closer to God. We are incarnated as egos, stepping-stones to evolution."

After he left, I lay down on the sofa and turned on my drumming tape to take a shamanic journey, as I'd learned many years ago with Michael Harner at Esalen. I asked for guidance about my healing. An old woman in black appeared and said, "Yours is an empty, cold illness, which started in your back from exhaustion. It can be cured by rest and love—by loving yourself."

I knew I did need rest, but I felt as much in need of love. I had a strong community of friends in New York and wanted to spend time with them. I'd bought a new apartment on the East Side after Arthur and I divorced. I spent the next few months shuttling between New York, where the rheumatologist and the holistic doctors were, and Mill Valley, where Ram Dass and my puppies were. It could hardly have been called rest.

To escape a foggy San Francisco summer and reestablish old friendships, I rented a cottage in rainy East Hampton and took my new Lhasa apso, Snowball, with me. Basho and Tashi had both died in Mill Valley: first Tashi, of an illness, and then Basho, perhaps of a broken heart.

The summer began badly, and it got worse. On the plane, in a desperate effort to escape, Snowball chewed a hole in his carry-on bag and sunk his canine into my hand when I pushed his head back inside. Afraid I'd be arrested for having a vicious dog onboard, I wrapped my hat band around the wound and spent the trip with my hand in the air to stanch the flow of blood. I have a callus on my hand to this day.

My rented cottage stood between Peter Matthiessen's zendo, where he conducted meditation sessions each day, and Kurt Vonnegut and photographer Jill Krementz's house, which was usually full of interesting people. Old friends lived across the street, and Indiana Nelson, my painter friend from Arizona, had rented a house near the beach. It didn't take long to be in the Hampton swim—although it rained a lot and I often sat on the white guesthouse sofa with Snowball, feeling sorry for myself. Then I'd rally myself and have a dinner party.

It proved to be a cozy summer, although it took a bit to get off the ground. Soon after I arrived, I found myself hostess to a funeral. My landlady's daughter died after a long and tormented illness, and I felt the least I could do was offer the family back their house for the reception.

Meanwhile my own family life, if it deserved such a euphemism, was even more depressing. I was just another pawn in the chess game Mummy played against death. From her point of view, eternal life was represented by her plantation. She fantasized the land would serve as a living memorial, and the house, a legacy through which she would live on and be worshipped by all who visited. It's not unusual for people to think that physical monuments create a kind of immortality. Public institutions benefit from this generous fallacy all the time; however, it's not possible to control what happens beyond the grave. As the 1990s drew to a close, which were also Mummy's nineties (she was born in 1902), she was in heavy control mode. Felled by a series of strokes, she spent most of her days in bed changing her will according to the fluctuations of her affections toward her various children and grandchildren.

I don't know about her exchanges with my relatives, but though she was spending the summer at her house on Fishers Island, she communicated to me through her lawyer. The phone rang one damp afternoon in East Hampton as Snowball and I tried to keep warm on the living room sofa in the guesthouse, where there was an excellent heater. It was Mummy's lawyer, Andy Reagan. "Your mother has decided to ask you to run the plantation," he said. "Please meet us in our offices on Thursday."

At 10:00 a.m. I arrived at Andy's office at Shearman & Sterling in New York, to find him neatly garbed in a navy suit, chatting with Mummy, who was dressed in an all-black suit and hat with her hands resting firmly on a large wooden cane. She looked like an angry spider.

"Your mother has decided that you will pay the bills and your nephew will run the plantation," the lawyer announced.

I was furious and at the same time didn't want the plantation, so it was easy to say, "I'm sorry, but I won't do that."

Mummy stamped her cane. "That is what I want."

"Sorry, no," I said.

It went on like that. I knew she couldn't believe that I didn't care a hoot about her fondest treasure—an echo, perhaps, of her throwing away things I cared about, from stuffed animals to some of my favorite costumes. I went back to East Hampton and Snowball.

A couple of months went by. At the end of the summer, the phone rang. It was Andy Reagan. "Your mother wants to have a meeting at Fishers," he said.

"All right," I said. "But I'm not interested in the plantation unless I run it alone. No one else involved."

"I've explained that to her," he replied.

"Then I'll bring Michael, my financial consultant," I told him. "It's a big enterprise, and I'll need advice."

"Fine," he replied.

The phone rang half an hour later. It was Mummy's secretary, Doris.

"Your mother is on the line," she announced.

"Why are you bringing Michael?" Mummy asked angrily.

"Because I know nothing about the business of running Medway or how much it costs, and I'll need advice," I replied.

"Well," she said, "if you are bringing a second, I'll have one too."

"Really?" I said. "I didn't know it was a duel. Why didn't you call me yourself instead of having the lawyer do it?"

She hung up.

I took the ferry from Long Island to New London opposite Fishers Island, where I caught the Fishers Island ferry. On the ride over, the smell of the sea brought back the sweet bitterness of summer vacations. Home from Foxcroft for the summer, I'd looked forward to a jolly home and friends (how silly of me—*Dream on*, I thought). Then came to the jarring realization that "home" was the chauffeur who picked me up and the cook who gave me a tray alone in the dining room because Mummy had gone out to dinner with friends.

As I looked around the ferry, I noticed two handsome young men in blue blazers, blue Brooks Brothers shirts, neatly creased khaki pants, and Gucci loafers with no socks. The world was their oyster: girls, money, fabulous houses, and their own relaxed enjoyment of life. They knew they belonged and were entitled to power, to having a good time, to being "at home" anywhere. Meanwhile I sat alone on the ferry bench in white pants, a blue blazer, Gucci loafers, and gold bracelets. Where and with whom did I belong?

I was right to wonder. The chauffeur met me at the dock. Mummy had gone out, and a tray and a couple of her dogs awaited me in the living room.

The following morning Michael arrived from his home in Massachusetts, in shorts and espadrilles. We went swimming, and afterward we all had lunch on the lawn under a yellow umbrella. Mummy was wrapped in wool socks and shawls; the lawyer wore a black suit and pointy laced shoes. I was wearing a dry bathing suit and sarong, and Michael, shorts and a sports shirt. As sailboats coasted by in the sea, the butler brought us lobsters, salad, and white wine, while Mummy drank consommé and vodka and scowled at my recalcitrance.

"I want you to pay for the plantation and Sandy to run it," she said. "You have plenty of money with all that dough you inherited from Janie."

"Well, I don't want to spend 'all that dough' on Medway. In fact, I'm creating a foundation. It's called the Tara Foundation, after the Tibetan bodhisattva of compassion."

"If you've got so much money you don't know what to do with it, give some to me or at least to Sandy to run the plantation."

The lawyer said, "This is what your mother wants."

"I hear that," I said coldly. "I just don't agree."

Michael looked askance at us both, thinking, I imagined, *Do these people really carry on like this?* But he knew we did. He knew all the stories about Mummy keeping the little Volkswagen she'd given me when I borrowed money to go on a trip to Africa, and saying, when I returned, that I couldn't have it back.

She looked like an old lady wrapped in shawls, but she was a demon in disguise.

"Mummy," I said, "I don't want the plantation. I'm keeping my money, and Michael is here so I completely understand any suggestions you make financially. But I don't think there *are* any I care about understanding better."

"So how do you plan to keep Medway going?" she asked.

"I don't plan to unless I have complete control over it, and that's the whole story."

Mummy sat steaming.

Michael took the afternoon ferry and drove home. I spent the night but went out for dinner with friends and let off some steam myself. I left for New York after offering Mummy—who acted as if nothing had happened—a kiss good-bye.

Months passed. I was back in Mill Valley painting and hiking the next time Mummy's lawyer called. "Mrs. Legendre has decided to have you take over Medway," he said.

Well, I thought, *I won that round.* I was beginning to look at dealings with Mummy as a prizefight, which was how she looked at dealings in general. *You always get what you don't want*, I thought. I wanted to win; I didn't really want Medway, but in the end I made a go of it.

"Then I may as well try out having some conferences there," I replied.

I certainly wasn't planning to take up shooting.

I put together a conference on flying saucers and aliens, which Laurance Rockefeller had suggested. The Tara Foundation would now support a conference. I invited Mr. Rockefeller and a lot of scientists and environmentalists and scholars. It was a great success.

Mummy had rallied enough from her strokes to show up each evening for dinner dressed in brilliant brocades and silk tea gowns. Stirred perhaps by the presence of Rockefeller and a few others, she regarded my up-till-then boring idea of a conference as something fun to attend ... at least the dinners. That was all that tempted her. She was thrilled there were so many men.

"Put me next to the astronaut," she demanded as I arranged the dinner seating. She meant Edgar Mitchell, the Apollo 14 astronaut who had founded the Institute of Noetic Sciences after experiencing a spiritual moment of universal oneness in the space capsule during his return voyage to Earth. She dismissed all spiritual and shamanic evidence of other dimensions, but she adored the idea of flying saucers and aliens.

The day after everyone left, a friend of Mummy's arrived for the weekend, a sporting woman from Virginia in heavy tweeds and brogues and full of no-nonsense opinions. Over lunch, she and Mummy discussed the woman's daughter, Pamela.

"Such taste; you can't imagine," the woman declared. "Pamela chose pink-and-blue tablecloths for the hunt ball. *So* lovely; *so* original."

"Oh!" gasped Mummy. "Pamela is so clever. What taste!"

Then she looked at me and said, out of the blue, "I hate Andy Warhol."

"Oh," her tweed friend replied," I can't stand him. I can't stand intellectuals."

"Neither can I," said Mummy, glowering at me.

I excused myself, giving up any thought of mentioning what I'd been doing during the past week. I didn't expect compliments, but I was surprised to be completely ignored. I can't think why I was so naive.

I didn't spend much time at Medway over the next year, only going down to host a couple of three-day conferences—for which Mummy appeared for dinner and never mentioned anything about them.

One weekend I invited Ram Dass. He stayed for three days, during which Mummy never directed a single word to him; nor did she acknowledge anything he said. It was the first time in my life I'd seen her be overtly rude to anyone except her own family. Just before he left he said, "Bo, with your mother I have to leave my personality at the door. There's no one in the room but her. She fills up all the space."

His observation, simple and direct as always, confirmed for me that I'd had good reason to believe I did not exist.

Oddly, or perhaps not so oddly, in the end it was claiming Medway for my own and making it mine that convinced me that I did exist; for after Mummy died, it took three years, but I banished her ghost. The place became, not a memorial to Gertrude Legendre, but a place where she once lived, and where many other people had lived too: including a governor, an architect, slaves, and Democrats, artists, and writers. After I hosted several conferences—on the environment, the arts, and spirituality, among other subjects—I decided to use Medway as a writing retreat. I was on the board of *The Paris Review*, and I thought writers would benefit from a quiet place to work in the country. With the help of George Plimpton, at that time editor of *The Review*, and Robert Silvers, editor of *The New York Review of Books*, we made lists of deserving writers. For several years, groups of very interesting people came to live and work at Medway for a month at a time. I felt happy that many of them mentioned Medway as a place of peace and inspiration on the flyleaves of their books. Looking back at the generations of all the people who'd lived there, I fantasized that the twisted gray moss, sinister with ancient longings and loves, was curling around our present anxieties and laughter.

The next time I saw Mummy was when I stopped at Medway just before heading off to Uruguay to visit my best friend from San Francisco, an Argentinian woman who had a house in Punte del Este. I decided my back pain might vanish in the heat and the diversions, as Argentines are particularly good at having fun. Mummy said plaintively she had never been to Uruguay, but she was hardly in a condition to go. It was a cold November day, and she told me it was an unusually warm and flower-filled spring. She said angrily that I would never speak French when we traveled in France with her friend Ellen Ordway. When I pointed out that it was my sister who'd gone with her, she got even angrier.

I realized there was no point arguing with my ancient and dying mother, and I changed the subject, saying it was nice to hear that she was conversing with spirits. (Her secretary, Doris, had told me this. I hadn't realized Doris had such a nonchalant attitude toward spirits. She and Mummy must have talked about them a lot—unbeknownst to me!)

"It's a perfectly natural and normal thing," she replied.

As I left her room, she said, "I love you, darling."

"I love you too," I said.

That was the last time I saw her.

In Uruguay I had fun—which was the point. We lay on the grainy sand beaches and baked ourselves golden brown. We went to parties and danced and wore extravagant dresses; and we sat home by the pool and gossiped. The challenge was the unusual schedule: going to bed at four and trying to sleep through the afternoon and stay up all night.

A few weeks later, back in New York from Uruguay, I had a flash that Mummy had died. It was about eleven o'clock in the evening, and I was riding home in a taxi from a film award ceremony. When I got home, there was a message on my answering machine from Doris saying, "Mrs. Legendre died at 7:05 tonight in her sleep."

It was March 8th—the exact same day my father had died. Later, Oneathea, the cook who served as her nurse, told me that she had been close to death for a long time before that, and she believed Mummy had waited to die on that day.

I rang Doris. "I sat with her in the afternoon," she told me. "And she sent me a psychic message saying, 'I am looking beyond to a place you cannot see. I don't want to go, but it is time.'"

I knew that Mummy believed in ghosts and spirits—but the power of dying, of waiting to die, perhaps for the same moment Daddy had died, was undeniably the fulfillment of a psychic wish on her part. And then the message to Doris, her secretary, and in the end, her best friend …

"When shall we have the funeral?" she asked.

It was Wednesday night. "Sunday," I replied. That seemed a good day for a funeral.

I called my sister and said, "Mummy died tonight, and we'll have the funeral Sunday. Do you want to help organize it?"

"I'm not coming to the funeral," she said. "I have a bad back."

Landine had refused to visit Mummy at all for several years, so it didn't surprise me she wasn't coming now.

"Look, I know Mummy was impossible, but we've got to go to her funeral."

"Not me," she said. "I have a bad back."

I did, too, but that was hardly the point. Anyway, I felt strangely energized by the sudden responsibility. Landine's eldest son didn't come either. *Demonstrating against the dead makes a point with the living*, I thought, *but probably not with the deceased.*

I packed alternative funeral outfits: a black silk Givenchy pantsuit if it was hot; a black wool Hanae Mori suit with a skirt if it was cold; and a black linen sleeveless dress in case it was boiling. I caught a plane down to Charleston the next morning at dawn.

211

That afternoon I sat in the sun on the porch at Medway planning the funeral with Doris and Robert Hortman, who had managed Medway for years. It was eighty degrees, the pear trees snowed their blossoms on the lawn, and the bushes were pink with camellias; everything was green. Mummy had died at the best time of year.

Afterward, I took a walk through the woods and thought how unappealing I found this country. *I prefer the mountains of Big Sur*, I thought, *but now this is mine.* I felt a deep relief in my body, as one does after a good cry or when one stops doing strenuous exercise. Maybe Mummy had been stealing my energy in these last few months to keep herself alive. I suddenly had boundless energy and no pain.

During the night Spunky, Mummy's springer spaniel, realized his mistress was gone. Perhaps it had taken that long for him to believe she wasn't coming back. The dog whined and panted and restlessly prowled the guest rooms. Finally, at about three in the morning, I sat down on the floor with my statue of Tara and my other sacred objects, and meditated on lifting Mummy's spirit into the next world. As I prayed for her to join the spirits of her friends, I saw a vision in my mind of Daddy meeting her, and she was so happy. They didn't look back as they disappeared into the light. Spunky lay down outside Mummy's door and went to sleep for a while. A few hours later he was up and whimpering again.

In the morning Erica, the German housekeeper, came in to ask about menus. "Twenty houseguests and over a hundred for the funeral," she announced.

Mummy had been close to being blind during the last few years, her eyes dimmed with age, and the house had fallen apart: no fresh flowers in the rooms, empty flowerpots on the terrace, bedspreads missing from the beds. I flushed the maids from their seemingly permanent morning coffee break, and we went into high gear.

Michael—my friend and financial advisor, who had been helping me through the rough terrain of inheriting Medway—called his father, who we figured knew about such things, to learn about the elements that go into a funeral service. We called Michael's wife to fax down her "funeral folder" of appropriate poems and quotations.

I'd sent word to everyone that the funeral would be at eleven o'clock on Sunday—which is, of course, when every minister in creation is busy. It said something about my church attendance that I didn't know this. I dispatched Doris to call retired ministers.

Senator Strom Thurmond called to say he was putting Mummy's death in the Capitol Record. Torn between the chance to tell him what I thought of the border patrol at target practice next door, and saying thank you, my upbringing prevailed. I'm sure Mummy had been complaining for years about the border patrol anyway.

Sunday dawned windy and sunny. I was exhausted. After breakfast I gave out the poems I'd selected to my nieces and nephews who *did* attend, so they could be part of the funeral. The minister, who had never seen any of us before, said, "Call me Joe," and he had just the right sense of humor for an eccentric funeral. I'd had a podium set up on the lawn by Daddy's grave between two mounted elephant tusks. Mounted elephant feet from the same poor beast held palm trees. I put Mummy's ashes in a huge silver racing trophy that her father had won at the 1916 Kentucky Derby. Spiritual singers in old-fashioned costumes stood under a nearby oak poised to sing "Old Time Religion" and "Swing Low, Sweet Chariot" between the eulogies and poems.

I wore my new black wool Hanae Mori suit, as the weather was sunny but cool, and my mother's black felt fedora to cover my strawlike hair, which had suddenly turned orange while I was in Uruguay the week before. I'd had no time for the hairdresser since I'd returned from Punta del Este. It was lucky, one of the guests said: one should always wear something belonging to the person whose power one needs to carry at a certain occasion.

For the most part, everyone did what was expected. My various nieces and nephews managed to each present their poems and eulogies with aplomb. Then Ann Armstrong—my "political" cousin, who had been a Democrat until she shifted parties and became Nixon's ambassador to London—spoke solely about herself and her career, mentioning only by way of an introduction that Mummy was her beloved aunt. Since she became an ambassador, she was the most esteemed of all of us in

Mummy's eyes. If there was one thing Mummy liked, it was titles … ideally, royal ones. I remembered that when Ann was ambassador, I'd stayed at the embassy and gone to parties in glittering dresses with nary a thought that she was staying home having dinner alone with her children. I guess I'd thought an ambassador would know at least as many people in London as me! But listening to her funeral oration I also felt no guilt.

And then it was my turn. I remembered joining in the singing at Daddy's funeral and then being sent home. Not so today: I wore Mummy's hat, literally and figuratively.

I walked nervously up to the podium and looked out at the assembled company. There were more than a hundred people on folding white chairs on the lawn next to the horse pasture. A strong wind swept the Spanish moss sideways, and people held onto their hats. My family sat in the first row. Directly behind them were some of our old retainers, including Lizzie and Candace, the cook and chambermaid with whom I had grown up, dressed in beautiful dresses and hats with satin bows. Next to them were friends of Mummy's, people who worked on the plantation now, and friends from neighboring plantations in a variety of outfits ranging from tweed jackets and slacks to dark suits. The women were particularly eclectic—some dressed for a party, others for a country hike. There weren't enough chairs, and many people had to stand. Their heels must have been sinking into the soft earth.

My voice cracked, not from sadness, but with a sense of the enormity of the moment. Mummy was gone, and I was standing in her place. I thought I might cry. Then I pulled myself together and gave a eulogy about my adventurous and original mother. Oddly, despite a history of problems, I was also friends with her—and rather good, if I say so myself, at writing little speeches. So I whisked through it, having tried it out on the housekeeper and Doris.

When I finished, my nieces and nephew helped me pour Mummy's ashes from the silver racing trophy into the hole dug beside my father's grave as Sam, the butler, fired off her shotgun. The urn was so heavy, it was quite hard to manage; and the wind blew the ashes about so we had to work to avoid Mummy's being blown in our faces. I'd asked the spiritual singers I'd hired to sing "I Got Plenty of Nothing" from *Porgy and Bess*, as a sort of joke, and we all walked down to the log cabin for lunch to the strains of "Nothing is plenty for me ..."

Many people said, "You look and sound just like your mother." or "It was like listening to Gertie." All the old retainers said, "You are jes' like your mother," which they all meant as a compliment.

Around four in the afternoon, slightly tight from the white wine we'd had at lunch, my childhood friend Carola and I took the silver urn with the rest of Mummy's ashes into Grandmother's Garden on the right side of the main house, where we sprinkled them in the azalea bushes. They're supposedly good fertilizer.

That evening a number of guests told dreary and inappropriate stories at dinner, but I just sat back in my mother's chair and not caring what they did—because, I thought, *They will all go away, and I can do what I want. I'm free.*

After everyone went home, I lay awake in bed, my heart racing. *Medway is like owning a shark*, I thought. *Anything I have, it will take. Why is the Valium in New York, the Vioxx in California?*

The trouble was, I lived in too many places and now I lived in one more.

Jungle Cure

I redid Medway. I switched the dining room and the living room the day after the funeral. All the men on the place moved furniture. I painted the living room pale pink and had the sofas and chairs reupholstered in pink and blue and yellow. The dining room became a cozy paneled library full of books, with turquoise curtains and a turquoise Bukhara rug. I bought new furniture for the gun room and turned the brown-and-black motif, full of spears and masks, into a bright blue-and-red, welcoming library with a huge Tibetan *thangka* to push the evil spirits out.

Finally I attacked the inner sanctum. I painted Mummy's cypress-paneled bedroom white with pale blue moldings. I thought she might return from her grave or the staff might rebel, but happily everyone loved it.

Nevertheless, when I spent the first night there, a fire erupted in the bedroom fireplace and the sconces fell off the walls. Sam, the butler, rushed in and saved the house, but I had to do the bedroom over. He said he saw Mummy in the smoke! The Christmas tree fell over three times during the night. "She's back," everyone said—and I thought so, too.

A few weeks later, on a windless day, a parasol rose from its base on the log cabin porch and blew onto the roof. To retrieve it, the men had to get a ladder from the gatehouse. When they got there, they saw a fire blazing in the woods. If they hadn't gone for the ladder and caught it in time, that fire might have burned the woods down.

"She's on our side now," said Sam, meaning my mother. "She's taking care of us. It's okay."

Meanwhile I got sicker and sicker, with brief periods of health— or at least periods in which the pain was less intense because I took Vioxx. I continued looking for cures. One day a friend came up with a suggestion just exotic enough for me to accept. Jeremy Narby, an anthropologist who studies the tribes in Peru, suggested I go and see if the shaman's medicine, *ayahuasca*, could help me. Brewed from Amazon jungle vines and leaves, it is a known hallucinogen, but it is also a serious medicine said to have cured many illnesses, from AIDS to cancer. When I divulged this plan to my long-suffering rheumatologist in New York, he said, "If you get cured by a witch doctor, I'll write a paper about it."

That was all the encouragement I needed. I planned a trip to the shamans in the Amazon immediately.

In the spirit of Paul Theroux, who went to India to cure a cold, I was on my way to the Amazon to seek a cure for my fusing spine. I couldn't even roll over in bed anymore without clinging to the edge of the mattress and pulling myself slowly over to my side. I felt too exhausted for love and too ugly to flirt. Pain had become a fact of life, like getting up and brushing my teeth in the morning.

Ralph Metzner had written a book, *Ayahuasca: Human Consciousness and the Spirits of Nature*, about the *ayahuasqueros* I was going to visit. In it, he said,

> The fact that Westerners will seek out a foul-tasting jungle medicine, in a faraway environment and culture, a medicine which frequently leads to violent purging and can include terrifying visions, is a remarkable paradox, and yet an overwhelming majority of people who try it find in it the deepest spiritual realizations of their life as well as profoundly healing changes.

Jeremy Narby had told me that taking ayahuasca had healed his back, but I think it was a minor problem. Optimistically, I thought it might heal mine. I was also curious and terrified to discover if I might have a profound spiritual awakening; physical healing or emotional transformation, I wanted it all. Perhaps the old Foxcroft motto would come true for me: *Mens sana in corpore sano.*

Dark clouds formed huge gray dragons in the orange cauldron of dawn as the spine of the Andes sliced through the permanent fog bank shrouding Lima. I am a dragon according to Chinese astrology, and I was glad to see this powerful ally as I headed for scary visions in an alien environment.

Lima was freezing cold, a mass of rotting concrete buildings. It was October 2000, and the government was in total confusion. As a result of corruption and election scandals, President Fujimori was preparing to flee.

In the huge Marriott Hotel lobby, walls of glass revealed the clammy gray blanket of fog surrounding everything. I descended to the lobby to meet Tirso, my translator for the trip. He was a total stranger on whom I would be completely dependent. Jeremy had originally recommended another translator, Mark, whom I had met and liked; but the day before I left for Peru, Jeremy called to say Mark had canceled and Tirso would replace him. I later discovered Mark had committed suicide, but Jeremy didn't want to tell me and possibly freak me out. It wasn't exactly an auspicious beginning.

A man in his forties strode confidently toward me, an envelope in his hand. His face was smooth and golden-colored, and he wore an orange baseball cap with a large *T* on it. His faded pink cotton sweater reminded me of golfers at Fishers Island.

"You must be Bo," he said. "I brought you something."

Inside the envelope was a birthday card.

"It felt like the right thing," he said proudly.

I accepted the card in the spirit of starting a new life.

We had a terrible lunch of dried-up fish and overcooked vegetables from the hotel buffet, the contents of which I suspected had been there since yesterday. Tirso confided that he was a potato expert, hoping for a Hindu cure for his depression by listening to the tapes of Deepak Chopra. I had a ghastly feeling we typified those foolish and desperate souls who believe foreign cures for the body and spirit are more worthy than the ones at home.

Tirso had taken ayahuasca many times, and he showed me pictures of his shaman, who was wearing a long blue robe and a huge feather crown. Just my kind of shaman: dressed for the part, looking peaceful and powerful. Unfortunately, we were going to see a different shaman. I explained that we would be in the jungle for only a week, as I planned to go to see Machu Picchu. We agreed to meet at the airport the next day to go to Iquitos, where Francisco, the shaman Jeremy had recommended, would initiate me into the visions of ayahuasca.

I took a brief shopping tour at a mall across from the hotel in the hopes that shopping would calm my nerves. Bits of greasy paper blew about among shops selling incense and Chinese jogging shoes. I saw a sign over a hamburger joint that said, in English, "Living Is Dreaming, Dreaming Is Becoming." *What kind of country is this, with a spiritual junk-food place?* I wondered. I went back to lie down in my all-beige room.

Tirso and I spent the next night at a hotel in Iquitos, which was like fairyland compared to everything around it. The town consisted for the most part of rattletrap buildings, dirty kiosks selling bolts of cheap cloth and bunches of bananas, and broken bicycles piled against each other along a wire fence. Our hotel had air-conditioning, a swimming pool, ice, and edible food.

The next morning at seven-thirty our shaman, Francisco, appeared. He was dressed like a gangster in a baseball cap, green fatigues, huge dark glasses, and brown suede hiking boots—undoubtedly the latest fashion in Iquitos.

"I knew when I read your e-mail you were an impatient woman," he chastised me, practically before we said hello. Although he lived without electricity, gas, or running water, he was apparently a hotshot with the computer. That's not quite what I had imagined my shaman doing after hours.

The street outside the hotel was a tangle of bicycle rickshaws appropriately called "mosquitoes," as they buzzed around clipping the heels of prospective clients like mosquitoes buzz around one's head. We headed for the jungle in a forlorn-looking gray taxi with ripped flannel seats. During the hour-and-a-half drive, Francisco and Tirso kept up a running dialogue in Spanish. I felt disappointed and deflated; as usual, this was not what I had expected. I had imagined riding donkeys or perhaps paddling a canoe up the Amazon to our camp—something a bit romantic and exotic—and, what's more, I'd expected my shaman to pay attention to me.

The cab stopped on a bit of empty road, bordered by thick jungle on both sides. Tirso returned immediately to Iquitos in the taxi to make a phone call, leaving me without a translator and the distinct sense I was not in control of this trip. There were no explanations from either of them about Tirso's desertion.

Francisco gathered up some bags and led the way up a steep muddy path. I carried a canvas bag of wilting Kleenex and toilet paper. It was neither hot nor buggy, which I had expected; in fact, the monkeys had cute babies hanging onto them as they leapt from tree to tree.

Francisco paused in our climb to release a butterfly caught in a spiderweb. Despite my lifelong loathing of butterflies, I suggested this was a good omen signifying that I might be set free of my illness, and he agreed. He understood a bit of English, it seemed. After an hour of steady walking and climbing, we reached the camp, called Sach'amama after an Incan mythological figure, a two-headed serpent known as "the mother of the forests." When she surfaces, she becomes the tree of life: one head eats its tail, and the other points to the sky.

My temporary new home was a huge hut made of logs and palm-leaf matting, with a palm-leaf roof. Like all the huts in the camp, it was built on stilts to avoid the rainy season floods. Rows of wooden cots covered by mosquito nets lined the sides and back wall, and hammocks were strung around the center of the room. The toilet was at the end of a long porch, separated by a crooked blue plastic curtain. There was no seat, nor any privacy. *Calm down*, I told myself. *It's going to be all right. Hang on. Be in the present.* Though really, I'd rather have pitched a tent in the woods and peed under the trees than share this windy dormitory.

Francisco showed me around the camp: the brown stream down the hill where we could bathe ("without soap," he said sternly); the dining room, with long wood backless benches; a couple of other huts; and a "school" he was building. Indeed, the building went on for the entire month I was there, buzz saws going full time.

Over a lunch of tomatoes, cucumbers, and rice, he said, "I will take ayahuasca tonight and do a diagnosis of you. You must come to the ceremony, but no ayahuasca for you yet."

As night fell, we slogged up a small mountain to the ayahuasca hut—the "temple" of this kind of shamanism—where we sat on uncomfortable wooden benches. A candle melted to a table glowed faintly at one end of the space. A hot breeze breathed on us and rattled the palm-leaf fans hanging from the roof. The jungle leaned in from every side, squeaking and grunting.

I sat on that bench for five hours in the dark listening to the *icaros*, songs the shamans sing to the plants to beg for their cooperation. I thought of my mother's safaris to wild countries. She'd had cocktails watching the sunset before dinner while sitting on comfy Abercrombie & Fitch canvas chairs. In contrast, I was sitting on a hard bench in the dark, listening to people throw up. Ayahuasca supposedly doesn't "work" until after one throws up, unless one has taken a great deal of it for years.

At breakfast the next morning, Tirso showed up from Iquitos ready to take on his role as translator. It appeared he had called his nephew, Cesar, who would soon join us at the camp to participate in the cure. Nobody bothered to ask how I might feel or react to this. Tirso ate a copious amount of food and supposedly translated what Francisco said. As our time together wore on, I realized I wasn't always getting the full story in these translations, so I was never sure what parts were left out.

"Francisco says that physically you are like a car that is cold and we have to start it up slowly with medicine and purges. You have to have patience."

"So physically I'm a ruined jalopy. What else did he learn?"

"There are black dots like ice around you."

"What does that mean?"

"He saw a black hand come over your face, and a voice said, 'She's mine.' He said, 'Let me see this creature,' but it covered your face."

"So?"

"Someone has cursed you."

"Who?"

"It's not useful for you to know. Don't think about it," Francisco interrupted, in English; and then he relented. "A young man."

Sorcery! I was "cursed" by a young man; maybe my last lover had called on evil spirits when we broke up in 1995. I'd been increasingly sick ever since, and here, where the worlds of "reality" and "altered reality" overlapped, it seemed quite normal that Francisco should "see" the curses I had intuited in the breakup. Perhaps, I hoped, the shaman's magic would reverse this spell.

I returned to my hammock with ghastly recollections of that love affair, and all my love affairs and all the mistakes I had made in my life. A woman with a German accent entered without seeing me buried in the hammock, and she had a long conversation with two Peruvian men about arranging to stay in a hut called Ita Runa. I hadn't known it existed, but now I wanted it. The idea of a small, private hut was delicious after this windy, depressing room lined with cots.

After they left, Tirso arrived to say my purge was ready. Purge! No one had mentioned a purge. I told Tirso to arrange for me to stay in Ita Runa, but he peremptorily hurried me up the hill to the ceremonial hut. There Francisco's assistant, Francisco Dos, gave me a bitter drink accompanied by much smoke blowing, *chakapa* rattling, and repetitions of "Gracieux Seigneur."

Nothing happened.

"Do you feel dizzy or sick?" asked Tirso, who was to be the ever-present audience of my misery.

"No," I said.

Francisco gave me another dose of medicine, which burned into my guts like acid. He told me to strip to the waist and then poured foul-smelling liquid over me, which he spread around with his chakapa, beating my torso with palm leaves. I sweated and froze and hung over the back of the wooden bench retching and gasping. Tirso and Francisco Dos looked on pityingly. I was more than ready to return to my cot afterward.

Over what was turning out to be a very repetitive diet of white rice and sliced tomatoes or cucumbers, I met Barbara, whom I'd heard discussing huts while I was lying in my hammock. She was a German psychiatrist and physician who had come to study the plants. I liked her immediately. She had a huge smile, an easy manner, and a lilting voice full of humor. I felt we were together in our plight. What's more, she was an old hand and had already spent a month at this camp earlier in the year.

Francisco sat down at the table, and Carmen, the cook, brought him a plate of fish and potatoes, which we looked at with envy. "Bo will move into Ita Runa," he said, "which 'means spirit of the sun,' because it is the dieters' hut and she needs to diet and heal. Barbara will move into Rupert's ayahuasca hut. This is an honor for her, because she has been here before and is now a shaman, a serious student of the plants."

Francisco was a great manipulator. He knew we both wanted Ita Runa, but he had a way of arranging conflicts so that everyone was silenced. He turned to me. "Money is not important to shamans," he said. "Shamanism is not a way to be rich, but to share spiritual knowledge. Barbara is on the path, and now you are too. You'll see you will soon start to learn."

He called her "Barr-bar-ra," rolling the *r*'s.

When people say they don't care about money, that is invariably an indication they care a great deal about it. I felt torn about Francisco. I wanted to trust him as my healer and shaman, yet I saw he was all too human.

He led the way to our huts. Ita Runa consisted of a roof resting on four poles on a wood floor. It had a South Sea island charm, although

I correctly worried about what would happen when it rained. Barbara's hut was identical to mine, however. Smoke from the ayahuasca fire, the ashes of which were outside, had blackened everything.

At Ita Runa there were two wood cots with a rough table between. I hung my hammock between the sustaining poles. Barbara arrived, and we headed for the bath hole in the stream. While we scooped yellow mud out of a calabash and rubbed it all over ourselves, Barbara told me her psychiatric practice was in Cologne.

"The doctors send patients to me when they've tried everything else. I use very alternative methods. That's why I'm interested in the plants. When I go back, I'm going to start life new." She grinned. "I hope with someone. I am fifty, and men like younger women; but even more to the point, I'm a strong woman." She laughed and looked at me. "Like you."

"Well, don't look at me. I am a total failure at relationship. It may be one of the reasons I got sick."

We used a small white plastic pail hanging on a branch to throw water over ourselves until we were clean; then we dried in the sun with our arms straight out as though crucified, like George Segal statues.

"What is wrong with your neck?" she asked.

"It's called Bechereff's disease in German," I replied.

"Oh, that is hard. You should take up yoga and belly dancing."

"I've done a little yoga," I said. "I've always been terrified of physical pain, so what did the universe give me? It's leading me to try all sorts of things—like coming here."

At breakfast the next morning Francisco said, "Bo will take ayahuasca. Everyone starts with ayahuasca, which is a vine. Barbara, you will start dieting with *ajo sacha*. All shamans must begin with it after they have taken ayahuasca."

He led us into the jungle to look for ajo sacha, which is considered magical and capable of driving away dark spirits. I was quite relieved to hear that it would have that capability. I frankly didn't trust Francisco to drive them away. The first tree he hit with his machete was, he said, "asleep." From the next one, he cut a small branch and blew cigarette smoke on it in thanks.

The next afternoon, as I as was getting settled with Proust in the hammock, Panchita, Francisco's assistant, appeared lugging a primitive form of steam bath: a wooden tub of recently boiled water. He sang songs to maintain the spiritual mood, while I sat under a blanket in ninety-degree heat leaning over the steaming tub.

"No bath," Tirso, who had been observing this torture, announced when I was covered with sweat. "Straight into bed now."

I lay in bed all night soaking wet, furious, feeling sticky and stinky.

Francisco showed up at dawn to say I couldn't have a bath until the next day. "Pray that your mistakes and imperfections will be transmuted into healing," he advised.

A couple of days of passed. I had barely recovered from the purges and the sweat when—as night fell—Francisco arrived at my hut along with Panchita and Tirso and an iron pot of smoking copal. "This will help cure you," Francisco said. He lit a candle and melted it to a stone on the table. Panchita sat on the spare cot. Tirso occupied the steps.

"Francisco wants you to sit on the stool and fan the smoke toward you," said Tirso. Then he motioned me to stand up and pushed the pot between my legs. I was half-naked, wrapped in a loose sarong, a wild witch astride a fiery perfumed cauldron in the dead of night.

Tirso watched through half-closed eyes. "The copal will purify you," he said.

The night was filled with shadow spirits and jungle whispers. As incense smoke rose between my bare thighs, Francisco sang *icaros* to ask the plants to heal me while beating my bare back with flower perfume in which he had dipped his chakapa. Afterward, Panchita gave me a massage with oil he said was made from snakes and electric fish. He told me it would recharge my body.   It smelled of old fish, not so much healing as sick-making. And what, pray tell, were electric fish?

Francisco was a *perfumero*, a shaman who heals with perfume, he informed me—rather a surprise after so many bad-smelling "healings." This evening, he'd brought a huge calabash of perfume in which tiny yellow flowers floated. The scent was subtle and intoxicating, delicious after all the disgusting smells I'd had to suffer.

When they left, I lay in the hammock listening to the whizzing and buzzing and croaking of the jungle. Maybe Francisco was healing the bitterness of my life with the sweetness of flowers and incense, literally lubricating my creaking bones with proverbial snake oil. I spent the night in the unfounded sense of security created by the cheesecloth tent of my mosquito net. This flimsy gauze web gave the impression of being as solid as wood, because if I turned the flashlight on inside it, the light was reflected back from its white walls and there seemed to be no "outside." Flashlights carried by others in the camp as they passed illuminated the net as well, which also made it appear as a solid wall.

Tuesday was ayahuasca day. Francisco woke us at five. The earlier one does rituals, the better, it seemed. Barbara, Francisco, and I picked three hundred glossy-green *chacruna* leaves, taking care not to step on any living plants. He led us into the jungle, now and then stopping to tap a vine with his machete. Finding one he liked, he was about to cut it when a tiny bird appeared and peeped *chichua chichua*, which Francisco said meant "No." We went on searching. Francisco tapped another vine, and this time the chichua bird—for that is what it's called—peeped *chris chris*, which Francisco said meant "Yes."

"How do the shamans know which plant to combine with which?" I queried Francisco.

"Many years ago," he explained, "a king of the Incas died, and in the place he was buried, the ayahuasca vine grew at his head and the chacruna bush at his feet. A member of his tribe had a dream in which he boiled the two plants together, and when he drank the brew it imparted important visions to him. Ever since, the shamans have drunk this potion and learned from the visions it induces."

When we returned to the camp, Francisco and Panchita built a small bonfire to cook the ayahuasca. The thick brown bubbling stew was covered with evil-looking yellow foam. Barbara came to my hut to escape the smoke and try to teach me my *icaro*, the perfumero's song. Never musical, I seemed to have become tone-deaf in the Amazon. She gave up after a while and recorded the song on my tape recorder for me to memorize. We wandered over to her hut to check on the ayahuasca. We found an Italian man who looked about thirty years old. Dressed in a white gauzy Indian costume, he was leaning against the hut, watching the ayahuasca bubble.

"I am Dino," he said. "I met a fat woman in England from the fourth dimension who told me to organize tours to the rain forest."

Apparently he was alone on this tour.

It seemed he was joining our healing circle. At eight thirty, he trooped along with Barbara and me up to the ceremonial hut. The ayahuasca was a bitter, disgustingly thick brown liquid. Francisco handed me a cup, and I drank most of it.

Francisco looked in the cup. "All," he said.

I finished it. Nothing happened. Hours seemed to pass, and still nothing happened. I knew it. *I'm a total failure at this*, I thought.

After a small eternity—perhaps an hour or so—Dino suddenly screamed, "*La luce, dov'è la luce?*" And, switching to English, "I am bad, bad, bad man."

The noisier and crazier he got, the more morbidly rocklike was my perch on the wooden bench. No longer interested in visions in this chaotic atmosphere, now I was dedicated to sanity; this was something of an oxymoron in an ayahuasca ceremony. Around midnight I got up and sat on the bench behind Dino and rubbed his back.

"*Dov'è la luce?*" he moaned.

"The light is in you," I said soothingly.

"It is?" he said, surprised.

"Yes," I said firmly.

"The ceremony is over," Francisco announced, sounding somewhat peeved.

But now that the commotion had stopped, I began to feel the drug. There were sepia serpents crawling across a sepia landscape.

"I'm spending the night on this bench," I said, lying down. "I can't move."

"I will spend the night here with you," said Francisco.

"So will I," said Barbara.

Several hours later it occurred to me that I was in the jungle with no mosquito net. More terrified of malaria than deadened by ayahuasca, I staggered down the hill to the communal hut.

In the early morning my mouth was ashen, but my mind was diamond clear. *I am part of the Big Mind*, I thought. *Everything I have learned from the Buddhists is true. Like facets of a vast glass prism we are each faces of the same reality reflecting individual colors and personalities of the whole.* Just as I was feeling pleased about this, I realized there was another aspect to my personality: I didn't trust anyone, so I kept myself safe by controlling everything.

Francisco, unaware of my enlightening experience, arrived with grapefruit sections.

"Oh, good," I said. "Grapefruit for breakfast!"

But no, he had brought the fruit to rub on my face and arms to cool the ayahuasca spirits. While he was doing this, I demanded, "Barbara and I must be your only clients. While we're here, no one else can come. I'll pay the expenses of the camp to make sure there are no other guests."

I had decided to take over. I wanted his attention, and I didn't want other people like Dino strolling into our sessions. I had not come for a jungle ayahuasca cocktail party. If money would do it, fine. It wasn't generosity; it was desperation.

"Also," I added, "we must get chairs and a toilet seat."

I fell back exhausted on my pillow, my hair matted with grapefruit and sweat. Barbara arrived about half an hour later with a distinctly unappetizing plate of white rice and sliced tomatoes. She had had a powerful ayahuasca journey in which the goddess of ayahuasca had told her not to take any more of the medicine.

"But this is the first week of a four-week stay in ayahuasca country," I said. "Isn't that disturbing news?"

"In return, the goddess promised to find me a relationship," Barbara replied. "You know, that ayahuasca was way too strong last night. Very careless of Francisco."

"I've thrown money around like an ugly American and told Francisco he can't have anyone else in the camp," I admitted sheepishly.

"I hope it works," said Barbara cheerily.

Barbara went to the river for a bath, and I got up to take one myself. When I came back, I visited Francisco in the dining hut, our general meeting place. "You are a difficult case," he informed me. "It will take longer. You must stay a month at least. I am sending for my uncle Ruperto, the *Banco* shaman."

"A month! Why a month? I was going to Machu Picchu!"

My voice trailed away in the face of Francisco's seriousness.

"A Banco is the highest level of power in the shamanic hierarchy," he explained. "He will come from the jungle, and we will work together on your cure."

Barbara was presently living in his house. I wondered where he'd put her when the Banco arrived.

Francisco left for Iquitos that afternoon with money and instructions from me, and he returned the next day with a French girl, despite my ban on guests. He also brought me a padded plastic toilet seat with flowers painted on it and six green plastic chairs. He sat us down on our new plastic chairs and gave us the quintessential multicultural explanation for disregarding my request. "This is the sacred violet month, and three women have come to Sach'amama. You three represent the points of the spiritual triangle, the mothers of air, earth, and water. Jesus stands above the triangle blessing you. This is a very good omen for our work together."

This little speech was delivered in Spanish and broken English, and translated by Tirso. (Apparently, when the missionaries came here, the shamans and their followers kept right on worshipping the sacred turtle, which they believed gave them life—and thoughtfully added the halo of Christ above it to keep the priests happy.)

Corinne, the French girl, turned out to be an avant-garde composer come to record the icaros for English radio. Francisco appeared to have forgotten that he'd told us several times that we couldn't record the icaros, because making them public would steal the magic from them.

Ruperto, the powerful Banco shaman, arrived two days later. He was distressed to find Barbara in his house, and he hung around it like a like a hungry dog, trying to seduce her. He had long yellow teeth and didn't speak a word of English. That evening, I had my first session with him in the ceremonial hut. Tirso explained that he healed by sucking the bad spirits out of the ill person, a process he'd learned from a plant that gave him his *mariri*. A mariri is a serpent spirit, which is activated by smoking tobacco and healing people. When he sucked on my skin, supposedly the mariri came into his throat, and its invisible breath of flame trapped the bad spirit, which he spat out.

While Ruperto performed this ritual, I had a clear vision of a supercilious, tough young man in his thirties. I knew who it was. "Get out!" I yelled, but he just laughed. "The shamans will get you out!" I shouted.

Barbara, the witness to all my sufferings, told me later as we were rehashing the night, that she saw a black animal spirit come out of my back.

The next day Francisco put me on the ajo sacha diet for the week. "What will it do?" I queried.

"The plant will tell you what it's good for when you drink it," he said. "It is known to be good for snakebites, arthritis, and depression."

I supposed arthritis was a pretty close match for what ailed me, but it didn't sound like a sure cure. At 4:00 a.m. Francisco brought me my cup of ajo sacha, because that was the appropriate time to drink it. I went back to sleep and had a dream in which the queen of ajo sacha came dressed in white, with branches for arms. She showed me her old wrinkled face from three different angles.

When I told Francisco about my dream, he said, "The spirit of ajo sacha has accepted you. Its 'genii' is in your body. You only have to touch it to recall its power. Plants have their own type of consciousness, which they impart to us when we consume them."

That afternoon, Francisco invited Barbara, Corrine, and me to the dining hut to talk about dreams. "Dreams are even more effective than visions," he said. "What have you been dreaming about?"

"I dreamed that there were several straw huts, each one housing a cyclone that told the future," I told him.

He was delighted, but as was so often the case, he didn't throw much light on the experience. Perhaps he didn't know how to translate it into a story he thought I might understand.

Ayahuasca night arrived again the very next night. Three hours to zero. I was afraid of needing to vomit, because my frozen back made it impossible. Sneezing and even yawning were difficult. A solid wall existed where normally my ribs should expand.

After we gathered in the ceremonial hut, Francisco gave me a brimming coconut cup of ayahuasca. I drank it all down and then sat cross-legged feeling deathly ill for ages, sweating, and freezing. Suddenly a huge chartreuse snake appeared, coiled above me batting long black eyelashes over its blue eyes.

"I will clean every corner of your body," it said.

I was mesmerized before it, the mongoose before the snake. The next moment I was plunged into soap bubbles and swirling water, tossed about like laundry. I'd become a washing machine. The machine roared in my guts.

I tried to get up to go outside.

"Don't move," said Barbara, who was taking my pulse. "Your circulation has slowed way down, and you mustn't move."

The back of my bench disappeared. I couldn't find the floor. I was made of rubber, a baby with no control, no sense of who or where I was. After an aeon of insecurity, the pale green anaconda gave me a little squeeze as it blinked its huge blue eyes rimmed with black mascara. "I am your friend," she said. I loved her.

I was just enjoying my ayahuasca trip when Francisco said, "The ceremony is over," and yawned noisily.

I couldn't move.

"Where is the ground?" I asked.

"You are on it," said Barbara.

I seemed to have lost my sight. Everything was a blur of light.

Francisco, Francisco Dos, and Barbara rolled me into a hammock and carried me down the hill. My head hit trees as the hammock swung. They laid me on the floor of the communal hut, and I promptly had diarrhea. Carmenchita, Francisco's general servant, who cooked and did laundry, arrived with a pail of water, which she unceremoniously poured over me. I was too sick to notice.

During the night Barbara dragged me onto a mattress and spent the night watching over me. "You could have died," she said. "Francisco is most irresponsible."

"I'm so glad you're here," I purred.

I meant it with all my heart. She'd saved my life.

In the late afternoon we gathered in the dining hut to debrief with Francisco and Tirso. Cleverly, Francisco took the lead, averting arguments by saying, "Barbara was wonderful. It was good we had Barbara"—which took the wind out of her sails.

"We succeeded almost 100 percent in taking out the negative forces," he added.

"Have you had similar experiences with other people?" I asked.

"Oh, yes … happens all the time," he said. "Not usually as sick as you, but occasionally, even worse."

Somehow I doubted that.

"You turned into an angel with feathered wings," he continued encouragingly. "You will have a long happy life."

I thought, *He's relieved I'm still here.*

"You needed to have the old medicines you took washed out so your healing can begin," he explained. "Your body was very toxic. We are using the ayahuasca as medicine for you. We will do a brainwashing to get rid of your thoughts."

We returned to my hut, and he instructed me to sit on a stool and stare at a candle without blinking for fifteen minutes. I did it for nine and blinked, and didn't admit it.

I cheated at brainwashing.

After he left, I lay in my hammock cursing myself for not being a better meditator. After all the time I'd spent on Buddhist retreats, I wasn't the hotshot spiritual person I thought I was. In the middle of the night, however, I woke to an incredibly beautiful symphony. The music surged around me on all sides, a stereophonic concert from the jungle. In the warm night, it seemed quite normal that the plants should be singing, and I was relieved to finally be included in their society.

When I told Francisco the next morning, he said in a matter-of-fact way, "Yes, you heard the music of the jungle spirits. It was good you heard them."

In the seventies, Christopher Bird and Peter Tompkins had written a book called *The Secret Life of Plants*, in which they measured the reactions of plants to different kinds of sounds and found they had distinct musical tastes. They made no mention of the plants singing!

When I finally left Sach'amama (after not quite a month, more like three weeks), my spine wasn't more flexible, but I had experienced a deep healing—if one can call the torture of increased self-awareness "healing," which is what the mystics say it is. I saw that, on the one hand, I wasn't meditating enough or with the best concentration. But on the other hand, I was strong in a good way—perhaps forcing Francisco to be a little more considerate than he otherwise would have been. He had actually conceded to my requests that made the camp more comfortable.

For the average health-seeker, a brush with death in the jungle might seem enough, but I thought perhaps there were more possibilities to be squeezed from the ayahuasca vine. So two years later, when Jeremy Narby suggested I join him and a couple of Swiss rock musicians to visit his shaman, Juan Flores, in Mayantuyacu, Peru, I got right in the canoe.

We disembarked on a sheer bank of wet mud, which everyone zipped up except me. Then we hiked for an hour—or maybe it was two—uphill through the mud to the camp: an assortment of palm-leaf huts, with the main one hung with purple crepe-paper decorations. I'd never seen a river literally boiling like water on a stove before; but here a steaming green river rushed by a few feet away, and the cook made tea straight from its waters.

I moved into a blue hut covered with paintings of snakes and vines. The mosquitoes were thicker than jam, so even taking a shower was an invitation to itching. We stood in the clouds of vapor coming off the river and had "steam baths" instead.

Dinner was Marrakesh in the sixties. There were two Frenchmen, a Swede, and an Italian—spiritual seekers who were sophisticated, well traveled, multilingual, and very hip. My pilgrimages are always parties too!

233

Juan Flores led our first ayahuasca ceremony that night. I felt wrapped in a soft blanket of love and care. There were beautiful songs and comfy mats, and a man to help us if we needed to go out; but above all, there was a sense of safety. I dared to let the medicine take me away and was rewarded by a brilliantly colored jungle world of animals and plants, followed by a series of deep insights. I heard Ram Dass say, "Do what you do, but keep your heart open." I understood that my mother was so traumatized by her own life that she could not deal with a child, and that I was blessed that she found me so wonderful a nanny as Mamie. I saw chicken wrapped in plastic at a supermarket and knew I should not eat such things.

At breakfast the next morning, Juan Flores said, "The beginning of the journey is always hard, as at first one frequently meets death. The plants make us humble. Ayahuasca opens the knowledge of people, and we work to bring positive thoughts to all the world."

His words reminded me of Dodrupchen Rinpoche on my first trip to Sikkim, when he said, "This is the time to practice for humanity, not one's individual goals."

"What happens to the ayahuasca inside of us?" I asked. "Does it experience being human as we experience the spirit of the plants?"

He laughed. "It does. They also learn from us. It is their life's purpose to cure us."

I liked the idea that the magic went both ways, and I felt somehow more part of things, now that I had begun to understand how the jungle spirits worked.

A few days after we arrived, the weather turned cold and a gray drizzle fell. I lay in the hammock exhausted from the strict diet that is part of an ayahuasca cure (on which one eats only rice and cucumbers), the medicines, and the mud, which was so thick my boots now weighed twice their original weight. The fifty-foot walk between my hut and the *maruka*, the name for the hut where we took the ayahuasca cure, had become a dangerous swampland.

One day, when Jeremy and I were discussing how these experiences could be useful to Westerners, Juan said he wanted to build a simple laboratory where scientists and shamans could work side by side to develop plant medicines that could stand the test of travel. I had dreamed of such a place when I was at Sach'amama—the Institute of Indigenous Science and Wisdom, where the science of plant medicines and the understanding of their spiritual aspects might be studied. I urged him to do this and promised I would help.

During the next ayahuasca journey, three days later, a voice in my head said, "Do you want to see your death?"

"Well, if it's not too scary," I said, rather unenthusiastically.

"You must decide where you want to die and who you want with you," the voice demanded.

Where? Who? I couldn't think. *Who would hold my hand?*

"When you die, you cannot hold anyone's hand," it continued inexorably. "Don't hold on to anything; it will only hold you back."

Death arrived in a vision. It was a great vacuum of love into which one's consciousness is drawn. The difficult moment, I saw, was the last exhalation, as the soul is released through the head. At that moment, the soul becomes disoriented. It doesn't know how to steer, because there is no breath. There is no breath on which to reenter the body, and the soul flutters like a feather in the wind. The feather is borne here and there by the wind until it allows itself to be drawn into the great golden vacuum of love, of oneness.

Somewhat buoyed by this vision, I asked for an experience of what death felt like. As I held the question in my mind, everything stopped. Completely stopped. There was nothing—total emptiness. Then the "movie" of my vision would start again. The "stop" was the experience of death.

I remembered my Dzogchen training, in which one looks for the gap between the thoughts to the experience of emptiness. The Tibetans say the most important practice at the moment of death is non-clinging. In the total emptiness we experience at that moment, it's important to not let the mind slide back into its earthly habit of attaching to thoughts. I felt that, like a helium balloon, one releases; the "self" rises into the sky, no longer confused. The same was true with soul, in my vision. The state of our minds at the moment of death is crucial not only to our experience of rebirth, but also to our experience of death.

When I asked Juan Flores about my vision, he said, "Death is love. After death you see normally as you do in this world. You see actual people in this world as spirits. What you do in this life determines your next life." He sounded like a Buddhist. "If you rectify your mistakes, you move on. If not, you will have to live another life to do it."

Listening to him, I realized the truth of what Tulku Thinley Norbu, the lama I'd visited with Harold in New York, had said: "When you get old and the body is deteriorating, if you have done this meditation you will have the inner awareness to rely on. But, if you waste your energy with going here and there, doing many things, you will go around trying to have it all back again."

The dark side of my bright life was that when I found a way of being—whether in marriage or in spiritual practice—that could address my loneliness, my yearning for meaning, my feelings of abandonment, fear, and doubt, I became panicked. I resisted the discipline it would take and the huge fear I felt at looking at myself, even in a reality that might well make it better. Adrift, unsettled, unanchored, in a state of fear, I couldn't do it. Surely I couldn't blame this on my mother. As my shrink had said years earlier when I was struggling in my marriage to Arthur, perhaps there was some deep hole in my personality that kept me from being able to put a correct value on things.

During our last ayahuasca session, I was overwhelmed by the tremendous evil and cruel materialism of so many of the world's governments, including our own. I saw that leaders of religions everywhere must get their flocks of whatever persuasion to pray for peace and wisdom in the world. After that, I got distracted trying to mentally move my furniture around in my new apartment in New York. Annoyed with myself, I shifted to the Buddhist team and asked Tara to give me some teaching.

She arrived in a blaze of golden light and said, "Your teaching is gentleness. Be gentle with yourself and others."

"What else?" I asked greedily.

"That's enough," she said wisely.

But there was more. The jungle still had a message for me. The colored snakes conducted me to their spirit world, a clearing in the jungle where bulldozers were running over the colorful plant spirit snakes. They were crying out, their mouths open in agony as they were crushed to death by the heavy machinery. The trees bent down and said, "These are our children. Our family is being murdered every day. You must save them."

My burdens seemed to be increasing by the day. Since I'm not much of an activist myself, I made sure when I returned home that I gave all the money I could to organizations that actually save the rain forests.

When I got back to the little town of Pucalpa, I was able to rectify one thing that had driven me crazy throughout the whole trip. I had been dressed like my mother in an old-fashioned safari outfit. I headed for the local general store, where I found a pair of bright red, skin-tight elastic jeans. They were a perfect fit, but about three inches too long. The salesgirl said, "You can get them hemmed in the bank."

I stood in line with everyone cashing traveler's checks, and when it was my turn I said, "I would like my pants hemmed." The clerk came out of his little cage, led me into the inner sanctum, and said I could change behind the desk. Afterward he put a "closed" sign on the cashier's cage and walked to his sewing machine next to it, where I left him stuttering away and headed to a beauty salon to have my hair done. It was looking as though it had been done by a monkey in the jungle.

I thought I looked pretty nifty with freshly shampooed hair and red jeans. However, when the bellboy at the Marriott saw me, he asked, "Has madame been in the jungle?"

CHAPTER

Letting Go

Resettled in my seaside cottage in Mill Valley after my first trip to the Amazon, when I conversed with plants via the shamans and their drugs, I felt a new freedom. It wasn't that I was healed physically, but I had changed my psychological attitude and felt better and more accepting of the way I was. I erased the bitter taste of the ayahuasca by writing a monologue about the experience called *Tobacco's Mother*—because, in their hierarchy of plants that can confer wisdom, the shamans consider tobacco the child of ayahuasca. I performed it in San Francisco, Los Angeles, and New York; in fact, I still perform it occasionally.

My experience at Sach'amama had made it easier to be with my bodily pain and rigidity without getting so upset. Hunger and ayahuasca had weakened my body but strengthened my spirit—maybe because I had seen death, and an electric storm that had hung out at the shores of my consciousness had lifted a little. Consuming no salt or sugar had been good for me, but that was not something I was prepared to continue.

Shortly after I returned from Peru, I had a dream that I was in a store trying on all sorts of glamorous silk dresses, none of which fit. Perhaps I had finished with costumes for roles that were no longer mine.

One role, to which I'd been particularly attached, was that of being "special." I thought that if my life wasn't special and out of the ordinary, it was worth nothing, possibly because my family's life seemed so exotic.

I felt exceptionally ordinary on a Tuesday in May 2003. I had had my regular yoga lesson in the morning and afterward decided it was time to clean out my closets. That is something I almost never do. I consider it a waste of time, a supremely mundane undertaking; and anyway, one of these days I might need that gypsy skirt or leather-fringed shaman's jacket, or the elaborate beaded satin ball gown.

I called a service that picks up donations for a cancer charity to collect my things. I was throwing away at least a bit of my old life: the sweater with purple hearts I bought skiing in Aspen; sequined leotards from The Golden Door health spa; an African safari suit, leftover from a trip in the sixties when I interviewed Rhodesian Prime Minister Ian Smith; two hideous leopard print velour jackets, presents from Mummy on successive Christmases; red cowboy boots from a summer in Santa Fe; worn-out satin dancing slippers; and the white fur après-ski boots I'd taken to Bhutan. No, I couldn't do the fur boots after all; they looked too much like puppies.

As I went through this exorcism of the past, I was forced to notice my life had been going on for some time—sixty-three years, actually. Apparently, I hadn't been noticing. I sat down in shock. I'd been waiting for my life to start, but I'd already been living it without quite acknowledging it. I'd thought it would begin when I got thin, then when I fell in love, then when I was in a "good" relationship, then when I wrote a play—on and on. Each time it was something else. I remembered the dream I'd told Ram Dass about a long hike up a mountain to a sea, and the sea was death. That was enough to make one sit down.

On Wednesday the truck carried away the detritus of memory. Ram Dass came for dinner that night, and we smoked a little hash. He had on a tan felt hat, which was quite fetching; I told him to keep it on for dinner. As I looked at him, I had the sense that we'd moved into another reality—separate from the one I knew every day. I was so high, or Ram

Dass' presence while high was so strong, that suddenly, I was terribly afraid. When I told Ram Dass, he said, "Just stay in the present."

The fear vanished, and suddenly I had an experience of being one with everything. "Everything is self," I said, stunned. "Being alone in nature makes me feel this way sometimes."

I remembered sitting on a windless hill above the sea: rolling, golden hills around me; the huge, blue Pacific before me; and the sense that, like a hawk floating in the wind, I, too, was swept into the rhythms of the wind and the land. With Ram Dass I felt a unity with him and at the same time with "everything." This feeling demonstrated itself as an all-enveloping sense of safety and happiness.

I looked at Ram Dass in the felt hat and felt pure love and gratefulness to have a friend who could help me along the road of understanding. He smiled and nodded. "It's always here," he said, referring to the feeling of oneness.

Ramana Maharshi, a great Hindu sage, had said, "The best is silence, aloneness. But there is no reason to give up the idea of realization because you are in the world."

A few months after my conversation with Ram Dass, I took a long hike up Mount Tamalpais, a beautiful mountain that is ten minutes from my house in Mill Valley. Walking on the dry, golden hills of August, I wondered if I was too much in the world when I was in New York. Perhaps those days of parties and people, all the hours whirling through the social scene, should give way to more time in nature—and ideally, to spiritual practice. I vacillated. The twelve years I'd spent in Big Sur, mostly in the hills, had been a positive change for me. What now? A new chapter should begin, I thought.

One day in my seaside cottage in Mill Valley, I spent the afternoon weeping for no particular reason. To figure out what was going on to cause such sadness, I went to my little art studio and took up my brushes. When I paint, I often discover what is really going on in my deepest mind. I painted a wolf. When I stepped back from the canvas, I saw the wolf stood on a ledge—the edge of a mountain. My wolf had moved up the mountain.

In the fall of 2004 I sold my apartment in New York, although I'd lived there in one apartment or another since 1958—forty-five years—and bought a house on Mount Tamalpais. Oddly, I had no pangs about the decision. I knew I could go back and see my New York friends anytime, and I didn't want to live in concrete canyons anymore. It was important to be close to the earth and get used to the idea that I was ultimately going to end up in the ground, no matter what.

By the spring of 2005 I had filled my new house with all my furniture from New York, which fit perfectly, and I started looking around for a community. I wanted an extended family, a tribe. *There must be one*, I thought. *I just haven't been invited to belong.*

I invited about twenty-five of the most wonderful people living nearby for dinner on the terrace as the sun set. Afterward we sat in a circle in the living room, and I said, "This is a gathering of the Tamalpais Tribe. I'm afraid no one will bring me roses and chicken soup when I am old and dying, so I want you to gather here every so often so we can be a part of a tribe. I've always wanted to be part of a tribe, a community, and here we all are!" I raised my glass to them all, and they toasted me in return.

I looked around the room full of shamans, meditation teachers, writers, doctors, and ecologists, with many of whom I'd taken workshops: Sandra and Michael Harner, author and founder of the Foundation for Shamanic Studies; authors Christina and Stan Grof (an expert on psychedelic therapy), who created the International Transpersonal Association; Dr. Larry Brilliant and his wife, Girija, who led the team that stopped the smallpox epidemic in India; Randy Hayes, the founder of the Rainforest Action Network, and his wife, Lauren; and Jack Kornfield, who cofounded the Insight Meditation Center in Massachusetts and went on to found the Spirit Rock Meditation Center in California. I'd gathered the people who had started the New Age movement and now were mostly senior citizens. How could their wisdom help transform a world that since 9/11 had been falling apart?

"I thought perhaps we could all say something about the cutting edge of what's transforming our lives," I suggested.

As I waited, it occurred to me that I'd been cooking dinner for interesting people for years for an ever-changing cast of characters—from journalists and politicians, to artists and writers, to spiritual masters and consciousness experts—and it would keep changing and mixing, and soon I put them all together. It would be like that fabulous Southern stew called a jambalaya. This was a big difference from my parties in the seventies and eighties. For years, I'd held the image of being the provider for others whose talent made them worthy to contribute to society. Now I was a participant.

The Tam Tribe was a public way of bringing my two lives together, the hostess and the seeker; or as a friend of mine once joked, the debutante and the "shamanette." As the evening progressed, the conversation gradually shifted from purely personal considerations to how we might contribute to other organizations trying to raise people's consciousness—about the environment, women's rights, oil, or whatever. The Tam Tribe was a group of people who lived in the same area and held a state of mind that explored the responsibility of conscious people to bring positive change to a world craving safety, community, and spiritual sustenance.

I thought, *The people of America are like frogs in slowly boiling water: they will have lost their freedom or be dead by the time they realize the seriousness of the situation. How can we help them to be more aware?* That was really the question I felt we should consider.

I worried that my interest in so many spiritual disciplines and careers represented a series of shallow wells. A swami in India had once told me about a monk and a pupil who kept trying different things. The pupil noticed that the monk was digging a little hole and asked him what it was.

"A well," the monk replied.

Each time the pupil went to see him, he was digging a hole in a different place. "That is no way to dig a well," said the pupil. "You have to dig in one place."

"But that is what you are doing, running from teacher to teacher," the monk replied.

However, I felt and still feel that community is the great well that feeds all others; it provides the sense of support and friendship most of us need to go forward with our projects. I decided that pilgrimage was my practice and the pursuit of many forms of creative expression was my particular path. It dawned on me that my habit of endless self-criticism was just that: a habit. In some ways a good habit. I want never to be one of those comfortable people convinced of their own "rightness." On the other hand, I had been hanging out with some pretty evolved people, both spiritually and politically—if one thinks of ecologists and people into "saving the world" as political. Something must have rubbed off.

I was still a little stunned by my chutzpah, asking so many of my "teachers" to rally round my Tam Tribe circle, and I noticed they loved it. Several people said to me in different ways that perhaps my greatest talent was bringing people together. My "Bobo parties" had turned into more useful get-togethers; but they were right: it was the same energy or skill—bringing people together. Out of my solitary walks on the mountains of Big Sur and Marin had come the realization that I could use old skills for a new purpose. As Ramana Maharishi had said, "I am in the world."

I put this new understanding into practice by launching into a new project, a television series for Link TV, *Lunch with Bokara*: thirteen interviews with spiritual masters, scientists, and philosophers. I cooked lunch for my guests while I introduced them, and then we chatted over lunch.

The kernel of the idea for the project came about during a fund-raising lunch with Harry Belafonte at Chez Panisse in Berkeley. My friend Mark Hertsgaard, the author of *Hot* and other books about ecology and climate change, invited me on some pretext or other. The head of Link TV happened to be there, and I suggested some short segments with spiritual teachers.

"Five minutes," he said firmly.

Soon it was half an hour, and then it turned into a series of thirteen hour-long episodes. My intention, which grew out of my vision of the tree of Truth in Morocco so long ago, was to show that, when one takes away the practices and the costumes, all fingers of spirituality point to the same eternal truths. I brought together women and men of every belief system: a Hindu with a Buddhist; a philosopher with a bishop; a cosmologist with a Confucian scholar; Ram Dass and Huston Smith; an African shaman with a Zen teacher. Link thought it might run a year. People loved it. We did a series at the Rubin Museum, too, showing the films and interviewing people to talk about them. I think it's still running online on Link TV today.

However television policy, concocted in this case by men with super-male egos, raised its ugly head. Although the show made enough friends and money for the station so that they could start a whole stream of spiritual and philosophical programming still going on, the network's management replaced me with a man; stole my guest list, addresses, and ideas; and never bothered to tell me I was fired. I just read in *The New York Times* one day that Link TV was announcing a new series of programs on spiritual and philosophical content. No mention of me.

When I talked to the head of programming and said I was amazed at this wanton stealing of my idea and dismissal of me, he just said, "Well, I hear you are upset." He never even offered an apology.

Later, using my contacts at the Rubin, they filled my old niche there, too. I was hurt, horrified, and jaded enough to think, *That's TV—unlike most creative mediums, it seems to have no conscience, or is it just Link TV?*

It took nearly five years to make up for the lost time and get my "show on the road," as my mother would have said. And by then it was a different show, not even on television.

Since my life in California seemed so definite, so sure, I thought I would be there forever, and I decided to put Medway on the market. When was I ever going to get to South Carolina? Though beautiful, the place was still redolent of past family pain, and I'd discovered that putting on conferences and organizing writers' retreats was a lot of trouble. In addition, there was the enormous financial strain of managing the plantation. I hadn't fully appreciated the difficulties. Medway's main source of revenue, timber, had never fully recovered from damage inflicted by Hurricane Hugo in 1989. My financial advisor was adamant that I couldn't afford it. In the spring of 2006,

Robert, the manager who had worked there for years, first for Mummy and then for me, called to say it was sold.

I invited some of my close friends from New York for "the last hurrah," which proved to be a complete "aha" for me. The blanket of anxiety, which usually dropped over me when I was at Medway, dissolved in the pleasure of being with my friends at a beautiful, luxurious place where we all were having a good time.

Robert said, "You're so relaxed. Everyone on the place is wondering what happened to you."

I looked at him, astonished. They'd noticed?

"Medway is fun!" I said.

"That's good," he replied, "because the buyer fell through."

"Oh, good!" I heard myself say. "I can bring friends for more weekends."

It was a reprieve. I wasn't going to lose my newfound relationship with Medway quite yet. It was also a newfound relationship with myself. Coming to terms with that place of childhood fear, anxiety, and loneliness released me into a new level of confidence in who I was. It was almost Chekhovian in its impact. I accepted the land, and the land accepted me. I was this person, and I was also many others—we all are—but something profoundly liberating began to happen that spring. It felt like a disguise was slipping off my shoulders and I was finding a comfortableness in my body and soul that I had never known.

Back on Mount Tamalpais I walked the trails every day and thought about what I was destined to do in this last chapter of my life. It felt like the most important time ever. My personal world had come together. The bigger world was falling apart. We had ten years until environmental D-Day, and the majority of Americans were so phlegmatic and uninterested in knowing about current events that they blindly resigned their freedom and their lives to madmen. What did I have to offer now, and what had I learned from all the journeys I'd taken? The universe, I understood, exists in some kind of balance between spirit and form, and the challenge of conscious life is for each person to find his or her particular balance. Mine had been a balance between being a maypole for people to join and a solitary spiritual seeker. And now?

That question became academic in June 2006, when I had a bad relapse of ankylosing spondylitis. For me, it always started emotionally and then moved into my body. I was shocked at some business mistakes I had made, and this tiny inroad of anxiety made me vulnerable to the ever-present pressure of the illness. I was in so much pain I could hardly go up and down stairs. One morning I couldn't hold my hand tight enough to squeeze the toothpaste. Then I couldn't get down the stairs to make coffee in the morning. I was all alone. It took ages to get to the kitchen hanging onto the stair rail. I tried not to reascend for a while. Why, I wondered, had I bought a tall, thin house with five floors, with one, or at the most two, rooms on each floor?

I knew I had to let the emotional part go, and I did after a while; but the body is slower to respond to a change of heart than the mind. I remembered something my very first boyfriend, a German artist, had written on a picture for me: "Strange how long it takes the mind, the heart to see."

Larry and Girija Brilliant, who lived down the hill, sent me to Dr. Sacks. Larry is a doctor and a spiritual seeker, and he knew from strange illnesses and good doctors. Dr. Sacks said Enbrel would help. He was kind and patient and not at all scary. He didn't tell me I was about to die of something awful, but he did say I would have to give myself shots.

Shots!!!

How awful.

However, I liked him right away.

He said, "Bo, when you are ready for Enbrel, just call my nurse Darlene, and she'll teach you how to give yourself a shot."

"I can't," I said firmly. "I'm terrified of needles."

"It looks like a ballpoint pen. Lots of my patients are afraid, and they all learn to do it. Whenever you're ready. No rush."

My health did not improve. I was in horrible pain, and pain is depressing and very wearing. I felt worn down to a shred. I had to cancel a much-anticipated trip to Maine in August. Yoga had become a study in pain tolerance. Finally I called Darlene. She gave me a syringe that looked like a ballpoint pen and a foam pad to practice on. One doesn't see the needle. I pushed the button.

"That's it," she said.

"Can't I try again?"

"No, it only has one try in it."

"You do it this once," I said, and I held out my arm.

"We do it in the leg or the stomach," she said. "Wherever there's fat."

All my life I had fought fat; how could it be that now I was thin and had to look for fat? *Truly this proves that life can be unfair,* I thought.

The first time I did it on my own, I asked my acupuncturist to watch. Inexplicably, my right thumb became terribly weak, and I couldn't push the button. He pushed it for me. "I see your mind," he said. "'I must! I must! No! No! No!'"

The next week I went back to the acupuncturist and said, "I'm doing it."

And I did. It was easy. It didn't hurt—just a little burn-sting for thirty seconds. What was all the fuss about? Why did I keep having to relearn the lesson that imagination is so much worse than the reality—the dentist, the illness, the boredom. I remember Ram Dass once said he thought having a stroke and being incapacitated would be the worst thing. Then he was incapacitated. Suddenly he said, "I'm just doing 'having a stroke.'"

I found that, too. I thought I couldn't tolerate pain. But I'd had pain for fifteen years, every day, and gone right on living my life—just with pain. One gets used to it and stops fussing. "Living with pain." "Having a stroke." "Stuff happens."

The Enbrel took away a lot of the pain, and my energy started coming back. I hadn't known how bad I felt until I felt better; but if someone had told me when I was twenty that I would spend fifteen years in pain I wouldn't have imagined it impossible.

Then I had another kind of healing. After I inherited Medway, my best friend in South Carolina had been a Trappist abbot called Francis Kline. In August, just after I canceled my trip to Maine because I was too ill to go, I got a call from one of the monks at Mepkin Abbey, Father

Francis's monastery. He said Father Francis, who had had non-Hodgkin's lymphoma for some time, was going to die in the next two days.

"He asked me to invite you to his funeral," the monk said.

"His funeral!" I gasped. "How much longer can he live?"

"Maybe a couple of days," came the answer.

"Don't let him die before tomorrow evening," I said.

I suddenly felt strong and determined. I caught a plane to Charleston the next day and was at the monastery by five thirty. I had never chartered a plane big enough to fly across the county before. It wasn't as though I had the money; but, I explained to my astonished money manager, this was an emergency.

In the monastery hall, Father Francis's brother, Ron, and I chatted. He said Father Francis was "holding on" because he was uneasy about how the monks in his monastery would fare without him.

After what felt like an eternity but was probably half an hour, I said, "I must leave. I'll come back tomorrow."

"No," Ron said. "You must wait. He sometimes feels better after they prepare him for the night."

After what seemed another small eternity, a monk took us inside the room and said, "Bobo came to see you."

Father Francis took my hands and held them to his face. "Bobo, Bobo," he whispered.

I sat with Father Francis and his brother and one of the monks. Father Francis lay breathing slowly and with difficulty. He saw nothing nor did he speak. He was somewhere else. Before I was going to leave, I stood up beside his bed, and against the white wall behind him, I "saw" Jesus with his arms extended toward Father Francis. It was like one of those ancient paintings one sees in the museums in Rome. But it was also "real."

I leaned down close to him and said, "I've come to wish you a good journey and to remind you that you have done everything you ever needed to do and you can let go. I can see them waiting for you."

Father Francis half-sat up and said, "Bobo, how wonderful!" He took both my hands in his and kissed them and mumbled a prayer over them.

The next day he was too ill to see anyone. I had to fly immediately back to California because that way the plane rental counted as "one trip" with "turnaround time" for the crew. When I called the monastery, I learned that he died as I was landing in San Francisco. That evening I felt his presence in my shrine room and knew he was sending me some healing and wisdom. I knew it was time to let life take its course and just accept guidance from above. As I left the shrine room, I opened a book by my friend Brother David Steindl-Rast. In it, he quoted T. S. Eliot: "Recollection is concentration without elimination." Every spiritual discipline I knew anything about had some version of that truth. There is the fine, one-pointed focus of mind, and the simultaneous acceptance and awareness of the all.

The next day I climbed up Mount Tamalpais. The sun was hot at noon, and I slipped into a grove of redwoods to sit on a rock by a tiny rivulet. It pattered down between the dry needles and crumbling twigs, and I dipped my hand in it where it formed a four-inch pond and blessed my face with its coolness. *Nature is my family*, I thought. *The emptiness in me is the water evaporating as it reaches the sun. Here I am connected to my soul. Like the rock I am sitting on, I have been misshapen by the rolls of fate.*

I remembered the story about the monk and his pupil that the swami had told me. *Oh, God*, I thought. *He told me the story because it's about me.* Then I had a new thing to worry about, and I wondered how to choose. As was so often the case, Bob Thurman saved me. "You practice many things," he said.

Retired somewhat against my will from television, I took to painting again and tried my hand at some new monologues. I wasted a couple of years. I fell into my old habits of giving dinner parties and traveling. I sold the big house on Mount Tamalpais and returned to my favorite— everyone's favorite—little cottage by the sea. Home for me was there. I enjoyed Medway, but I certainly didn't need it.

CHAPTER

16

Moving On

I decided that for my seventieth birthday I needed to reflect on my life so far with wise friends. I had lunch with Mike Murphy, a true mystic who was a student of Sri Aurobindo. "I don't want a traditional party," I told him. "I want to have a ritual to find out who I really am, in a deeper sense. I want some constructive reflections from my friends on how to live the wisest life I can."

"Well," he replied, "I'll lead a séance to find out what everybody thinks about your life."

"Wonderful!" I said.

Next, I had lunch with my dear friend Angeles Arrien, a Basque shaman who actually shares my birthday. In her Four-Fold Way program she teaches how to walk the mystical path with practical feet. Ironically, she was teaching a workshop on her marvelous book *The Second Half of Life*, which examines the very dilemma I was facing.

An experienced Tarot card reader, she offered to read mine as a birthday present. The cards said that it was time to give birth to new forms, to shed my old masks and past skins—like a snake—and allow myself to be seen as who I really was. I thought of the painting I had done recently of a woman with masks falling off her face and how right that felt. Angie said I had entered the cycle of the hierophant, the Great or Holy Mother, in 2004 and that it would extend until 2013. She suggested that this would be the best time to get in touch with what had real meaning for me, and she predicted I would sell both Medway and my Fifth Avenue apartment. This turned out to be true.

She suggested that my "service" in the world would always be tied to my creativity. "At seventy," she said, "we can just be who we are, do what we want, and it will be right for us." One of her best pieces of advice (which is pretty much a life-suggestion for anyone) was, "If you don't feel thrilled about something, don't do it. Always follow your heart." Angie always advises to do things that have "heart and meaning" for oneself.

The other Angie in my life, Angie Thieriot, offered me a reflection by phone from Argentina. "You push people away when they become intimate," she said. "It's from our mothers not giving us milk and making us feel unlovable."

Erica, my yoga teacher, also said I pushed people away, and that gave me pause. Was I afraid to be close, the very thing I most wanted? Yes, maybe I had been; but we wouldn't be talking about it if I wasn't changing, would we?

Eleven of my favorite people accepted my invitation to my birthday ritual: Jack Kornfield; Mike and Dulce Murphy; Erica; Daidie Donnelley, Don Johnson and his wife, Barbara Hollifield; Susan Griffin; Christopher Miles, a brilliant psychic and healer; Ty Cashman, a philosopher and ecologist; and Wes Nisker, a meditation teacher, writer, and performer.

My friends wanted to make it a party, but I said no; they insisted, though, even offering to bring food. I started thinking about little cardboard cartons scattered around my kitchen, and my heart sank. I realized that some things just don't change. So I hired a cook and a butler, and I did end up giving a party.

But it was a very special party.

The morning of my birthday, I took a hike up Mount Tamalpais.

251

The fog lay like a woolly white blanket across the sea to the foot of the dry hills, creating a cool breeze that blew up the mountain. The September sun beat down with the intensity of August. All morning the phrase from the old Irish song, "I'll take the high road, and you take the low road, and I'll be in Scotland afore ye," was running through my head. *What significance does this have for me*, I wondered. *What is my Scotland?*

The long, dry grass, bent under its own weight, hid the start of the downhill path I meant to take, so I took the uphill path by mistake. It was hot, and I felt tired after half an hour—most unusual for me. Above me on the hill I noticed a spreading bay tree overhanging a huge boulder. I climbed up the slippery incline and sat down on a small rock and leaned against the tree. I was far above the sea of fog and the rolling gold hills clotted with navy-green clusters of oaks and bay. It was amazingly comfortable, and I sat for a long while letting the warm, bay-scented wind bring back memories of my life. Yet I felt queasy from a great sadness that filled my heart, and I was very tired.

I remembered a teacher at a meditation retreat telling us that sometimes people on retreats think they are having a heart attack, when what's really happening is that their hearts are breaking open. I knew I needed to open my heart.

Lying down would feel good. I looked about me and noticed there was a flat place next to the huge boulder protecting a spot just behind a low branch of the bay tree. I climbed over the branch and spread my denim vest on the dry leaves and put my water bottle under my head. I kept my knees bent for fear of slipping down the hill.

Above, the fingers of the bay's branches shook their vast plume of bright, scented leaves, which glittered like the caps of ocean waves in the sun. I smelled the warm wind and sank into the cushion of dry, scented leaves. I befriended the boulder at my side and sank into a deep flow of recollections. After a while I realized the hill would support me, and I stretched out my legs with no fear of sliding away. Something told me this support existed in my life, too, if I would relax and feel it.

Despite the lulling comfort of the leaves beneath me, the warm wind, and the scent of the bay, I continued to be troubled by the immediacy of death. I became obsessed with death, regardless of my efforts to rationalize that I was unlikely to die on this day under this tree. Nonetheless the obsession permeated my dreams and reflections for the next couple of hours. I didn't sleep, but rather was transported to that nether region one sometimes visits on waking, at the edge of falling sleep, or in a deep meditation.

As I lay there, my mind drifted to my mother, who had died ten years earlier, and our rather rough relationship. I was moving closer to deciding to sell her beloved plantation, which she'd left in my care. I knew she would have been opposed to it, as she wished for it to stay in the family for future generations to inherit. None of us were able to afford it, however—a fact that apparently had not occurred to her. A friend had suggested that she might actually be preventing me from selling it in some way from another dimension of time.

This put me into my family story, and I closed my eyes to the flickering sun and saw a family polarized with jealousy and lack of love. Mummy had set us all against each other in her desire to control us, and now her fondest dream was ruined because we could never get together. *It matters less what happens to the place than what happens in the family,* I thought, and I vowed to do my best to heal the tatters of our relationships.

These reflections led to a reevaluation of my own life, and tears flowed down my cheeks as I thought about my failed marriages, the ill-considered love affairs, the illnesses, and the sense that my life was an unmitigated disaster. My heart ached so, I thought it would break.

Yet for some reason, the contemplation of death and loss opened a space for me to release the sodden clouds and let in a ray of light, a recognition of what was good about my life—my wonderful friends and the things I had done.

A couple of hours had passed, but although I wasn't hungry, I thought I'd better eat something just to ground myself. I unwrapped my sandwich, had a few bites, and looked around at what had become a sacred place for me. Leaning against the tree that had sheltered me was a little wooden plaque almost hidden in the leaves. It bore a woman's name on it and a brief epitaph: "Born in 1930 and died October 15,

1990"—almost twenty years ago that very day! I had been lying on her remains, which according to the plaque were "buried near this tree."

No wonder the veil between my own life and death had become so permeable and loneliness had swept over me. I reminded myself to stay in the moment, to be here now, to stay grounded in what was true for me this minute.

The rocks were my friends, and the bay tree and the mountain. Nature was always here to heal me. Nature was my family. I remembered that again at night when the stars and planets sparkled and reflected in the sea by my house. Everything reflected the great universe of galaxies. I was part of the rocks and the trees, the very earth of our planet. We all are. Nature is our mother and our home.

Eventually, I pried myself off the ground and padded down the mountain to my car, and went home to wade through my closet for a birthday outfit. As my guests arrived we gathered in the garden, watching the sun set and the light change on the water as we drank flutes of champagne. Then we went inside for dinner. Over dessert I gave a toast, offering my thanks to each person for the role they played in my life and for their unique gifts as individuals.

Don had arrived wearing a huge neck brace, having recently survived falling down a mountain onto rocks in a stream at the age of seventy-four; so he was tired, to say the least, and Barbara took him home right after dinner. Dulce suddenly developed a terrible stomachache and also had to leave. Nine of us were left after a very gay dinner with lots of wine and champagne.

Mike Murphy announced that his gift would be to lead a meditation "séance" in which my guests would say what they appreciated about me. I sat next to Mike on the sofa, and the minute he went into his powerful meditation, I dropped in, too, sober as a judge despite the wine I'd drunk and how high I felt. I couldn't believe it. The whole room had the same reaction.

He started off by saying, "Bo's great contribution is bringing people together, which she puts down as just 'social' and frivolous. But look at tonight and who is here and what the conversation has been. She gave parties for our Russian guests in New York, bringing Norman Mailer together with Boris Yeltsin. She brings writers and thinkers together. She gathers people and sets the context for their conversations. She sees deeply who they are, as she did at dinner, and creates family wherever she goes."

Susan said she envisioned my soul flying away at night to explore the world and learn things I want to know. Erica said that when I went around the table at dinner, I reminded her of who she really is and what she has to offer the world. It went on like that in a way that my birthday was about what I had wished for: a deeper understanding, a reassurance that I was on the right path and could give people something helpful for them. It momentarily dispelled my lifelong worries about not being "enough." These people, whom I respected, thought I was enough and loved me.

I had a family and a home. They'd been there all along.

I went back to Medway after a while. I liked being there alone more and more. It actually felt like "home," not least because of my redecoration of the house, filling it with color after its long incarnation in green and beige. Perhaps, too, the spirit of the place had changed a little, with all the creative and spiritual people who had visited me. Also, I felt loved there now; I discovered I had a "family" with Oneathea, the cook who had been Mummy's nurse during her final years of illness; Wanda, the housekeeper; and Sam, the multifaceted butler. Some of my friends in Charleston had become like family, too, and some actually *were*. Pierre Manigault, my nephew, had become a regular at Medway, and we had long chats as we walked through the woods. His ex-wife Lee and their two children, India and Gigi, felt like a new family.

I treated Medway like Big Sur, converting Mummy's painting studio into my studio and turning her bedroom into a blue-and-white, summery retreat. I had people to take care of me and cook dinner for my friends, and that's not to be sneezed at. I really appreciated it.

There's something about having a place like that which *demands* one fill it with people. They all enjoyed it so much, I felt mean not to share it. But more and more I didn't feel like entertaining. I wanted to get back to my writing and painting and live the way I had in Big Sur, where I just created art and exercised.

In 2010 I gave two house parties, one at Thanksgiving and one at Christmas, and I got a terrible flu and went to bed for a week after each. Oneathea, who was fast becoming one of my best friends, nursed me back to health, but we both realized this wasn't an ideal way for me to live.

The recession hadn't let up since the market had crashed a few years earlier. In the spring of 2011, Michael, my financial consultant, came to call. We both knew it was time to sell the plantation. It was costing me a fortune, which up till then had been paid by a foundation I started; but the foundation had gone defunct in the financial crash. I wrote doggerel for him about his visit, during which we discussed money and spiritual life.

> The money master came to lunch;
> It's always fun we laughed a bunch.
> He said it's time to make a choice,
> I heard a slight change in his voice—
> "In seven years you will be
> Dead or in penury."
>
> "Oh that" I said," I died last year.
> But strangely I am still quite here.
> I think the jewels will save the day
> Or else to death I must give way."
>
> "And by the bye in case I die
> A spiritual thought is not an ought—
> And kindness is a lot more fun
> Improves the soul, I think, a ton.
>
> He gathered up his paper files
> And left me wreathed in sunny smiles.

It had been a while since I practiced my shamanic skills, but I felt like a little rock-grinding might clear my head. I took a shamanic journey by directing my attention inward and calling on one of my animal spirits to accompany me. Call it imagination, meditation, fantasy—what you will—it works for most people who have practiced it a bit.

I flew with my owl to a bay grove on a hill in Big Sur where my special rock is. The rock looked like a frog and had a frog spirit, which said I must learn to swim in the waters of wisdom now. I saw the importance of rocks and nature in my life. I had to be in nature to practice my spiritual work in a relaxed way, supported and inspired by it. The frog represented the amphibian side of my personality, the side that lived in two worlds. The message of the journey I had with the rock was that I could live in both worlds.

Several weeks after this shamanic journey, the phone rang and it was Harold, my guide to lamas and the best martini maker ever. I felt that I'd dropped off from my commitment to practicing Tibetan Buddhism, but I hoped it was deeply instilled enough so I wouldn't lose the spiritual connection. We sank into our old conversation about looking at the mind and seeing all our silly thoughts and slowly realizing that beneath it all the mind is a still place.

I am an inveterate jokester of what is silly and serious at the same time. I made up doggerel for Harold, because Buddhists are taught to find—that is, watch—the mind. I'd learned from Dodrupchen Rinpoche years earlier to look for the gap, that moment of "no mind" when thoughts stop, as they do when you sneeze. Seeing that gap, or that moment of still emptiness, is the point of meditation. When the mind stops, it is called "the view" according to the Nyingma school of Tibetan Buddhism.

The lama said, "Please find your mind."
I noticed that I had gone blind.
Sitting there on my zafu
I gave a little a-a-choo!
He said, now you're in the *gap*!
I fell into a little *nap*!

"And how was that?" the lama said.
"I like it better in my bed."
"No, the emptiness which you saw
That is the mainstay of this lore."

"Where, where??" I cried.
"I missed the *view!*"
No wonder I am in a stew!

Shortly after this conversation, I returned to California. I wanted, among other things, to reassess living there, as, if Medway was sold, California would be a much bigger chunk of my life. I went walking through the woods on Mount Tamalpais one day, thinking about personal evolution and how it was all just about facing one's deepest fears and going on to the next thing. My life was just *nothing* like what I expected.

Suddenly, after a hiatus, I seemed to be in the throes of telling stories again. It was if life had suddenly taken on a new energy again. My children's book, *The Dragon's Gift*, which was for grown-ups and children alike, was published. I had done the illustrations years earlier in Big Sur, after a vision I'd seen during a guided meditation session with Thelma Moss. It's about a frog and a little girl who seek the secrets of the universe, which the dragon happens to know all about. In the Chinese astrological calendar I am a dragon. Perhaps letting go of the plantation would free me for something new. I began to feel totally excited about my life!

CHAPTER

17

Not What I Expected

After a few months of dithering about price and timing, the buyer who was interested in Medway made an offer that I accepted. On December 23, 2011, leaning over the coffee table in the plantation living room, I signed the contract to sell Medway without even sitting down. I felt relief and a sense of accomplishment. The decision was made, and there was no turning back. Shilly-shallying, a character weakness my mother deplored, and a state I found myself in quite frequently, was no longer an option.

Medway had defined seventy-five years of my mother's life and twelve of my own. Like death, the big changes are often over in no time. Sixty seconds was all it took to let go of the place.

My last Christmas there was delightful. I invited a mix of family and friends, along with several Medway regulars who always came to lunch at Christmas and Easter. The day was balmy enough to eat on the log cabin terrace by the lake. When it turned chilly and started raining, we moved inside and had dessert by a roaring fire. We laughed and told stories. My two little great-nieces were there: thirteen-year-old India, who loves dragons and wizards, and ten-year-old Gigi, who is absorbed in horses. India is about ideas and writing, and doesn't much care what she looks like, but Gigi adores clothes and immediately put on the sequined dress I gave her and wore it over her tights all day. They are the first children in the family to whom I'd felt connected, and I really enjoyed having them around.

For New Year's Eve, I decided I was not going to bend, as I so often do, to pleasing others and resisted the temptation to do one last New Year's Eve party at Medway, Mummy-style, with an opulent costume ball. Mummy's parties had been as legendary as they were lavish. She adored parties (although she loved shooting more). One year, she rode in on an elephant that our friend David Balding was keeping at his circus nearby. He'd driven it over in a huge truck; Mummy was thrilled. At midnight Mummy fired her shotgun over the lake, after which there was a grand march, prizes for the best costumes, and a traditional midnight meal of Hoppin' John, a combination of rice and black-eyed peas that was supposed to bring good luck in the coming year.

So on this, my last New Year's Eve at Medway, Carola—whom I'd known all my life—and I kept my favorite tradition. We wrote our wishes for the coming year on pieces of paper, which we threw into the flames in the fireplace. We hoped the smoke would carry our secret desires to the spirit world where they'd be honored. My most fervent wish was for my creative work to become the first priority in my life.

As I lay in bed that night, I remembered Medway when I was a little girl, making up stories and pretending to be Heidi. I was too afraid of Mummy to ever let her know what I was really thinking or feeling. Now some sixty years later, I was sleeping in her bed and selling her plantation.

Change often comes in tiny increments, as my friend Bob Thurman recently reminded me. When I ask for affection and don't get it, I don't have a fit of despondency. I learned that from Snowball, who at dinner parties went around the room putting his paw delicately on each person's knee. If they patted him, he was happy; if they didn't, he withdrew his paw and calmly offered it to the next person. I have suffered enormous and scary pain from ankylosing spondylitis without making everyone around me suffer by hearing about it, so I must have learned discipline, a quality Mummy used to emphasize I lacked completely.

Packing up Medway would take huge daily discipline, and a colossal effort to remain cheerful and calm in the face of exhaustion, sleeplessness, and grief. I unpacked trunks of family memorabilia I'd never seen and sent them to a museum or other family members. I found Victrola records that Oneathea said were worth lots of money, but the sheer volume of decisions and the amount of "stuff" I had to deal with were so overwhelming that I just gave them to the poor, hoping they had record players.

Ancient clothes, smelling of mothballs, had to be sorted out: my parents' war uniforms, stiff with age; elaborate costumes for the many costume balls Mummy had attended; legions of hunting outfits; trunks of satin slippers in every hue to match as many evening dresses. I found Mummy had Vuitton trunks that stood up and were nothing but shelves for shoes! It reminded me that everyone in the old days traveled by steamer across the sea, and they could travel with dozens of trunks if they wanted. Packing up Medway was not only breathlessly exhausting, calling on every grain of self-discipline I had, but it was also a walk through time—flipping through generations at the click of a trunk lock or a clothes bag zipper.

On New Year's Day, I left Medway and went to California for a shot of calm reality, yoga, friends, and hiking. I didn't go back until the middle of February, giving myself a scant six weeks to pack up decades of life on the plantation.

Sam met me at the airport in his white butler's jacket, black pants, and a black bow tie, immaculate as ever. We'd been having the same conversation for decades.

"How are you, Sam?"

"Fine, ma'am."

"How's your family?"

"They fine too."

"Have you been fishing?"

"No, ma'am."

"Anything new at Medway?"

"No, ma'am."

My friend Mirabai Bush, who cofounded The Center for Contemplative Mind in Society, arrived to help with the packing. Mirabai is a calm, meditative sort of person who went to India in the early days and studied with the great Indian saint Neem Karoli Baba. She later taught meditation and coauthored a book with Ram Dass.

Mirabai was the perfect friend, plunging right in, clearing out the bookcases in Spring Grove, one of the seven houses on the plantation grounds. She went through endless *bibelots* with decisiveness: "Bo, this is broken; throw it out!" She tackled huge cardboard boxes packed with a strange number of things wrapped in aging yellow newspapers. "Out!" she'd say, unless it was really good. It was wonderful to have someone helping me make decisions.

All day long we opened trunks filled with dusty papers, old records, long-discarded ski clothes, cabinets of china, and racks of my canvases. We voted on which of my own paintings were worth keeping and piled the rest in a bedroom to be thrown out. We are all attached to our creations, but these are not children. I was ruthless. There wasn't enough space to keep any but the best. Other artists had told me they did the same.

Oneathea and Wanda were right by my side, dragging trunks around, throwing out papers, helping decide what to keep and what to toss right along with Mirabai. We came across family photographs from so long ago that the images were in silvery film. There were pictures of relatives I didn't know existed dressed in bustles, their hair piled high with combs and crowned with lace parasols. Everything in the family collection was sent to the College of Charleston to be preserved in its historical archives.

After Mirabai left, I took my latest puppies, Rishi and Usha, for a walk in the woods. The late afternoon sun slanted through the pine trees on the soft, needle-covered path. The low country had never appealed to me, because the land was all of a piece—flat pine forests, ponds lined with tall dry reeds, and windy, dusty roads snaking through woods. But over the years, as I'd made Medway my own, there were new and happier memories to stand beside the old. Redecorating the plantation in my own palette was one of the ways I laid claim to it. The writing retreats and conferences I'd organized had made Medway fun and worthwhile for me, and they had helped nurture and inspire numerous artists and authors.

I'd also found peace there: being alone, walking in the woods, lying by the pool reading, painting in Mummy's old studio, writing—living my own life in solitude, with a few friends coming out from Charleston for meals when I felt like it. The transformation had taken about five years, but I'd finally felt comfortable at the plantation, especially lying on the white sofa in the pink living room reading in the late afternoon, listening to music while a fire crackled in the fireplace. I no longer sat stiffly in the dining room, all alone while Sam served me dinner. I had a tray in the Gun Room—now decorated in red-and-blue oriental prints with a huge Tibetan thangka hanging where spears and ancient guns had once hung—and watched TV while I ate.

I was letting it all go, and my departure loomed. Endings always come faster than one imagines, I find: a trip, a meal, a relationship— suddenly what happened? It's over.

March eighth was a full moon, the last full moon of winter. That year, the moon coincided with the arrival of Mars, bringing what astrologers call the grand trine of earth signs believed to usher in a time of abundance.

March eighth was also the date my mother and father had both died—fifty-two years apart. I went out to my parents' grave early in the night when the moon was huge and low on the horizon, its shimmering reflection in the black lake lighting up the lawns and silhouetting the oaks against the luminous sky. It was a night of soft wind and billowing shadows.

I took a small votive candle and put it on Daddy's gravestone. The frogs were peeping and making a whooshy croak that reminded me of the frogs I used to listen to by the lake in Big Sur. I told Daddy I hoped he was near me and that I was sorry beyond words we did not know each other. I thanked him for giving me his humor and the desire to write. I imagined both my parents together and happy, wishing they could have been closer to me. I thanked them for my time at Medway and explained why I had to sell it. I knew they'd been happy there, and eventually so had I; but now it was time to let go. I prayed for their support as I started my new life.

The official closing of the sale of Medway took place just before Easter. I had always invited friends to enjoy the holiday with me. It is usually a gorgeous time of year. This spring, every azalea and camellia was in bloom, and the cherry trees looked like cancan dancers. Wisteria filled the gardens with its fragile fragrance, and roses were beginning to bloom. Tiny green strawberries were starting to bud, and wildflowers had appeared in the woods. White roses were reflected in the lake.

None of my friends in New York thought to call and see what I was going to be doing at Easter. I wondered if, from now on, when I wasn't inviting guests, I would disappear from their sight. The last time I had been in New York, a woman I knew only slightly said, "How can you sell Medway when I haven't been there yet?!"

Since I couldn't face spending the holiday alone, I decided to take things into my own hands and called up Ashton Hawkins, an old friend and a Medway regular. "I have nowhere to spend Easter," I said. "I'll have just sold Medway and may be depressed. Can I come visit?"

It was the first time in my life I'd ever asked someone to do something for *me*.

Ashton stepped right up and not only invited me and my dogs for the weekend but also planned lunches and dinners for me in an effort to make it fun. This was a revelation! Ask and it shall be given! *From now on, this is the new Bo*, I thought. *I'm going to ask as well as offer.* It sounded like the opposite of all the spiritual teachings I'd heard or read, but we all have different lessons to learn. On the other hand, I could hear Mummy's rasping voice saying, "Give, give, give" when she wanted me to entertain her guests with the hula!

I had thought all these years that I hadn't learned anything or developed much from retreats and gurus. Now I realized that, in selling Medway and changing my life radically, I had gone through a really difficult time; and what got me through it were the tools I'd learned during my spiritual quests. I had the discipline not to get mad and to stay cheerful, and I'd learned to be more patient and less judgmental. Somewhere, underneath all this, I was beginning to trust myself.

Suddenly and unexpectedly, Oneathea said it was time for the good-bye staff party on the log cabin terrace. *Oh, my God,* I thought, *the party!* Oneathea had had the presence of mind to order sandwiches and fruit and chips from somewhere, and Sam had gotten the drinks together. They were taking care of me even at the party for *themselves!*

I put on a clean shirt but hadn't time to do my hair or put on makeup. I certainly didn't look like a plantation owner—more like a stable girl who curries the horses. What would I say in my good-bye speech? *God!* I thought. *A good-bye speech!* I hadn't had time to think that through.

I chatted with each person who worked at Medway, and then I climbed on the lowest log cabin step and presented them all with gifts. They came up one by one, and I embraced them and gave them their gift, while Robert, the manager, took our picture with his cell phone.

I made one terrible gaffe. Since Wanda and Oneathea had been working with me every day for weeks packing the closets and trunks, I had simply given them things they especially wanted as we went along, so I had nothing special for them. It was too late when I realized they didn't have their moment to walk up and get a present. But they came up and had their pictures taken just the same.

Then it was time for my speech. *Thank God I have a gift for monologues,* I thought. I just made one up as I went along. I told everyone how much I would miss them and how much their care and work had made my years at Medway wonderful. It was long and quite heartfelt, and everyone felt happy about it. I had tears in my throat for the first time.

March 28th was to be my final day at Medway. Lying on the floor by my bed was a book of wisdom sayings. The reading for that day was weirdly appropriate. It was from the great Indian teacher Krishnamurti:

You are now alone because you are full of the memories, all the conditioning, all the mutterings of yesterday, your mind is never clear of all the rubbish it has accumulated … To be alone you must die to the past … when you are alone there is a sense of being an outsider, the man alone is innocent and that frees the mind from Sorrow.

That is what I wanted: to be free from the past. In letting Medway go, I was letting go of a big piece of my physical past; in forgiving Mummy, I would let the psychological past go to a great extent—unless Faulkner was right when he wrote, "The past is never dead, it's not even past." My experience is that it *is* past, but it's not dead.

I madly packed last-minute things—vitamins, lipsticks, my favorite sweater, a forgotten scarf. Just then, Dean, the lawyer for the buyer, arrived from New York with Trenholm, my attorney, for an inspection tour to make sure that I'd left all the furniture and china as promised. Dean had a thick book of photographs, which he checked off against the contents of the house. It felt rude and invasive, but once he realized that Trenholm and I were nice people, he began to chat with us about his wife and baby, despite continuing with his list. I talked him into letting me keep a rug and a chair, but otherwise it was quite surprising what the buyer, a wildly rich man, insisted on keeping: the portable disc player from Best Buy; dried-up zebra rugs, the skins nearly furless; hundreds of plates and demitasse cups—things that it seemed unlikely anyone who could buy Tiepolo's would really use. (I knew this because, when I was in New York, I had called his secretary and said I'd like to meet him. He invited me for a drink and proved to have in his apartment—and, he assured me, in several storage houses—an art collection worthy of a major museum.)

After Dean left, I took a walk around the grounds and down to the lake in the golden twilight. An alligator slithered from the bank into the dark water. I watched from a rickety dock, where my favorite oak tree bent over the lake. Walking farther along, I found a deer antler beneath another oak. In shamanic lore a deer antler symbolizes the magic of change. How encouraging that a Medway deer was helping me move into my new life.

When I got back to the house, I was surprised to learn I was expected to attend the final closing the next morning. I was already booked on a flight at the same time, but Wanda scrambled and managed to rebook me on a later plane.

The date of the closing, March 29th, would have been Mummy's 110th birthday. I think she would have been pleased that the new owner, a shipping tycoon, was planning to use the plantation for quail and duck hunting. I'd halted all hunting when I took over Medway, much to the chagrin of some of Mummy's friends, and particularly the plantation manager.

When I woke up that morning, I realized I had to look like a serious person selling a plantation. Wanda retrieved a linen jacket from a wardrobe box that had already been sealed, and Oneathea unearthed from my suitcase a cotton blouse that was only slightly creased. No one knew where my shoes had been packed, so I wore my scruffy loafers under my clean khaki pants.

The closing, which was in John Haggerty's law office, was rather unusual. Haggerty, a handsome man in is fifties with a ready smile and lots of Southern charm, represented the buyer. He was an old friend of Mummy's and a new friend of mine, who'd recently come to Medway for dinner with me. He wore a pink Brooks Brothers shirt with the top button undone and no tie or jacket. Trenholm, my lawyer, looked more official in a gray suit and tie and acted very serious, although he still had his usual twinkle. Dean wore a navy suit and dotted tie. He was quite shaken up by the whole experience and promptly lost his files in his laptop. He kept muttering, "I know they are here somewhere." John comforted him by saying he had all the files anyway.

I signed a snowfall of papers Trenholm handed me. All the lawyers looked a bit depressed. I asked if maybe I couldn't have Oneathea with me at Martha's Vineyard for the summer, since no one stays at plantations except those who work in the woods and grounds and maintain the houses in the heat and dampness of summer. Dean looked doubtful. It was the only time I nearly cried. I knew Dean thought his boss would not be interested in helping me out.

As I was signing papers, John said, "I'm so sorry about this. I have had so many good times at Medway."

"That is such a beautiful place," Dean said suddenly. "It must be hard to give it up."

Trenholm held himself together with a serious demeanor, although I knew he was terribly sad and overcome by his years of memories and happy times at Medway with me.

Dean insisted on having his picture taken alone with me before we took a group picture. I told Dean he'd had been kind and sympathetic. "I'm a very sensitive man," he said, and he showed us more pictures of his pregnant wife and baby. We all *ooh-ed* and *ahh-ed* appropriately.

Suddenly the closing had become a tearful parting of friends joined by a mutual feeling that this closing was painful and sad. I doubt there had ever been such a real estate deal before, nor a bunch of lawyers all together at a transaction so moved. It felt like a funeral. The lawyers all hugged me good-bye and urged me to hurry back to Charleston.

But for the moment, I hurried back to Medway and rushed to the swimming pool in the golf cart for a final dip in the warm turquoise water. I lay for a moment in the sun and then got dressed to rush back and have a last salad on the porch before we left for the airport at three o'clock. The dogs had departed earlier in the morning with Sam, who was driving them to New York in my car.

Oneathea and I hopped in the plantation's car to head for the airport. As we drove down the road, she said, "I think we should go back for Wanda." I agreed, and we scooted back for her. Then we raced pell-mell to the airport. No one said what she was thinking. None of us wanted to be the one who broke down. The end had come.

As we went through the front gate at Medway, an owl swooped down over the car, which is extraordinarily rare in daylight. Owls are keepers of sacred knowledge in the shamanic world, as well as representing status and intelligence. Like the deer it's a symbol of transition, and of course it is the symbol of wisdom. The owl felt like a final blessing.

At the airport we hugged good-bye hastily because we thought the plane was leaving in a few minutes. I waved good-bye as they started the silver Volvo, now the new owner's silver Volvo. They were working for him now; all of my physical connections to Medway departed for Medway. The plane turned out to be two and a half hours late. We could have had a more leisurely good-bye.

To my amazement, when I found my limo at the airport in New York, there was a sign on the back of the front passenger seat: "It's not about avoiding the storm, but learning to dance in the rain." Limos are *never* allowed to have signs in them. That was odd, considering what I'd just done.

Home is not real estate; it's community, a group of people among whom there are trust, friendship, and loyalty. I'd found this in Mill Valley in the most immediate sense of a group of friends whom I see regularly. I'd found companions in spiritual centers around the world; in underground cafes and new friends' homes in Eastern Europe; in summer resorts like Martha's Vineyard and Fishers Island; and in artistic enclaves where painters, actors, and writers congregated.

I thought of the year I'd gone to Dudjom Rinpoche's funeral in Nepal and discovered a group of people—Andrew, Lavinia, and Vivian, among others. For a couple of weeks we had taken teachings, eaten meals, and explored Kathmandu as a little family. In Bucharest, through Joanna Ciorrana, I'd met a group of writers, poets, painters, and revolutionaries who became so much like family that one of them drew a picture of us with ribbons coming out of our mouths and circling the globe. In Tangiers with Betty Vreeland and her best friends, Joe and John, I'd found a group of empathetic people among some truly wonderful writers and painters, like Paul Bowles and Brion Gysin. I'd found empathetic society in the theater, when I did summer stock and we'd all lived near each other and worked and eaten together; and again among the painters De had introduced me to back in the sixties. I remembered the press corps on Robert Kennedy's campaign, and the generosity of veteran reporters who'd given me tips and explained things.

There had been the gatherings in New York over the years, often bringing well-known writers and politicians to speak and hang out with groups of interesting people. In California, there'd been the Tam Tribe, where I'd gathered movers and shakers in the worlds of consciousness, spirituality, shamanism, sociology, and psychology. On the TV series *Lunch with Bokara*, I'd brought together people who might never have met otherwise and shared that community with a television audience.

I'd worried all my all my life that I didn't have a home. Now I saw that I'd been bringing amazing people to each other's attention the whole time, having gatherings where like-minded people discovered each other. The pilgrimages and destinations all blended together in one long stream of experience that unfurled from my past and extends into the future, a continuing path of societies and confederacies that are momentarily home.